CYCLING
IN IRELAND

2nd Edition

All photos by David Flanagan except
those credited on page 272.
Cover: The Scarplands Loop, see page
206.

Disclaimer

CYCLING
IN IRELAND

The Scarplands Loop, Fermanagh, see page 206

CONTENTS

Cross Lake, Erris, Mayo, see page 180

INTRODUCTION

This book documents the best cycling that Ireland has to offer. With ninety-six routes spread across the entire island there is something for everyone; from gentle, traffic-free cycles ideal for the whole family to long challenging routes packed with relentless climbs. The emphasis throughout the book is on quiet roads and beautiful landscapes.

Even though Ireland is a small country and one of the least densely populated in Europe, it has a massive 100,000 kilometre road network. The vast majority consists of local roads, little travelled and sometimes a bit rough, they offer a unique and peaceful way to experience the Irish countryside.

This book caters for as many cyclists as possible, featuring routes on everything from smooth tarmac roads to rough mountain paths, there is plenty for riders of all levels of fitness and commitment. With this in mind, each route description contains details of worthwhile shortcuts, extensions and diversions.

In addition to the ninety-six routes described in detail, there is a chapter dedicated to long-distance routes suitable for cycle touring. There is also a chapter focussing on the Wild Atlantic Way, the 2,500 kilometre route that runs the length of the west coast.

The popularity of cycling in Ireland is growing at a huge rate, particularly since Covid, and every weekend the roads and trails are busy with cyclists. Currently, our infrastructure is lagging behind this demand, and it's only recently that 'the powers that be' have started to appreciate the benefits of cycling as a means of transport, recreation, exercise and as a tourist attraction. However, the future looks promising as there are plenty of plans for more signposted road routes, greenways and mountain bike trails.

Hopefully, this book will help visiting cyclists experience some of Ireland's best cycling and inspire locals to discover new and interesting routes across the country.

NOTES ON THE SECOND EDITION

This, the second edition of the guide, follows just over five years after the first, which was published in May 2018. The most significant update is the addition of sixteen new routes, evenly spread across the four provinces. There are also some more subtle changes including plenty of new photos, tweaks to the maps and the addition of photo captions.

The majority of the new routes are off-road, with six gravel, five mountain bike, four road and one greenway route.

Gravel, which was in its infancy in 2018, has gained a lot of traction in the last five years and is now established as a distinct discipline. Bridging the gap between road and mountain bikes, gravel bikes are ideally suited to Ireland's rough roads and enable varied routes that combine road sections with tracks and paths.

In the last few years a number of mountain trail centres have opened and many of the exiting ones have been significantly extended. Most of these centres now offer a wide range of trails for all abilities.

Unfortunately, the rate of development of new greenways has been slow. However, there are a number in the planning and construction phase so hopefully the third edition will include the Connemara Greenway, the South East Greenway and the South Kerry Greenway among others.

The west side of Ballaghbeama Gap in Kerry, part of the Tour of Iveragh, see page 128

ROUTE TABLE

REGION	COUNTY	NAME	DISTANCE	HEIGHT GAIN	SURFACE	PAGE
East	Louth	Cooley Mountains	42km	790m	Road	46
East	Meath	Boyne Valley	35km	300m	Road	48
East	Westmeath/Longford	Royal Canal—Old Rail Trail	99km	320m	Gravel	50
East	Offaly	Lough Boora	22km	60m	Gravel	52
East	Offaly/Laois	Slieve Blooms	37km	770m	Road	54
East	Offaly/Laois	Slieve Blooms Trail Centres	52km	1,090m	MTB	56
East	Various	The Royal—Grand Canal	111km	300m	Gravel	58
East	Various	The Grand Canal—Barrow	168km	600m	Gravel	60
East	Kildare	Grand Canal Feeder Loop	48km	100m	Gravel	62
East	Dublin	Phoenix Park	10km	100m	Road	64
East	Dublin	Dublin Bay	37km	500m	Road	66
East	Dublin	Ticknock Trail Centre	11km	330m	MTB	68
East	Wicklow	Belmont and Bray Head	11km	210m	MTB	70
East	Wicklow	Blessington Reservoir	36km	340m	Road	72
East	Wicklow	West Wicklow	37km	860m	Road	74
East	Wicklow	Kippure	38km	960m	Road	76
East	Wicklow	Ballinastoe Trail Centre	11km	280m	MTB	78
East	Wicklow	Roundwood and Sally Gap	41km	730m	Road	80
East	Wicklow	Wicklow Coast	32km	170m	Gravel	82
East	Wicklow	Derrybawn	20km	760m	Gravel	84
East	Wicklow	Lugnaquilla	72km	1,570m	Road	86
East	Wicklow	The Military Road	79km	1,670m	Road	88
East	Carlow/Wexford	Mount Leinster	43km	1,090m	Road	90
East	Kilkenny	East Kilkenny	63km	750m	Road	92
South	Waterford	Waterford Greenway	41km	550m	Road	98
South	Waterford/Tipperary	North Comeraghs	72km	720m	Road	100
South	Tipperary/Waterford	The Knockmealdowns	47km	670m	Road	102
South	Limerick/Cork	Ballyhoura Trail Centre	51km	930m	MTB	104
South	Cork	Boggeragh Mountains	42km	800m	Road/Gravel	106
South	Cork	Mizen Head	54km	870m	Road	108
South	Cork	Sheep's Head	68km	1,190m	Road	110
South	Cork/Kerry	Priest's Leap and Borlin	55km	1,170m	Road	112
South	Cork	Gougane Barra	31km	550m	Road	114
South	Cork	Glengarriff Woods	11km	210m	Road	116
South	Cork/Kerry	Healy and Caha Pass	69km	1,410m	Road	119
South	Cork/Kerry	The Ring of Beara	139km	2,120m	Road	120
South	Kerry	Muckross Lake	10km	130m	Road	122
South	Kerry	Killarney Lakes	55km	820m	Road	124
South	Kerry	The Ring of Kerry	170km	1,680m	Road	127
South	Kerry	Tour of Iveragh	207km	2,780m	Road	128
South	Kerry	The Ring of the Reeks	68km	1,000m	Road	130
South	Kerry	Slea Head	43km	580m	Road	132
South	Kerry	Dingle Peninsula	67km	1,080m	Road	134
South	Limerick/Kerry	Limerick Greenway	49km	220m	Road	136
South	Tipperary	Silvermines	31km	400m	Road/Gravel	138
South	Clare	Loop Head	65km	570m	Road	140
South	Clare	The Burren	45km	630m	Road	142
South	Clare	Black Head	46km	500m	Road	144

REGION	COUNTY	NAME	DISTANCE	HEIGHT GAIN	SURFACE	PAGE
West	Galway	Portumna Trails	15km	70m	Gravel	150
West	Galway	Inishmore	28km	300m	Gravel	152
West	Galway	Galway Wind Park	41km	550m	Gravel	154
West	Galway	Casla	17km	110m	Gravel	157
West	Galway	Oughterard	65km	600m	Road	158
West	Galway	Derroura Trail Centre	16km	160m	MTB	160
West	Galway	Maamturks	62km	660m	Road	162
West	Galway	Sky Road	15km	280m	Road	164
West	Galway	Inishbofin	16km	180m	Gravel	166
West	Galway/Mayo	Cong and Clonbur	19km	170m	Gravel	168
West	Mayo	Sheeffry Hills	52km	440m	Road	170
West	Mayo	Owenwee Bog	16km	270m	MTB	172
West	Mayo	Great Western Greenway	44km	260m	Road	175
West	Mayo	North Clew Bay	35km	380m	Gravel	176
West	Mayo	Achill Island	82km	1,600m	Road	178
West	Mayo	Cross Lake	8km	40m	Gravel	180
West	Mayo	Rathlacken and Sralagagh	30km	510m	Gravel	182
West	Sligo	Ox Mountains	35km	590m	Road	184
West	Sligo	Coolaney Trail Centre	22km	460m	MTB	186
West	Sligo/Leitrim	Lough Gill	39km	450m	Road	188
West	Sligo/Leitrim	Benbulbin	55km	690m	Road	190
West	Sligo	Mullaghmore and Gleniff	30km	370m	Road	192
West	Leitrim	Glenaniff	25km	480m	Road	194
West	Leitrim	Drumshanbo	38km	540m	Road	196
North	Cavan	Cavan Lakes	32km	220m	Road	202
North	Monaghan/Tyrone	Slieve Beagh	44km	700m	Road	204
North	Fermanagh	Scarplands Loop	42km	560m	Gravel	206
North	Fermanagh	Navar Forest	20km	340m	Gravel	208
North	Donegal	Glencolmcille	66km	1,120m	Road	210
North	Donegal	Errigal	39km	560m	Road	212
North	Donegal	Glenveagh	32km	400m	Gravel	214
North	Donegal/Derry	Inishowen	164	2,260m	Road	216
North	Tyrone	The Sperrins	51km	790m	Road	218
North	Tyrone	Gortin Glen Trail Centre	17km	610m	MTB	220
North	Tyrone	Davagh Forest Trail Centre	11km	290m	MTB	222
North	Derry	Slieve Gallion	41km	580m	Road	224
North	Derry	Binevenagh and Benone	26km	460m	Road/Gravel	226
North	Antrim/Derry	Causeway Coast	155km	1,720m	Road	228
North	Antrim	Torr Head and Glendun	58km	1,070m	Road	230
North	Down	Strangford Lough	130km	1,180m	Road	232
North	Down	Castlewellan Trail Centre	15km	320m	MTB	234
North	Down	Mourne Mountains	43km	660m	Road	236
North	Down	Rostrevor Trail Centre	25km	700m	MTB	238
North	Down	The Western Mournes	28km	510m	Road	240
North	Down/Armagh	Newry Canal	32km	80m	Road	242
North	Various	Lough Neagh	180km	1,030m	Road	244
North	Armagh	Ring of Gullion	13.5km	370m	Road	246
North	Armagh	Tassagh	35km	500m	Road	248

ROUTE MAP

EAST

01 Cooley Mountains
02 Boyne Valley
03 Royal Canal–Old Rail Trail
04 Lough Boora
05 Slieve Blooms
06 Slieve Blooms Trail Centre
07 The Royal–Grand Canal
08 The Grand Canal–Barrow
09 Grand Canal Feeder Loop
10 Phoenix Park
11 Dublin Bay
12 Ticknock Trail Centre
13 Belmont and Bray Head
14 Blessington Reservoir
15 West Wicklow
16 Kippure
17 Ballinastoe Trail Centre
18 Roundwood and Sally Gap
19 Wicklow Coast
20 Derrybawn
21 Lugnaquilla
22 The Military Road
23 Mount Leinster
24 East Kilkenny

SOUTH

25 Waterford Greenway
26 North Comeraghs
27 The Knockmealdowns
28 Ballyhoura Trail Centre
29 Boggeragh Mountains
30 Mizen Head
31 Sheep's Head
32 Priest's Leap and Borlin
33 Gougane Barra
34 Glengarriff Woods
35 Healy and Caha Pass
36 The Ring of Beara
37 Muckross Lake
38 Killarney Lakes
39 The Ring of Kerry
40 Tour of Iveragh
41 The Ring of the Reeks
42 Slea Head
43 Dingle Peninsula
44 Limerick Greenway
45 Silvermines
46 Loop Head
47 The Burren
48 Black Head

WEST

49 Portumna Trails
50 Inishmore
51 Galway Wind Park
52 Casla
53 Oughterard
54 Derroura Trail Centre
55 Maamturks
56 Sky Road
57 Inishbofin
58 Cong and Clonbur
59 Sheeffry Hills
60 Owenwee Bog
61 Great Western Greenway
62 North Clew Bay
63 Achill Island
64 Cross Lake
65 Rathlacken and Sralagagh
66 Ox Mountains
67 Coolaney Trail Centre
68 Lough Gill
69 Benbulbin
70 Mullaghmore and Gleniff
71 Glenaniff
72 Drumshanbo

NORTH

73 Cavan Lakes
74 Slieve Beagh
75 Scarplands Loop
76 Navar Forest
77 Glencolmcille
78 Errigal
79 Glenveagh
80 Inishowen
81 The Sperrins
82 Gortin Glen Trail Centre
83 Davagh Forest Trail Centre
84 Slieve Gallion
85 Binevenagh and Benone
86 Causeway Coast
87 Torr Head and Glendun
88 Strangford Lough
89 Castlewellan Trail Centre
90 Mourne Mountains
91 Rostrevor Trail Centre
92 The Western Mournes
93 Newry Canal
94 Lough Neagh
95 Ring of Gullion
96 Tassagh

Derry

Belfast

Armagh

Galway

Dublin

Limerick

Kilkenny

Waterford

Cork

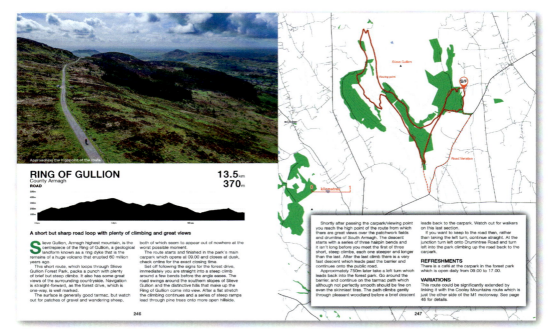

RING OF GULLION
County Armagh
ROAD

13.5 km
370 m

A short but sharp road loop with plenty of climbing and great views

Slieve Gullion, Armagh highest mountain, is the centrepiece of the Ring of Gullion, a geological landform known as a ring dyke that is the remains of a huge volcano that erupted 60 million years ago.

This short route, which loops through Slieve Gullion Forest Park, packs a punch with plenty of brief but sharp climbs. It also has some great views of the surrounding countryside. Navigation is straight-forward, as the forest drive, which is one-way, is well marked.

The surface is generally good tarmac, but watch out for patches of gravel and wandering sheep.

both of which seem to appear out of nowhere at the worst possible moment.

The route starts and finished in the park's main carpark which opens at 09.00 and closes at dusk, check online for the exact closing time.

Set off following the signs for the forest drive, immediately you are straight into a steep climb around a few bends before the angle eases. The road swings around the southern slopes of Slieve Gullion and the distinctive hills that make up the Ring of Gullion come into view. After a flat stretch the climbing continues and a series of steep ramps lead through pine trees onto more open hillside.

Shortly after passing the carpark/viewing point you reach the high point of the route from which there are great views over the patchwork fields and drumlins of South Armagh. The descent starts with a series of three hairpin bends and it isn't long before you meet the first of three short, steep climbs, each one steeper and longer than the last. After the last climb there is a very fast descent which leads past the barrier and continues onto the public road.

Approximately 750m later take a left turn which leads back into the forest park. Go around the barrier, and continue on the tarmac path which although not perfectly smooth should be fine on even the skinniest tires. The path climbs gently through pleasant woodland before a brief descent

leads back to the carpark. Watch out for walkers on this last section.

If you want to keep to the road then, rather than taking the left turn, continue straight. At the junction turn left onto Drumintree Road and turn left into the park climbing up the road back to the carpark.

REFRESHMENTS
There is a café at the carpark in the forest park which is open daily from 09.00 to 17.00.

VARIATIONS
This route could be significantly extended by linking it with the Cooley Mountains route which is just the other side of the M1 motorway. See page 46 for details.

246   247

HOW TO USE THIS BOOK

This book has been designed to be both a source for information for planning routes as well as actually following them. As such each route features a detailed map, a text overview of the route and, where practical, turn-by-turn directions. **GPX files for all of the routes in this book can be downloaded from threerockbooks.com/cycling.**

There are three approaches you can use to follow the routes in this book:

- Photocopy or photograph the relevant pages and print a copy to carry this with you or even pack the book in a pannier or rucksack.
- Take a photo of the relevant pages and refer to it on your phone.
- Download the route's GPX file onto your phone or GPS and use an app to navigate (see page 14 for more information about the various apps).

THE REGIONS

The book's 96 routes have been divided equally between the four regions: east, south, west and north. These correspond to the provinces of Leinster, Munster, Connacht and Ulster.

ROAD, GRAVEL OR MTB

Each route has been classified (see page 8) as either road, road/gravel, gravel or MTB.

A road route is one that is entirely on-road, but may also include well-surfaced bike paths or greenways. They are best suited to a road or hybrid bike with relatively narrow tyres.

Road/gravel routes feature rough roads and/or short sections of relatively gentle gravel. They should be manageable on most road bikes.

A gravel route features a significant portion of gravel tracks that are best suited to a gravel bike or a hybrid with wider tyres. These routes don't include technical terrain where the wider tires, lower gears and suspension of a MTB would be helpful.

A MTB route features rough, technical terrain that is only suitable for a mountain bike. The majority of the MTB routes in this book are found in trail centres which usually have a number of purpose-built trails with a range of difficulty.

Obviously these classifications are highly subjective and only serve as a rough guideline. It's a fine line between a challenging gravel route and a straightforward MTB route, largely dependant on the rider's skill and attitude.

The route descriptions contain more detail on the appropriate bike and will help you decide if a route is suitable for your skill level and bike.

THE ROUTES

Each route has a profile, text description and map. Generally, the given distance is very accurate, however, the height gain is derived from the map rather that measured on the route which means that the actual height gain can be up to 10% more.

The route profile shows the relief of the route with the distance (in kilometres) on the x-axis and the height (in metres) on the y-axis.

The description gives a general flavour of the route, mentioning points of interest, advising on bike choice, ground conditions and details of any notable shortcuts, extensions or variations. It also mentions where you can stop en-route or nearby for refreshments.

The maps are sufficiently detailed to use for navigation. The scale varies, it is marked on each map. The maps are oriented so that north is at the top of the page and the contour interval is 20m.

Most routes also have turn-by-turn directions. However, they have been omitted if the route is well signposted or very complicated. The more complicated routes (generally the gravel routes) are ideally suited to navigating using phone guidance.

While most routes can be ridden in either direction they has been described in the 'best' direction. This is determined by taking into account the topography and prevailing wind, as well as trying to get the harder climbs out of the way earlier.

The majority of the routes are loops, but there are also a few linear routes, many of which can be accessed by public transport. See page 34 for information on public transport.

MAPS

Even in this digital age paper maps still have an important role in planning and as backups. Consulting a large-scale map is still the best way to get the broad sense of a place and to make the initial decisions about how to approach a trip.

Ordnance Survey Ireland (osi.ie) and the Ordnance Survey of Northern Ireland (nidirect.gov.uk/OSNI) publish maps designed for tourists and recreational users in scales from 1:25,000 to 1:250,000.

Northern Ireland is covered by four (numbers 49, 50, 51, 52) cycling-specific maps at a scale of 1:110,000. They are produced by Sustrans, the sustainable transport charity, who also publish guides to a number of long-distance routes including the Sperrin Mountains (page 218), the Strangford Lough Cycle Trail (page 232), the North West Trail (page 251) and the Kingfisher Trail (page 252). These maps and guides are available online from sustrans.org.uk.

In the Republic the west coast is covered by a series of 1:100,000 maps published by Xploreit Maps (xploreit.ie) which contain plenty of useful information for the touring cyclist.

NAVIGATING BY PHONE

As most cyclists own a phone and carry it when cycling it makes sense to use it to navigate. And while some riders prefer a standalone GPS, the main advantage being longer battery life, for most people a phone is sufficient.

Loading a GPX file of a route into an app that offers turn-by-turn voice guidance means that you can get sit back and enjoy the ride without having to worry about navigating.

EXTENDING BATTERY LIFE
Setting your phone to flight mode (also known as airplane mode) will significantly conserve battery life. Lowering the screen brightness and turning off any apps running in the background will also help.

Remember to download the relevant maps and GPX files and fully charge your phone before you set off.

On longer rides it might be worth carrying a power pack. Be sure to keep some battery power in reserve in case of an emergency.

GPX
A GPX (GPs eXchange Format) is a digital file that describes a route as a sequence of longitude and latitude coordinates. They are compatible with most map applications so it's just a matter of loading a route's GPX file onto your phone or GPS and following the turn-by-turn directions.

To download the GPX files for the routes in this book visit threerockbooks.com/cycling. You will also find links to the routes on Strava and Komoot.

APPS
There are plenty of navigation apps, including Google Maps, Komoot, MapMyRide, OsmAnd, OutdoorActive (formerly ViewRanger) and Strava.

Performance-orientated cyclists might favour Strava while those more interested in touring, bikepacking and off-road riding might find Komoot a better fit. However, the best option in the author's opinion is OsmAnd, see the following page for more information.

BACKUPS
Obviously phones aren't 100% reliable, batteries can die etc. so it's a good idea to take a paper backup, particularly if you are following a remote route or one you are unfamiliar with.

OSMAND

OsmAnd has a number of advantages over the other apps: it is available for free for both Android and iOS, its open source maps contain excellent detail and it offers voice guidance.

Another major advantage is that it's possible to download a detailed map of the entire country when you install the app. This means that you can use your phone in flight mode, which will ensure the battery lasts a lot longer and don't have to rely on having a signal while you are on the ride.

Note the app is free but there is a small, once-off fee to download the contour information which is worth paying.

Once a GPX file is loaded into the app it's possible to follow the route using turn-by-turn audio directions. This is very convenient as you don't need to refer to the screen and can keep your phone in a pocket or bag.

INSTALLING THE APP

- Open the Apple App Store or the Google Play Store.
- Type in 'osmand' in the search bar at the top.
- Click on 'OsmAnd - Maps & GPS Offline' or 'OsmAnd Maps Travel & Navigate' (the icon is an orange doughnut).
- Click on 'Install' or 'Get'.

DOWNLOAD THE MAPS

Once the app is installed you need to download the maps so that they are available when your phone is offline. As the file is large (287MB) this should be done when connected to WiFi.

- Open OsmAnd.
- Click on the box in the bottom left corner.
- Click on 'Download maps' or 'Maps & Resources'.
- Click 'Europe' then 'Ireland' and select 'Standard map' or 'Map'.

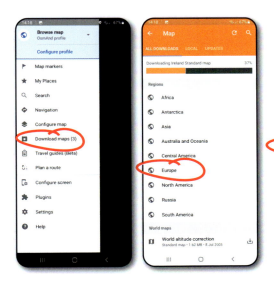

LOADING A GPX FILE

- Point your phone's browser at threerockbooks.com/cycling.
- Locate the route you are interested in and click the link to the GPX file. Click 'Download'.

FOLLOWING A ROUTE

- Go to your phone's download folder and click the file, it should then open in OsmAnd.
- In OsmAnd click on the box with the diamond shape and arrow on it.
- Click 'Start'.

ROAD CYCLING

Irish roads aren't known for the quality of their surfaces. Generally the only roads in Ireland with a really good surface are the busy main roads which aren't ideal for cycling.

A large proportion of Ireland's roads are boreens. These narrow roads are only wide enough for one car and typically have a strip of grass (or gravel or mud) running along the middle. Many are little more than tracks or laneways with little to no traffic. They are the perfect way to travel through the Irish countryside and the routes in this book follow them whenever possible.

RULES OF THE ROAD

If you are visiting from another country or haven't cycled in recent years then it might be worth familiarising yourself with the rules of the road. Cycling Ireland have produced a detailed document that outlines all aspects of cyclist behaviour, ranging from the Rules of the Road to advice on riding in a group. It can be downloaded from cyclingireland.ie/downloads/cyclingonroads.pdf.

ROAD NETWORK

In the Republic roads are identified by a letter followed by a number. Motorways are prefixed with M (cycling isn't permitted on motorways), national roads with N, regional roads with R and local roads with L. Local roads can vary hugely in quality, generally the more digits in the number the narrower and rougher they are.

In Northern Ireland motorways are also prefixed by M while other roads have a prefix of A,B or C (in descending order of importance).

Distances and speed limits in Northern Ireland are measured in miles while in the Republic kilometres are used (10km is 6.2 miles). The metric system is used throughout this book to avoid confusion.

Signposts in the Republic are in English as well as Irish, however in Gaeltacht (Irish-speaking) regions they may only be in Irish.

THE NATIONAL CYCLE NETWORK

Northern Ireland has a network of signposted cycle routes that form part of the UK-wide National Cycle Network. Designed for both commuters and leisure cyclists most of the routes are on-road with the exception of some urban areas with cycle paths or greenways.

The numbered routes connect major cities and towns. The North West Trail (page 251), the Kingfisher Trail (page 252), the Ballyshannon to Belfast (page 253) and the Ballyshannon to Larne (page 253) all follow sections of the NCN. For more details see sustrans.org.uk.

SPORTIVES

Sportives are organised, mass participation road rides that range in difficulty from shorter (50km), flatter events, suitable for the occasional cyclist, to the toughest events that combine long distances (up to about 200km) with massive amounts of climbing. The routes are designed to showcase an area's best riding, so sportives are a great way to discover new parts of the country.

Even through participants are usually timed, sportives are a personal challenge, not a race. Many cyclists use a sportive as a focus for their training, gradually building their endurance on their weekend rides.

In the last few years sportives have become very popular and there is normally at least one every weekend between March and September.

Usually the roads are open to other traffic during a sportive, but the route will be signposted and marshalled. There will be food and water stations and finishers may receive a memento such as a jersey or medal.

AUDAX

An audax is a long-distance event in which riders try to complete a long, tough route within a specified time. The time limits are reasonably generous, based on an average speed of 15km/h. The distances range from 200km up to multi-day events of 1,000km or more. For more information see audaxireland.org.

Mamore Gap, Donegal, see page 216

GRAVEL

Since the first edition of this book 'gravel' has emerged as a popular and distinct form of cycling. This edition contains over twenty routes in this style.

Gravel is best described as occupying the space between road riding and mountain biking. Usually gravel routes feature a variety of terrain such as forest roads, canal towpaths, double-track, laneways and easy singletrack and as well as some road. These routes aren't necessarily 100% off-road, and that in a way is the point, gravel bikes are equally at home on smooth tarmac and rough tracks.

Ultimately, the distinction between gravel and mountain biking is subjective, entirely dependant on the rider's bike and their skills.

A large part of the lure of gravel is exploring new areas and discovering new routes; getting away from busy roads is an added attraction. Gravel also offers somewhat technical riding without the extreme difficulty and risk of hardcore mountain biking.

Ireland has a vast network of local roads and boreens that possibly would be considered tracks in other countries. These quiet backroads, characterised by the grass strip that grows along the middle, can be combined with tracks and paths to create excellent gravel routes.

In the Republic the semi-state forestry company Coillte is the largest landowner, owning 7% of the country. These forests have a network of over 8000km of forest roads, built to allow access for harvesting timber, but also ideal for gravel riding.

Unfortunately, Coillte currently prohibits cycling outside of a relatively small number of designated areas. As a result it hasn't been possible to include as many gravel routes in this edition as I would have liked.

Hopefully, in the future Coillte will grant wider access to our forest roads and it will be possible to include significantly more gravel routes in the next edition.

The Slieve Aughty mountains in County Clare/Galway

Gortin Glen in Tyrone, see page 220

MOUNTAIN BIKING

The Irish landscape is well suited to off-road cycling in all its forms, from gentle spins along grassy towpaths to epic days in the mountains.

TERMINOLOGY

Sometimes the term off-road is used to describe cycle paths or greenways that are segregated from other traffic. In this book they are referred to as traffic-free, and the term off-road is reserved for unpaved tracks (such as towpaths or gravel roads). This book also makes a distinction between cycling off-road and mountain biking which is defined as more technical riding on rough tracks or singletrack.

MOUNTAIN BIKE TRAILS

The number of unsanctioned mountain bike trails, built by local riders for their own enjoyment, dwarfs that of official trails (page 23). These unofficial trails aren't documented due to the fear that publicising them they will attract the landowner's ire. This makes it very difficult for mountain bikers who are new to the sport or an area to find the best trails. Local knowledge is key, befriending other riders or joining a club are both good options. Failing that it's just a matter of getting out there and exploring.

FAT BIKING

A fat bike can go places a normal mountain bike cannot thanks to the incredible traction and flotation created by their wide (four inches or more) tyres. They are perfect for sand and soft, boggy ground. Although still a rare sight in Ireland they could become more common when people realise how well suited they are to Irish terrain and conditions.

If you want to give fat biking a go you can hire one from Fatbike Adventures (fatbikeadventures.ie) in Wicklow.

ACCESS

Unfortunately there is no legal right of access to the Irish countryside. All land in Ireland is in private or state ownership and those who enter onto land owned by others, for the purpose of recreation, do so thanks to the goodwill and tolerance of landowners.

Ideally you should seek permission before crossing land, however, in many cases, particularly in the uplands, this isn't practical.

For the most part this leaves cyclists in the same position as walkers with a few important exceptions. Coillte, the state forestry company, only permits cycling on designated cycling trails (page 23) and in our National Parks and Nature Reserves cycling is only permitted on gravel roads and tracks.

In practical terms there shouldn't be a problem sharing tracks and trails if cyclists behave appropriately and show respect for other users.

Finally, remember that a degree of risk is inherent in all outdoor activities including cycling and recreational users should be aware of and accept these risks, taking responsibility for their own actions.

BEHAVIOUR

In order to improve the access situation in Ireland it's vital that mountain bikers show respect for the environment and other trail users. The following suggestions are based on the International Mountain Bike Association (imba-europe.org) rules of the trail.

RESPECT THE LANDSCAPE

The soft ground of the Irish uplands is very sensitive to erosion, particularly in wet conditions. When the trail is soft, consider other riding options. Stay on existing trails and don't create new ones. Don't cut switchbacks and ride (or walk) technical features rather than going around them.

SHARE THE TRAIL

Mountain bikers should yield to horses and foot traffic. Descending riders should yield to climbing riders, unless the trail is clearly signposted as one-way or downhill-only.

RIDE OPEN, LEGAL TRAILS

Respect trail and road closures. Do not trespass on private land. Obtain permits or other authorisation as required.

RIDE IN CONTROL

If you need to pass another trail user, slow down, ring a bell or call out, and wait until they are out of the path. Be particularly careful on trails with poor sight lines or blind corners. Make sure that you can hear what's going on around you and ride within your limits.

DERRY

Garvagh Forest

Davagh Forest

Gortin Glen

Barnett Demesne

BELFAST

Craigavon Lakes

Blessingbourne

Stramore Park

Castle Ward

ARMAGH

Castlewellan

Tollymore

Coolaney

Rostrevor

Derroura

GALWAY

Ticknock

DUBLIN

Glencullen Adventure Park

Portunma

Ballinastoe

Slieve
Blooms

LIMERICK

KILKENNY

Ballyhoura

WATERFORD

CORK

0   Kilometres   100

PLAN AHEAD

Every mountain biker should carry everything they need for the ride they're undertaking, and know how to fix a puncture and make minor repairs. Download a GPS app onto your phone for navigation or carry a map when in unfamiliar locations. It's safer to mountain bike with a partner, but if you're heading out alone let someone know where you are going.

MIND THE ANIMALS

Animals are easily startled by an unannounced approach, a sudden movement or a loud noise. Give them plenty of room and time to adjust to you. When passing horses, take extra care and follow directions from the horseback riders (ask if uncertain).

TRAIL CENTRES

There are a small, but growing, number of purpose-built mountain bike trail centres spread across the island, north and south. The larger ones have a number of signposted trails of varying difficulty, as well as facilities such as showers, bike hire, café etc while the smaller centres may just have a single trail.

The trails are built with a quick-draining gravel base so that they can be ridden year-round. Many of them include man-made features such as rollers, berms (banked turns), rock gardens and, on the more advanced trails, jumps and drops.

GRADES

Trail centres assigned each trail a grade so that riders can choose the most suitable trail for their ability. Here is the most widely used system listed in order of difficulty:

- Green/Easy: suitable for total beginners and families. A hybrid will suffice on these relatively wide and flat trails.
- Blue/Moderate: suitable for intermediate riders. Expect plenty of singletrack and small obstacles.
- Red/Difficult: for proficient riders with good off-road skills. There will be lots of steep singletrack with plenty of challenging trail features.
- Black/Severe: for expert riders. Very steep trails with extremely challenging features.
- Orange/Extreme: for elite riders. Featuring huge jumps.

Note that grading can differ somewhat between trail centres, so choose cautiously. See mountainbikeni.com for more information.

NORTHERN IRELAND

Northern Ireland has a good number of trail centres of varying sizes located on private estates as well as on Forest Service and Council land. The three largest centres are of the highest quality. As they are reasonably close together, it's possible to ride them all in a weekend.

- Davagh Forest, Tyrone (page 222)
- Castlewellan, Down (page 234)
- Rostrevor, Down (page 238)

There are four regional trail centres that cater for beginner and intermediate riders:

- Blessingbourne, Tyrone (page 201)
- Barnett Demesne, Antrim (page 201)
- Castle Ward, Down (page 201)
- Garvagh Forest Park, Derry (page 201)
- Gortin Glen, Tyrone (page 220)

There are also a few other smaller facilities including:

- Tollymore skills course, Down (page 201)
- Stramore Park pump track, Down
- Craigavon Lakes mountain bike trail, Armagh (page 201)

For more information about mountain biking in Northern Ireland see mountainbikeni.com.

REPUBLIC OF IRELAND

The seven trail centres in the Republic are all on land owned by Coillte, the state forestry company.

- Slieve Blooms, Laois/Offaly (page 56)
- Ticknock, Dublin (page 68)
- Ballinastoe, Wicklow (page 78)
- Ballyhoura, Limerick (page 104)
- Portumna Forest Park, Galway (page 149)
- Derroura, Galway (page 160)
- Coolaney, Sligo (page 186)

There is currently one commercial mountain bike centre in the Republic, Glencullen Adventure Park in the Dublin Mountains (thegap.ie). It is more gravity focused than the trail centres with a number of relatively short downhill trails catering for all abilities. They also offer an uplift service in which a truck shuttles riders to the top of the hill regularly throughout the day.

DERRY

Ballyshannon
Cycle Hub

BELFAST
The Lagan and Lough
Cycleway

ARMAGH

Newry Canal

Belmullet
Cycle Hub

Achill Island
Cycle Hub

Great Western
Greenway

Louisburg
Cycle Hub

Westport
Cycle Hub

Cliden
Cycle Hub

Royal Canal

Mullingar
Cycle Hub

DUBLIN

Old Rail Trail

Dublin Bay

GALWAY

Doolin
Cycle Hub

Birr
Cycle Hub

Nenagh
Cycle Hub

Trail Kilkenny

LIMERICK

KILKENNY

Kilmallock
Cycle Hub

Limerick
Greenway

Wexford
Cycle Hub

Waterford
Greenway

WATERFORD

Dungarvan
Cycle Hub

CORK

Skibbereen
Cycle Hub

0   Kilometres   100

CYCLE HUBS

There are 15 cycle hubs spread across the country. Each hub consists of a number of signposted routes, the vast majority of these are loops, but there are also a few linear routes. The distances vary between 8km and 160km with most in the 30-50km range.

Generally the routes avoid busy roads but there are places when this isn't possible.

The routes are signposted in both directions by white signs with a blue border, a bicycle symbol and the relevant route number/s (see the photo on the following page).

Details of all the following routes including maps can be found at sportireland.ie/outdoors.

BALLYSHANNON
The town of Ballyshannon in the south of County Donegal has two routes.

The 39km Loop 1 heads west along the northern shore of Assaroe Lake before cutting cross country to Rossnowlagh. After cycling the length of the vast sandy beach the route returns to Ballyshannon along the coast road.

The 36km Loop 2 also follows the northern shore of Assaroe Lake before heading south and crossing the River Erne at Belleek. Continuing south it crosses the border a number of times before arriving at Lough Melvin. After following its shore west the route passes through the seaside town of Bundoran and the busy R267 leads back into Ballyshannon.

BELMULLET
The town of Belmullet, which occupies the thin strip of land that links the Erris Peninsula with the mainland, has two linear and two looped routes.

The 49km North Mayo Linear Route takes a direct route along the busy R314 that connects Belmullet and Ballycastle. A better option is the quieter 72km Rossport and Glinsk Linear Route, which includes a short loop around Rossport and follows some very scenic roads between Rossport and Belderg.

The Carrowmore Lake Loop is a gentle 37km circuit that follows the western shore of Carrowmore Lake.

The 50km Pullathomas Loop is a fairly flat route that follows the coast east with views over Broadhaven and Sruwaddacon Bay before meeting the R314 and following it back to Belmullet.

ACHILL ISLAND
The three routes on Achill Island start and finish in the village of Keel. Take care on the R319, the main road across the island, as it can be busy.

Loop 1 follows the coast around the southern end of the island. The 44km route is generally flat but has a few short steep sections. It's possible to take a shortcut at Ashleam.

The 28km Loop 2 follows quiet backroads north to Doogort, passing Silver Strand and Golden Strand, ideal places to stop for a swim, before returning along the main road.

Loop 3 is a short (12km) variation of the previous route. The deserted village is worth the short detour.

The three loops have been combined to create the route that is described in detail on page 178.

WESTPORT
Westport is home to three routes, a short linear trail and the Great Western Greenway (page 175).

The 24km Loop 1 does a circuit around the countryside north of the town.

Loop 2 is 14km and follows the coast road south before turning north and looping around the outskirts of the town.

Loop 3 is a shorter (8km) variation of the previous route that skips the northern section by following the Greenway.

The National Coastal Trail is a 9.2km cycle path that links Westport with the village of Murrisk at the foot of Croagh Patrick.

LOUISBURGH
The village of Louisburgh near the southern shore of Clew Bay has three routes.

The 19km Loop 1 heads west to Roonagh Pier, where the boat sails for Clare Island and Inishturk, before returning along a more inland route.

Loop 2 is a short (7km) route around Louisburgh, passing Turlin Strand.

Loop 3 is a more challenging 26km route through the Sheeffry Hills. With plenty of mountain scenery and quiet roads, there are even two streams to ford! It shares ground with the route on page 170.

CLIFDEN
Clifden, the capital of Connemara, has four routes.

The 16km Loop 1 takes in the Sky Road. A better variation of this route is described on page 164.

Loop 2, the 14km Errislannan Loop, heads south from Clifden and loops around the Errislannan Peninsula. En route you pass near the site of Alcock and Brown's crash landing after the first transatlantic flight. Watch out for the stretch of winding, narrow road just after Ardbear bridge.

The 33km Loop 3 heads north from Clifden passing the beautiful Omey Island, which you can cycle out to at low tide, and a number of other nice beaches as it loops around the headland. Shortly after passing through Cleggan the road climbs to meet the busy N59 which leads back to town.

Loop 4 is a 40km lap around Roundstone Bog, passing through Ballyconneely and the beautiful village of Roundstone before returning through the heart of the bog via the Old Bog Road.

DOOLIN

The busy tourist village of Doolin has four signposted routes.

Loop 1 is essentially a shorter (18km) variation of Loop 2. It heads south from Doolin towards the Cliffs of Moher before cutting inland and returning to Doolin.

Loop 2 is a 39km figure of eight that passes through the villages of Liscannor, Lahinch and Ennistymon.

The 43km Loop 3 heads inland through Kilfenora, passing Poulnabrone Dolmen before returning via Lisdoonvarna.

Loop 4 is another figure of eight. The 47km route heads north from Doolin climbing into the hills with spectacular views of the Aran Islands. It then descends to the coast before climbing through Caher Valley to Lisdoonvarna. This route shares some ground with the route described on page 144.

MULLINGAR

The town of Mullingar in the Midlands has three routes.

The 30km Loop 1 heads north from the town around Lough Owel. The roads are quiet with the exception of a stretch along the extremely busy N4.

The 49km Loop 2 follows Loop 1 northwest out of Mullingar before turning south and crossing the Royal Canal at Dolan Bridge. It then meets Loop 3 and follows it north into Mullingar.

The 30km Loop 3 does a circuit of Lough Ennell. En route it passes Lilliput, which was believed to be the inspiration for Swift's Gulliver's Travels, and Belvedere House.

BIRR

The town of Birr in County Offaly is home to five routes and a number of variations.

Loop 1 and 2 are short, traffic-free routes around Lough Boora Park. Both are part of the route described on page 52.

Loop 3 follows a 73km circuit around the countryside north of Birr. It passes through Banagher, Lough Boora Park and the village of Kinnitty on the edge of the Slieve Blooms. There are two variations: Loop 3A (16km) and Loop 3B (44km).

Loop 4 heads south on some busy roads to the outskirts of Roscrea before returning along the edge of the Slieve Blooms. Loop 4A is a slightly more direct variation (30km).

Loop 5 is a 49km figure of eight that passes through Banagher and Shannon Harbour. The 13km Loop 5A is based out of the village of Cloghan.

The 39km Loop 7 (there isn't a Loop 6) starts in Shinrone to the south of Birr and passes through the famous village of Moneygall.

Just to the north is the Pilgrim's Road. This 24km linear route links Ballycumber to the monastic site of Clonmacnoise following the crest of an esker, a ridge of sand and gravel that was formed by glaciers during the last ice age.

NENAGH
The town of Nenagh is a hub for three routes with a number of variations.

The 65km Loop 1 heads north along the eastern shores of Lough Derg passing through the lakeside villages of Dromineer and Terryglass before returning via Borrisokane. There are three shorter variations: 1A (11km), 1B (28km) and 1C (46km).

The 30km Loop 2 follows a network of leafy boreens along the shore of Lough Derg.

Loop 3 is a relatively flat 67km cycle that passes through Cloughjordan, Ireland's first ecovillage, before returning to Nenagh along quiet inland roads. Loop 3A is a shorter (46km) variation.

KILKENNY CITY
Kilkenny City has four routes. Detailed maps of them all can be downloaded from trailkilkenny.ie.

The 27km North Kilkenny Cycle Loop follows the River Nore north out of Kilkenny, passing Jenkinstown Park and Dunmore Caves before turning south to make its way back to the city.

The 82km North Kilkenny Cycle Route loops around the countryside northwest of the city. The best starting point is probably Castlecomer on the N78 north of Kilkenny.

The 41km South Kilkenny Cycle Loop follows the busy N10 south for some distance before following quieter roads back through the villages of Kells and Bennettsbridge.

The 63km East Kilkenny Cycle Route is described in detail on page 92.

WEXFORD TOWN
Wexford Town has three routes.

Loop 1 is the 53km Slaney Route. It follows the River Slaney north to Enniscorthy before turning south passing through Castlebridge and following the R741 back to the town.

Loop 2 also heads north to Castlebridge but veers east to Blackwater before turning south and following the coast past Curracloe beach and the Wexford Slobs, an important wildfowl reserve.

Loop 3 is a 78km loop around south Wexford with diversions to Rosslare village, Rosslare Harbour and the fishing village of Kilmore Quay.

DUNGARVAN
Dungarvan is home to four cycling routes as well as the Waterford Greenway (page 98) which links Dungarvan to Waterford City. Two of the routes tip their hat to the local cycling legend Sean Kelly. A native of Carrick-on-Suir, it was on the steep climbs of the Comeragh Mountains that Kelly laid the foundations for his amazing career.

The longest and hardest of the four routes is the 160km Kelly Comeragh Challenge. It takes in every hill worth climbing in the area and is a serious undertaking. The route on page 100 follows its northern section.

The Kelly Legacy is a 105km loop around the Comeraghs that avoids the worst of the climbing.

The 99km Heritage Route follows the coast southwest passing through Youghal before returning inland along the foot of the Knockmealdowns.

The Coastal Route is a 73km linear route that follows the Copper Coast from Dungarvan to Passage East near Waterford City.

The last route is the 13km Railway Loop which follows quiet roads along Dungarvan Bay.

KILMALLOCK
Kilmallock in County Limerick has four loops with a number of variations.

Loop 1 is a 70km circuit of the Ballyhoura Mountains. There is a tough climb over the pass between Glenosheen and Glenanaar. Loop 1A is a 22km variation.

The 83km Loop 2 heads east to the Glen of Aherlow. It's quite a hilly route with a very steep climb through the Glen of Aherlow. There are a number of shorter variations: Loop 2A (16km), Loop 2B: (41km), Loop 2C (64km).

Loop 3 is a 62km loop through the countryside north of Kilmallock. The route is generally quite flat but there are a few short but steep climbs between Lough Gur and Knockainey.

Loop 4 is a 50km spin around the pleasant wooded hills south of Kilfinnane. Much of it follows sections of Loop 1 and 2.

SKIBBEREEN
Skibbereen in County Cork is a hub for three routes.

The 24km Loop 1 explores the headlands and promontories south of the town.

The 35km Loop 2 combines a circuit with a long out and back section from Lough Hyne to the fishing village of Baltimore.

The 46km Loop 3 heads north looping around Mount Kid. It has some tough climbs but also some magnificent views across Roaringwater Bay.

Portumna Forest Park, Galway, see page 150

FAMILY CYCLING

Cycling is a great family activity and Ireland has a growing number of greenways (page 31) and other dedicated cycling trails that are ideal for young cyclists.

WHERE TO CYCLE?

Probably the best place for a child to safely develop their skills is a quiet park. Then, once they have mastered the basics, they can venture onto greenways and other traffic-free paths.

Many public parks allow cycling on their paths and some also have segregated cycling and walking routes. You should check if cycling is allowed before cycling in a public park.

For children that are too small to cycle themselves options include baby seats, trailers and tow bars. These are often available to hire from bike shops.

At the start of each region in the book there is a list of suitable cycling areas for children including parks, forests, and purpose-built trails.

- East, page 45
- South, page 97
- West, page 149
- North, page 201

SAFETY

There are a few important points to take into consideration when planning a cycle with your family:

- Everyone should wear a helmet and bright clothing.
- If you are out after dark make sure everyone has front and rear lights.
- Check that the children's bikes are suitable for their size and ability.
- Children should only cycle on the road when they are old enough to understand the rules of the road and can fully control their bike.
- If cycling with young or inexperienced cyclists keep to traffic-free tracks or very quiet country roads.
- Plan a route that is suitable for everyone in the group. Small children may struggle on steep hills so they are best avoided. Make sure that the route isn't too long and allow plenty of time for breaks, maybe include a stop at a playground for a picnic.

Carlingford Greenway, see page 46

GREENWAYS

There are a number of trails designated for shared use by cyclists and walkers, known as greenways, spread across the country. These traffic-free trails are very safe and ideal for families and small kids. The surfaces vary, some are fine gravel while others are smooth tarmac, and as most follow disused railway lines they tend to be very flat.

There are also a number of similar routes along the waterways known as Blueways (see page 32 for more information).

When using a greenway bear in mind that they are multi-use. Make sure you use your bell when overtaking, keep to a reasonable speed and watch out for children and dogs.

The following is a list of the longer greenways (see the map on page 24).

THE LAGAN AND LOUGH CYCLEWAY
The 34km cycleway runs south from Jordanstown along the western shore of Belfast Lough, through Belfast City and along the bank of the River Lagan to Lisburn.

THE NEWRY CANAL
This 32km route follows the towpath that runs alongside the canal between Newry and Portadown. The route is described in detail on page 242.

GREAT WESTERN GREENWAY
Ireland's flagship Greenway runs for 45km between Westport and Achill Island. See page 175 for more information.

CONNEMARA GREENWAY
Ultimately a 76km route will connect Galway City with Clifden. However, there are currently only two short sections in place. The first is near Ballynahinch and runs for 6km between Ballinafad (53.4559, -9.8143) and the Owenwee River (53.4542, -9.8675). A second stretch runs west from Clifden for 3.5km.

ROYAL CANAL
The 144km canal connects Dublin City with the River Shannon in Longford. For more details about the canals see page 32.

OLD RAIL TRAIL
The 40km Old Rail Trail follows the course of the Midland Great Western Railway between Athlone and Mullingar. See page 50 for a route that combines it with the Royal Canal.

BOYNE VALLEY TO LAKELANDS GREENWAY
Ultimately, this 30km greenway will link Navan in County Meath with Kingscourt in County Cavan. At the time of writing the 14.9km stretch between Navan and Nobber has been finished. There are also plans for the Boyne Greenway which will run east from Navan to Drogheda. Currently a 4km stretch is in place which links Drogheda with Battle of the Boyne Visitor Centre.

DUBLIN BAY
There is a large network of cycle paths and lanes in Dublin but most will only be of interest to commuters. The exception is the cycleway being developed along Dublin Bay between Sandycove and Sutton. Many sections are in place and work is ongoing. For more information see page 66.

TRALEE TO FENIT GREENWAY
This greenway runs west from Tralee Train Station for 13.6km to the seaside village of Fenit. The flat, traffic-free route have great views south across Tralee Bay to the mountains of the Dingle Peninsula. There are plans to extend the greenway to Listowel where it will join the North Kerry Greenway (see page 136). For more information see traleefenitgreenway.com.

WATERFORD GREENWAY
This 46km greenway links Dungarvan and Waterford City. See page 98 for details.

Work is ongoing on the South East (Kilkenny) Greenway which will start in New Ross and run south for 24km to meet the Waterford Greenway. There are also plans to connect St Mullins with the Waterford Greenway which will create a traffic-free cycle route between Dublin and Waterford City.

CORK GREENWAYS
There is great scope for a greenway that would run from Inniscarra Dam following the River Lee into and through Cork City and then along the shore of the harbour. Currently there are only a few disconnected sections of the route in place. Keep an eye on lee2sea.com for further developments.

To the west of the city is the Coachford Greenway runs for 5.6km along the north shore of Lough Inniscarra.

Carrigaline to Crosshaven Greenway is a 5km route that runs west from Carrigaline alongside the Owenabue River to Cork Harbour.

THE CANALS

Ireland has an extensive network of canals and waterways that were, in the era before trains, an important means of transporting goods.

The adjacent towpaths are ideal for cyclists as they are quiet, traffic-free, flat and pass through interesting countryside. They are suitable for both short spins and longer tours. Many of the towns that the canals pass through are served by train (and bus) so it's possible to cycle one direction and return by public transport.

The three waterways (the Royal Canal, Grand Canal and the Barrow Navigation) that have towpaths along their full length are of particular interest to the cyclist. All three are National Waymarked routes and you can download detailed maps of the Royal Canal Way, Grand Canal Way and Barrow Way from sportireland.ie/outdoors.

There is work ongoing to improve the surfaces of the towpaths so you may encounter sections of grass and mud between improved surfaces of gravel and tarmac. Currently the three waterways are rideable, if a little rough or muddy in places, on any bike with reasonably wide tyres (more than 35mm). A narrower tyre will struggle on the rougher sections particularly after wet weather. Inevitably the towpaths will all be paved, opening access for road bikes, but for the moment they retain a wild, unmanicured feel.

There is often maintenance work ongoing, particularly in winter, that may require the closure of short sections of the towpaths, however detouring around any works is usually straightforward. Check the Waterways Ireland website before setting off waterwaysireland.org.

In Northern Ireland there are a number of short stretches of towpath but the only long route is the Newry Canal which is described on page 242.

THE ROYAL CANAL

The 147km route that connects Dublin City with the River Shannon in Longford is the most developed of the three waterways. The majority of the towpath is surfaced with unbound stone but there are a few sections of grass. However it won't be long before the entire towpath is surfaced, see royalcanalgreenway.ie. See page 50 for a details of a route that links the Royal Canal with the Old Rail Trail. The Royal Canal forms part of EuroVelo 2 which traverses the continent from Moscow to Galway City, see page 255 for more information.

GRAND CANAL

The 132km Grand Canal is the southernmost of the two canals that connect Dublin with the River Shannon. It has a quieter, remoter feel than the Royal. The surface of the towpath is also less developed with longer, more frequent stretches of rough ground. See page 58 for a route that links the Royal and Grand Canals.

BARROW NAVIGATION

The 115km Barrow Navigation starts at the Grand Canal in Kildare before joining the River Barrow at Monasterevin and following it south to St. Mullins in Carlow where the river becomes tidal. The surface is variable with plenty of long stretches of grass. If the weather has been wet then anything less than a mountain bike will struggle.

Waterways Ireland have plans to upgrade the towpath, however there is considerable opposition from those who want it to remain in a more natural state. The full 168km route linking the Grand Canal and Barrow Navigation is described on page 60.

TOWPATH CYCLING

The towpaths are shared with other users and are narrow in places so slow down when approaching pedestrians and call out or ring your bell when passing. Take particular care when passing beneath bridges as the corners are often tight and blind.

BLUEWAYS

Waterways Ireland refers to both their land and water based trails as Blueways (bluewaysireland.org). Currently there are five Blueways designated for cycling.

The 16km Longford Town to Cloondara Cycle Trail follows the Royal Canal and the Longford Branch between the two towns.

The 14km Drumleague Lock Trail links Leitrim village and Drumshanbo. It is mostly towpath with a floating boardwalk at Acres Lake.

The Ballinamore Trail is a 4.5km loop that starts and finishes in the Leitrim town of Ballinamore following the Shannon-Erne before returning along the road.

The Ballyduff to Aghoo Bridge Trail is a 7km linear trail that runs along the Shannon-Erne from Ballyduff to Aghoo Bridge.

The 21km Suir Blueway runs along the River Suir from Clonmel to Carrick-on-Suir.

The Barrow Navigation, see page 60

TOURING AND BIKEPACKING

Cycle touring is a great way to see Ireland. The gentle pace and the daily rhythm of a long cycle allows you to see things that would be missed or unappreciated from the confines of a car. And while Ireland is a small country there is a huge amount to see and experience.

Depending on fitness and inclination some of the longer routes detailed in the main section of this book could make for interesting multi-day trips. Ireland also has over a dozen signposted long-distance (200km+) routes, see page 251.

COMMERCIAL TOURS
If you like the idea of touring, but aren't too keen on carrying all your own gear, then consider a commercial tour. There are plenty of companies that offer self-guided bike tours. They will suggest a route, arrange accommodation and shuttle your bags each day.

BIKEPACKING
Bikepacking is a new approach to bike travel in which cyclists swap racks and panniers for smaller fabric bags. Adopting much of the equipment and techniques used by lightweight backpackers allows bikepackers to lighten their load, enabling them to leave the roads for rougher, more challenging terrain.

In an Irish context a mountain bike lightly loaded with camping gear offers a huge amount of flexibility. The ability to take off-road variations and access remote campsites adds a whole new dimension to bike touring. Ireland's networks of trails and tracks offers huge scope for long, albeit unofficial, bikepacking routes. Read more about mountain biking in Ireland on page 21.

EQUIPMENT
The often damp Irish weather means it's vital to pack equipment in waterproof bags. It would be wise to pack critical gear, like electronics, spare clothes and sleeping bags in an additional drybag just in case.

Make sure that you are visible to other road users, carry good front and rear lights and wear bright clothing.

The combination of rain and wind, even when the air temperature is mild, can cool the body down very quickly. A good waterproof jacket is essential as are warm gloves, shoes and socks. Mudguards can also make a huge difference in wet weather.

Even if you aren't planning to leave your bike unattended in public it's worth carrying a good quality lock for peace of mind when you pop into a shop or if your accommodation doesn't offer secure storage.

PUBLIC TRANSPORT
In spite of the fact that public transport in Ireland doesn't cater particularly well for cyclists, it can still be quite useful.

In the Republic the train network is centred on Dublin with a number of lines connecting it to the larger towns and cities. Tickets can be booked and bike spaces reserved online. Some trains have a limited number of bike holders in the passenger compartment while on others bikes are taken in the goods wagon. On commuter trains and the DART bicycles are restricted to off-peak hours. See irishrail.ie for more information.

Bus Éireann runs an extensive bus network across the Republic. They will carry bikes if there is room in the luggage compartment but they can't be reserved in advance so it's a bit of a lottery. There may be a small charge.

In Northern Ireland the Translink Goldline buses (which serve the larger towns) and all trains carry bikes free of charge. Bikes aren't permitted before 09.30 between Monday and Friday. Each bus has room for two bikes and each train can take four. Space is allocated on a first come, first served basis and can't be reserved in advance. See translink.co.uk for more information.

WILD CAMPING
Wild camping is a great option, offering plenty of flexibility and independence, plus it's cheap. The Irish mountains and coast in particular have some great wild camping spots. If feasible ask permission to camp.

If you are discrete then no one will ever know you were there. Pitch your tent late, take it down early and don't make too much noise. If you are planning on lighting a fire choose suitable ground, minimise its effect on the landscape and remember to take all your rubbish away with you.

Between May and September beware the midge. The tiny flying insects can be a nuisance on calm, humid evenings especially near rivers, lakes or bog. The gentlest breeze will keep them at bay so choose an exposed spot away from any water or vegetation. It's also worth bringing insect repellent and a head net.

Climbing the north side of Conor Pass, Dingle, Kerry, see page 134

INFORMATION FOR VISITORS

GETTING HERE

The four main airports in Ireland are Dublin, Belfast, Shannon and Cork. Dublin is the largest, followed by Belfast, but Shannon and Cork are also worth considering. There are a number of other smaller airports including Farranfore in Kerry, Knock in Mayo, Carrickfinn in Donegal and Derry City.

The other alternative is to arrive by ferry from the UK and France. There are regular sailings to Dublin from Holyhead in Wales and Liverpool in England, and to Rosslare in Wexford and Cork City from South Wales and Brittany in France.

ACCOMMODATION

Finding accommodation usually isn't a problem, particularly in the more touristy parts of the country. During the summer it might be wise to book in advance. In the depths of winter you should also book ahead as some accommodation will be closed.

Camp sites and hostels are good budget options but it's also worth considering B+Bs and hotels. Some offer very good deals particularly during the off-season. Trip Advisor is the best starting point for researching accommodation.

FOOD AND DRINK

Practically every small village has a restaurant, café or pub serving food. Garages are a good option for a quick stop at lunchtime, most sell sandwiches and rolls as well as hot food.

Ireland is renowned for its pubs and they are a great place to retreat to during bad weather. Most will be happy for you to order a pot of tea or pint and sit beside the fire drying out for a few hours.

MONEY

The Republic of Ireland uses the Euro, while Northern Ireland uses the Pound sterling. If you are following one of the long-distance routes (page 251) that cross back and forth over the border you should carry both currencies. However most establishments in the area will accept either.

Generally Debit and credit cards are widely accepted. Larger towns have ATMs but most smaller villages don't, so carrying some cash.

WHEN TO VISIT?

The Irish climate is largely dictated by the weather systems that blow in from the Atlantic on the prevailing southwesterly winds. The strong winds make the weather very changeable and difficult to predict but the warm waters of the Gulf Stream keep the temperatures relatively high.

The wind can have a significant effect on a day's cycling so it's worth checking the forecast before setting off. If you are doing a loop think about the best direction to tackle it in given the forecast. Ideally you want a tailwind on the climbs and a headwind on the descents.

Good waterproof gear and a positive attitude are the best defences against inclement weather. If the forecast is bad, consider waiting a few hours for a clearing or taking a shorter, more sheltered route. The most important thing to remember is that it's rarely as bad as it looks.

Summer

As with any time of year the summer weather can be unpredictable. All that can be said with certainly is that the days are long, with more than 17 hours of daylight in June. Generally the weather will be mild but rarely uncomfortably hot.

Early summer (May and June) tends to be the sunniest but not necessarily the warmest time. June is relatively quiet, the high season is really just July and August. Even when the main tourist areas are busy it's easy to escape the hordes, you just need to venture slightly off the beaten track.

Be warned if you are planning to camp, midge (tiny, infuriating biting insects) can be a pest on still summer evenings.

Spring

In spring you will avoid the summer crowds, temperatures should be reasonable and the days will be lengthening. The weather, particularly in the second half of the spring, can be very good. It is often the driest time of year.

Autumn

Autumn shares many advantages with spring. Once the kids return to school in early September the popular destinations become quieter. This often coincides with a spell of settled weather.

Winter

As a cyclist you would be brave to come to Ireland for a holiday in the depths of winter. Granted it's very quiet but it's also cold and windy with very short days (there is only 7.5 hours of daylight in mid-December).

Heavy snow is rare but watch out on cold days for patches of ice or heavy frost, particularly in sheltered areas or at higher elevations.

The south side of Priest's Leap in County Cork, see page 112

WHAT BIKE?

This book contains a wide range of routes from technical mountain bike trails to flat, fast road rides, and there isn't one bike that can handle them all equally well. Selecting a bike always requires some compromise between versatility and performance. A bike that can handle a variety of terrain won't excel at any particular one while a specialised bike will struggle outside of its niche.

MOUNTAIN BIKING
For mountain biking it's a choice between full suspension or a hardtail. A full suspension bike is one with both front and rear suspension that is designed for rough, technical trails. Soaking up the bumps and keeping the wheels in contact with the ground allows the rider to go a lot faster. They are comfortable and fast, but heavier and more expensive than a hardtail.

Hardtails, which have front suspension only, are ideal for anyone starting out as they are great value and are well able for beginner/intermediate trails.

GRAVEL
A gravel bike lies somewhere between a mountain and road bike. Most have relatively wide tyres, disc brakes and a large range of gears, hence they are well suited to the rough Irish roads. Their versatility means they are fast enough on the road yet still able to cope with tracks and trails.

HYBRID
Hybrids, like gravel bikes, combine elements of both mountain and road bikes. They are intended mainly for the road but can also handle gentle off-road terrain. Hybrids typically have flat handlebars, relatively narrow tyres and room for luggage racks and mudguards.

ROAD
Road bikes are designed for riding on good quality surfaces as quickly and as efficiently as possible. They are characterised by drop handlebars, narrow tyres with minimal tread and a low, aerodynamic riding position. To some extent comfort is sacrificed for speed as the narrow tyres and crouched riding position can be hard on the body.

IRISH CLIMATE
What specific demands does the Irish climate and terrain make? The majority of Irish roads are rough, so a durable bike is essential. The weather is often wet so the ability to fit mudguards is useful. The terrain tends to be quite hilly and it is often windy so a wide range of gears will make life a lot easier.

EQUIPMENT

There is a small amount of essential equipment that every cyclist needs and should carry on every bike ride. Get into the habit of spending a few minutes packing and checking you have everything you need. As you can be sure that the one time you leave the tool kit at home you will get a puncture.

Mountain bikers tend to favour a small rucksack containing all their equipment and a hydration bladder. For short spins when you don't need much a small top tube or saddle bag will do the job. It can be left permanently on the bike meaning that you will never be without it.

On longer rides when you are carrying more food and spare clothing you will need something larger. Good options include a handlebar or frame bag.

SAFETY
If you are cycling on your own it's a good idea to let someone know the route you are planning to follow.

Carry a fully charged mobile, although you won't be guaranteed reception in some more remote areas. Make sure to download the relevant maps in advance in case you don't have a signal. If you are in an area that you don't know well it might be wise to carry a paper map as a backup. For more information about navigating using a smartphone see page 14.

While not mandatory in Ireland most cyclists wisely wear a helmet.

Good lights, front and rear, are essential after dark and high visibility clothing is a good idea at all times.

A bell is essential on multi-use trails to let other users know that you are passing.

During the summer remember to apply sunscreen before you set off.

Anyone cycling in remote areas should consider taking a few extra items such as a small first aid kit and an emergency blanket.

Put a €20 note in a ziplock bag and hide it away for emergencies.

FOOD AND WATER
Some cyclists consider the coffee and cake stop a fundamental part of every bike ride. Most of the routes in this book pass cafés and shops. Nevertheless it's a good idea, even on short rides, to carry a few snacks. There is nothing worse than being stuck completely drained of energy miles from home.

Likewise with water, carry more than you think you will need. Even on cold days you will need to drink regularly to stay hydrated.

TOOLS
Every rider should carry sufficient tools and spares to fix the most common problems. The following tools will fit in a jersey pocket or small saddle or top tube bag:

- Spare inner tube
- Puncture repair kit
- Pump
- Chain tool
- Tyre levers
- Small multi-tool
- A few quick-links

For longer or more remote rides it's worth taking a few cable ties and some duct tape (wrap a few metres around your pump). If you are unlucky enough to have a serious breakdown they might allow you make a temporary repair that will get you back to civilisation.

CLOTHING
The Irish weather is very changeable. And while the air temperature is usually reasonable, the real problem is the rain. Even in summer you will get very cold very quickly if you get soaked through.

In the winter cold feet and hands can ruin a cycle. Thick socks, overshoes or even plastic bags over your socks will help to keep your feet warm and a good pair of heavy gloves will make sure that you keep the feeling in your fingers.

Irrespective of the forecast it's a good idea to always carry a light waterproof jacket, it will keep you warm if you have a mechanical problem or injury. In winter you will need a heavier weight jacket and an extra layer or two.

It can take a bit of experimentation to figure out exactly how much to wear, as a rule it's preferable to be too warm than too cold.

BIKE SHOPS
Most large towns have a bike shop that offers repairs, sales and hire. If you find yourself stranded far from the nearest bike shop on a multi-day trip then one option could be to order the parts you need online for next day delivery, assuming that you have the tools and ability to fit them yourself.

TOP 10 CLIMBS

While Ireland doesn't have any climbs that can rival the sheer size of those found in the Alps, there are plenty of hard ascents that will challenge even the fittest cyclists.

The following list ranks the ten hardest climbs found on the 80 routes in this book. As the routes weren't designed solely to tackle as much climbing as possible this list doesn't include every hard climb in the country. If you want a definitive list of Ireland's hardest climbs then check out this very detailed spreadsheet goo.gl/8hTniy.

This list was created by ordering the climbs by height gain. Shorter steeper climbs were then pushed up the rankings above longer climbs with similar amounts of height gain.

A climb's difficulty can't really be encapsulated in a number. There are a couple of highly subjective factors, such as how the rider is feeling on the day, their fitness, the surface, the weather etc, that have a significant influence on how hard a climb feels.

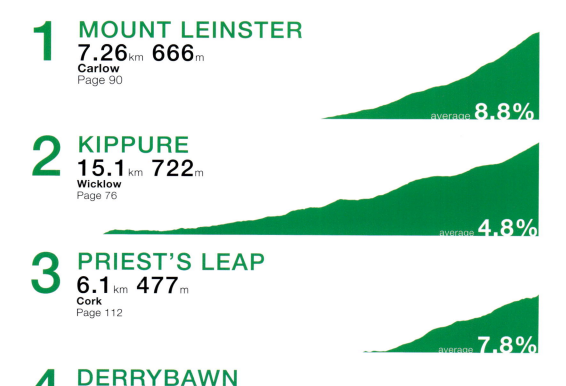

1 MOUNT LEINSTER
7.26km **666**m
Carlow
Page 90

average **8.8%**

2 KIPPURE
15.1km **722**m
Wicklow
Page 76

average **4.8%**

3 PRIEST'S LEAP
6.1km **477**m
Cork
Page 112

average **7.8%**

4 DERRYBAWN
3.9km **379**m
Wicklow
Page 84

average **9.7%**

5 **BLACK MOUNTAIN**
4.3km **350**m
Louth
Page 46

average **8.1%**

6 **CONNOR PASS**
7.9km **368**m
Kerry
Page 134

average **4.7%**

7 **WOLFTRAP**
9.0km **364**m
Offaly
Page 54

average **4.0%**

8 **BORLIN**
12.7km **379**m
Kerry
Page 112

average **3.0%**

9 **WICKLOW GAP**
6.7km **345**m
Wicklow
Page 86

average **5.2%**

10 **CAHA PASS**
6.6km **337**m
Cork
Page 119

average **5.1%**

EAST

The Military Road just south of Sally Gap, Wicklow, see page 88

FAMILY CYCLING IN THE EAST

The following routes are short, traffic-free and family-friendly.

LOUTH

1 CARLINGFORD GREENWAY *54.0518, -6.1928*
This 6.2km greenway follows a disused railway line along the southern shore of Carlingford Lough between Omeath and Carlingford village. See page 46 for a longer route that includes the greenway.

LONGFORD

2 LONGFORD CLONDRA GREENWAY *53.7224, -7.7974*
This 16km multi-use path follows a spur of the Royal Canal linking Longford Town with the Royal Canal proper and then follows it north to Clondra and the River Shannon.

KILDARE

3 DONADEA FOREST PARK *53.3420, -6.7450*
A 5.2km cycling loop around this 250 hectare mixed woodland near Maynooth in northwest Kildare.

OFFALY

4 LOUGH BOORA PARK *53.2247, -7.7281*
This former commercial bog is now a fascinating park with a number of signposted cycling routes. See page 52 for details.

DUBLIN

5 TOLKA VALLEY GREENWAY *53.3784, -6.2984*
A 4km off-road cycling and walking route linking Glasnevin, Cabra, Finglas and Ashtown on Dublin's northside.

6 PHOENIX PARK *53.3547, -6.3066*
The largest enclosed public park in Europe, Phoenix Park has an extensive network of cycle trails and paths. See page 64 for more information.

7 SLANG RIVER GREENWAY *53.2844, -6.2370*
This 4.6km multi-use path follows the River Slang from Sandyford Road in Dundrum to Marlay Park in Rathfarnham on Dublin's southside.

WICKLOW

8 AVONDALE FOREST PARK *52.9166, -6.2268*
Avondale Forest Park, just south of Rathdrum, is home to a number of multi-use trails through the estate's beautiful forestry.

WEXFORD

9 CARRICKDUFF BIKE SKILLS PARK *52.6571, -6.6630*
This basic pump track is an ideal place for small kids to develop their balance and bike control skills. It's beside the public swimming pool in the village of Bunclody.

10 RAVEN WOOD *52.3804, -6.3678*
Just behind the dunes at the southern end of Curracloe beach is Raven Wood. A nice track runs south through the forest to Raven Point.

11 JOHN F. KENNEDY MEMORIAL PARK *52.3213, -6.9346*
The 250 hectare park near New Ross is dedicated to the memory of JFK. It is home to over 4500 varieties of trees and there is plenty to see including a playground, a number of tree houses and a lake.

CARLOW

12 ST. MULLINS *52.4873, -6.9269*
The River Barrow runs from the Slieve Bloom mountains to the sea at Waterford. The most scenic section is at St. Mullins, a small hamlet on the Carlow side of the river. There is a wonderful cycle that follows the towpath upstream through the wooded valley. As the path is close to the water this cycle isn't suitable for very small children. For more about cycling the Barrow see page 60.

KILKENNY

13 NORE LINEAR PARK *52.6476, -7.2375*
Running alongside the River Nore as it makes its way through the centre of Kilkenny City this park has a number of easy cycling routes including the 2.6km Bishops Walk and the 1.7km Canal Walk. See visitkilkenny.ie for details.

The last stretch of the climb to the summit of Black Mountain

COOLEY MOUNTAINS
County Louth
ROAD

42km
790m

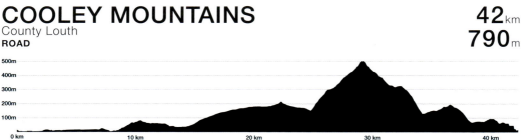

After the long hard climb up Black Mountain you are rewarded with spectacular views.

This route loops around the Cooley Peninsula starting gently along the Carlingford Greenway before tackling the climb to the top of Black Mountain (4.3km with an 8% average gradient).

From the village of Omeath (*54.0876, -6.2583*) on the southern shore of Carlingford Lough the route follows the Carlingford Greenway southeast for 6.2km to Carlingford. From the village follow the R173 south before swinging northwest, back on quieter roads, and climbing up the Glenmore valley.

Descending slightly after the Windy Gap (also known as Long Woman's Grave) there is a brief respite before the steep climb to the top of the Black Mountain.

At the saddle turn left and a final tough kilometre leads to the summit where there are great views across Carlingford to the Mourne Mountains and down the coast towards Dublin.

A narrow, gravelly road leads north through forest and open hillside to a t-junction where you turn right, crossing into Northern Ireland and climbing gently.

The road then swings east, running parallel to the Newry River as it makes its way down to the sea. A series of quiet backroads lead back into Omeath.

REFRESHMENTS
There are plenty of options in Omeath and Carlingford but there is nowhere along the route.

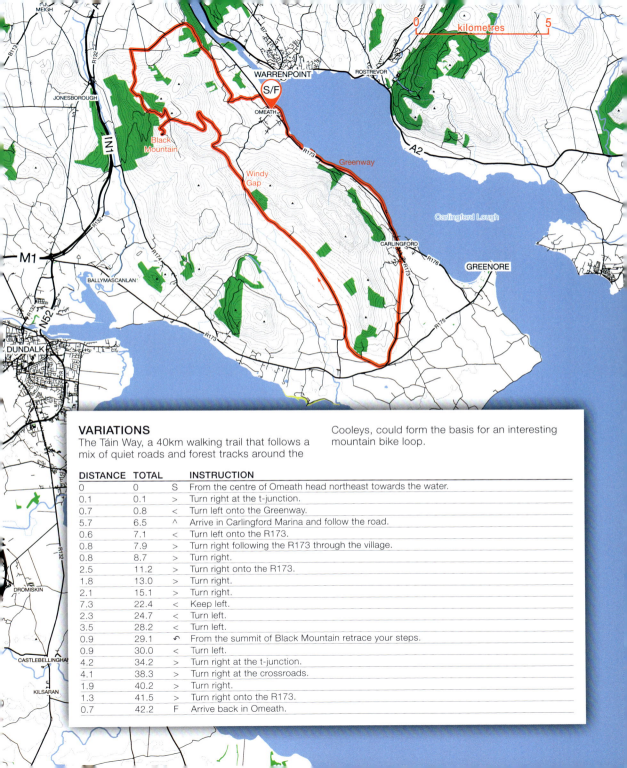

VARIATIONS

The Táin Way, a 40km walking trail that follows a mix of quiet roads and forest tracks around the Cooleys, could form the basis for an interesting mountain bike loop.

DISTANCE	TOTAL		INSTRUCTION
0	0	S	From the centre of Omeath head northeast towards the water.
0.1	0.1	>	Turn right at the t-junction.
0.7	0.8	<	Turn left onto the Greenway.
5.7	6.5	^	Arrive in Carlingford Marina and follow the road.
0.6	7.1	<	Turn left onto the R173.
0.8	7.9	>	Turn right following the R173 through the village.
0.8	8.7	>	Turn right.
2.5	11.2	>	Turn right onto the R173.
1.8	13.0	>	Turn right.
2.1	15.1	>	Turn right.
7.3	22.4	<	Keep left.
2.3	24.7	<	Turn left.
3.5	28.2	<	Turn left.
0.9	29.1	↶	From the summit of Black Mountain retrace your steps.
0.9	30.0	<	Turn left.
4.2	34.2	>	Turn right at the t-junction.
4.1	38.3	>	Turn right at the crossroads.
1.9	40.2	>	Turn right.
1.3	41.5	>	Turn right onto the R173.
0.7	42.2	F	Arrive back in Omeath.

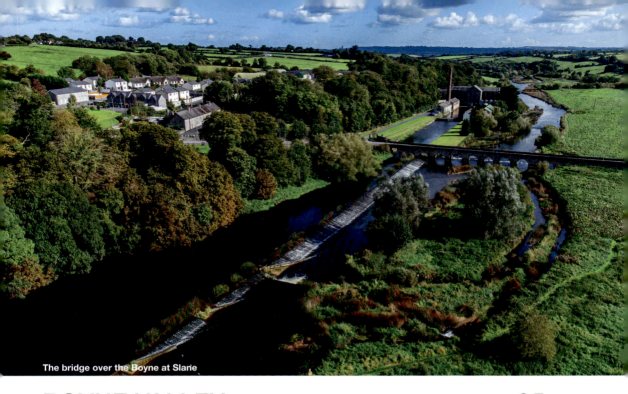

The bridge over the Boyne at Slane

BOYNE VALLEY
County Meath
ROAD

35km
300m

This route travels through the historic Boyne Valley past Newgrange, the world famous prehistoric monument.

The Boyne Valley is one of only three World Heritage sites in Ireland. There is a lot to see along this relatively short route and you could easily spend the day taking plenty of stops to sightsee along the way.

The route starts from the carpark (*53.7151, -6.3611*) beside the playground on the south bank of the Boyne in Drogheda Town. Follow the Ramparts Walkway, which is a little rough in places, upstream to Oldbridge Road and the start of the Boyne Greenway. The greenway continues along the bank of the river passing under the Mary McAleese

Bridge. The path then veers away from the river following the canal before joining the road.

Turn left at the junction and climb towards the pretty village of Donore.

After turning right in the village the road drops down past the Brú na Bóinne visitor centre. The road flattens out as it follows the river upstream and there are good views across the valley to Newgrange. Shortly after a short steep climb through the trees you turn right onto a quiet road. In the distance you can see the redbrick tower of the mill at Slane.

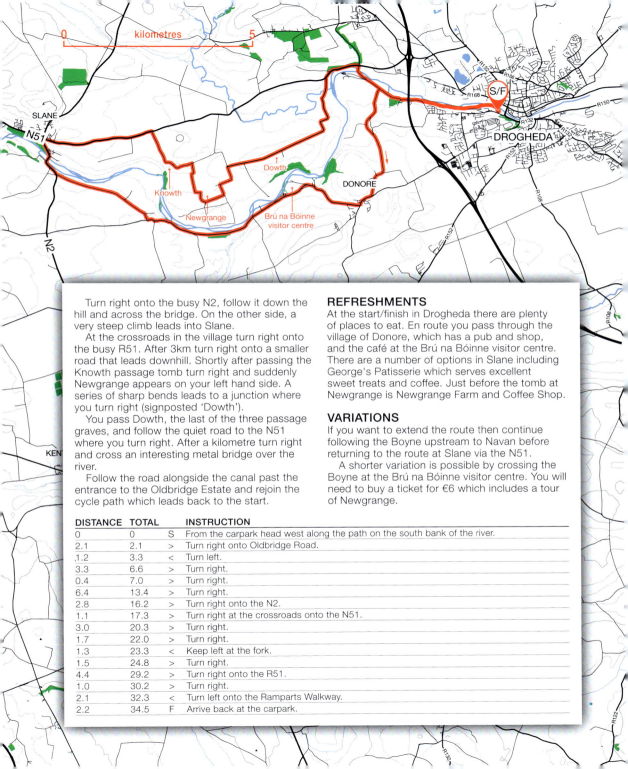

Turn right onto the busy N2, follow it down the hill and across the bridge. On the other side, a very steep climb leads into Slane.

At the crossroads in the village turn right onto the busy R51. After 3km turn right onto a smaller road that leads downhill. Shortly after passing the Knowth passage tomb turn right and suddenly Newgrange appears on your left hand side. A series of sharp bends leads to a junction where you turn right (signposted 'Dowth').

You pass Dowth, the last of the three passage graves, and follow the quiet road to the N51 where you turn right. After a kilometre turn right and cross an interesting metal bridge over the river.

Follow the road alongside the canal past the entrance to the Oldbridge Estate and rejoin the cycle path which leads back to the start.

REFRESHMENTS
At the start/finish in Drogheda there are plenty of places to eat. En route you pass through the village of Donore, which has a pub and shop, and the café at the Brú na Bóinne visitor centre. There are a number of options in Slane including George's Patisserie which serves excellent sweet treats and coffee. Just before the tomb at Newgrange is Newgrange Farm and Coffee Shop.

VARIATIONS
If you want to extend the route then continue following the Boyne upstream to Navan before returning to the route at Slane via the N51.

A shorter variation is possible by crossing the Boyne at the Brú na Bóinne visitor centre. You will need to buy a ticket for €6 which includes a tour of Newgrange.

DISTANCE	TOTAL		INSTRUCTION
0	0	S	From the carpark head west along the path on the south bank of the river.
2.1	2.1	>	Turn right onto Oldbridge Road.
1.2	3.3	<	Turn left.
3.3	6.6	>	Turn right.
0.4	7.0	>	Turn right.
6.4	13.4	>	Turn right.
2.8	16.2	>	Turn right onto the N2.
1.1	17.3	>	Turn right at the crossroads onto the N51.
3.0	20.3	>	Turn right.
1.7	22.0	>	Turn right.
1.3	23.3	<	Keep left at the fork.
1.5	24.8	>	Turn right.
4.4	29.2	>	Turn right onto the R51.
1.0	30.2	>	Turn right.
2.1	32.3	<	Turn left onto the Ramparts Walkway.
2.2	34.5	F	Arrive back at the carpark.

Lock 38 on the Royal Canal

ROYAL CANAL–OLD RAIL TRAIL

County Westmeath/Longford

ROAD

99km

320m

300m
200m
100m

0 km   20 km   40 km   60 km   80 km   100 km

A very flat and largely traffic-free route that follows the Royal Canal and the Old Rail Trail through the heart of the Midlands.

This route combines two greenways into a loop of just under 100km that is 80% traffic-free. The Royal Canal is a mix of tarmac and fine gravel while the Old Rail Trail has an excellent tarmac surface so this route is suitable for all bikes.

The route is described in an anti-clockwise direction starting from the Old Rail Trail carpark (*53.5171, -7.3632*) beside the R394 on the southwest side of Mullingar.

From the carpark cross the road, head down the track and turn right onto the Royal Canal Way. Follow the towpath for 36km, occasionally switching sides as it makes its way through the peaceful countryside.

At Archies Bridge leave the canal and follow a series of backroads south to Athlone. You pass close to Lough Ree and will get an occasional glimpse of it on the right.

After negotiating a number of roundabouts on the east side of Athlone you join the 40km Old Rail Trail which follows the course of the disused Midland Great Western Railway. The surface is very fast and there are good views across the beautiful rolling fields and it isn't long, especially if the wind is at your back, before you arrive back in Mullingar.

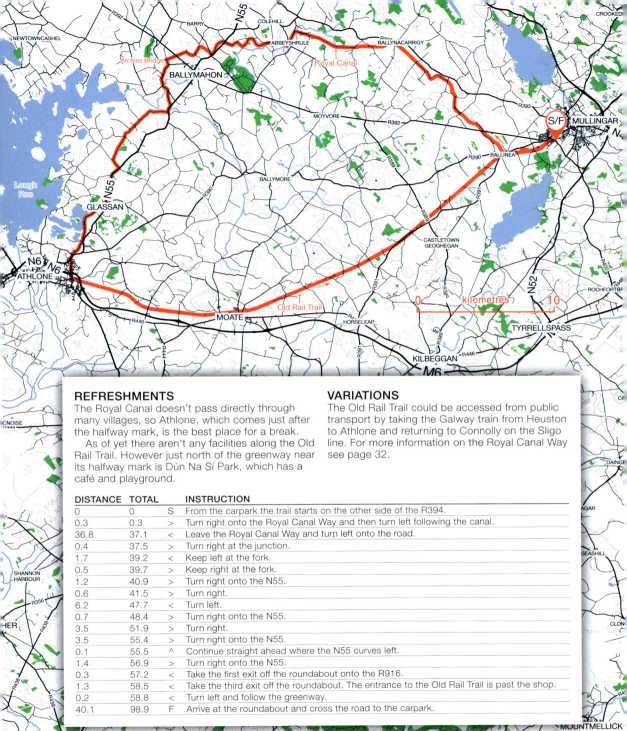

REFRESHMENTS

The Royal Canal doesn't pass directly through many villages, so Athlone, which comes just after the halfway mark, is the best place for a break.

As of yet there aren't any facilities along the Old Rail Trail. However just north of the greenway near its halfway mark is Dún Na Sí Park, which has a café and playground.

VARIATIONS

The Old Rail Trail could be accessed from public transport by taking the Galway train from Heuston to Athlone and returning to Connolly on the Sligo line. For more information on the Royal Canal Way see page 32.

DISTANCE	TOTAL		INSTRUCTION
0	0	S	From the carpark the trail starts on the other side of the R394.
0.3	0.3	>	Turn right onto the Royal Canal Way and then turn left following the canal.
36.8	37.1	<	Leave the Royal Canal Way and turn left onto the road.
0.4	37.5	>	Turn right at the junction.
1.7	39.2	<	Keep left at the fork.
0.5	39.7	>	Keep right at the fork.
1.2	40.9	>	Turn right onto the N55.
0.6	41.5	>	Turn right.
6.2	47.7	<	Turn left.
0.7	48.4	>	Turn right onto the N55.
3.5	51.9	>	Turn right.
3.5	55.4	>	Turn right onto the N55.
0.1	55.5	^	Continue straight ahead where the N55 curves left.
1.4	56.9	>	Turn right onto the N55.
0.3	57.2	<	Take the first exit off the roundabout onto the R916.
1.3	58.5	<	Take the third exit off the roundabout. The entrance to the Old Rail Trail is past the shop.
0.2	58.8	<	Turn left and follow the greenway.
40.1	98.9	F	Arrive at the roundabout and cross the road to the carpark.

Heading anti-clockwise on the Turraun Route

LOUGH BOORA
County Offaly
GRAVEL

22km
60m

300m				
200m				
100m				
0 km	5 km	10 km	15 km	20 km

This route follows a network of gravel tracks around the Lough Boora Discovery Park.

Lough Boora Discovery Park was once a commercial bog but nowadays the 2,000 hectare site is home to a sculpture park and over fifty kilometres of paths. The open bog is quickly being reclaimed by nature yet there are still plenty of reminders of the park's previous life including sections of cut bog and the narrow-gauge railway that was used to transport the turf.

Of the park's five trails, three are open for use by cyclists. The terrain is incredibly flat and most of the trails are traffic-free so they are ideal for families. The trails consist of fine gravel and are suitable for all types of bike.

Bike hire is available at the visitor centre with a range of bikes for children and adults as well as tandems and trailers. Ring 057 934 0011 to book.

The route, which combines the three cycling trails into a 22km clockwise circuit of the park, starts from the carpark (*53.2230, -7.7281*) beside the visitor centre. Head south around the west side of Boora Lake following the red arrows of the Mesolithic Route.

Passing the Sculpture Park with its 24 works of art the trail loops around the park to the Mesolithic Site, where the remains of ancient campfires and over a thousand artefacts dating from the Middle Stone Age were discovered.

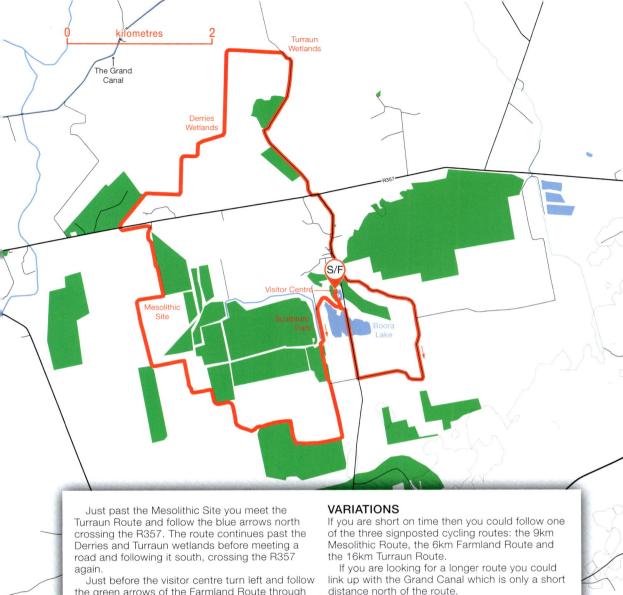

Just past the Mesolithic Site you meet the Turraun Route and follow the blue arrows north crossing the R357. The route continues past the Derries and Turraun wetlands before meeting a road and following it south, crossing the R357 again.

Just before the visitor centre turn left and follow the green arrows of the Farmland Route through the fields in a loop that leads back to the road. Turn right and follow the road back to the carpark.

REFRESHMENTS
The coffee shop in the visitor centre has a timber deck where you can sit overlooking Loch an Dochais and Boora Lake. For most of the year it's open daily apart from the winter months when it's only open at weekends. See loughboora.com for more information.

VARIATIONS
If you are short on time then you could follow one of the three signposted cycling routes: the 9km Mesolithic Route, the 6km Farmland Route and the 16km Turraun Route.

If you are looking for a longer route you could link up with the Grand Canal which is only a short distance north of the route.

On the R440 near the summit of Wolftrap

SLIEVE BLOOMS
County Offaly/Laois
ROAD

37 km
770 m

A tough tour through the Slieve Bloom Mountains.

The Slieve Blooms are a much overlooked mountain range. Even through they aren't particularly high or craggy, they have plenty to offer cyclists, specifically quiet roads and steep climbs.

This route links two of the Slieve Bloom's three big climbs. The roads are very quiet and the route is quite sheltered, only at the very top of the climbs do you leave the forests.

From the small village of Kinnitty (53.0978,-7.7213) head east onto the R440 and straight into the first climb of the day. Known as the Wolftrap, the 9.5km climb has 360m of height gain with an average gradient of 4%. Initially it climbs up the valley through pleasant woodland before emerging onto the open hillside. A final steep pull leads to the top of the broad ridge that connects Wolftrap Mountain and Stillbrook Hill.

At the bottom of the fast descent, shortly after crossing the bridge over the Delour River, turn right off the R440 onto a quiet back road that leads to the second climb.

Glendine, the tougher of the two climbs, is 6km long with 270m of height gain. The first half is little more than a warm up. The real climbing starts at the hairpin bends where you leave the valley floor and climb across the steep valley at an average gradient of 9%.

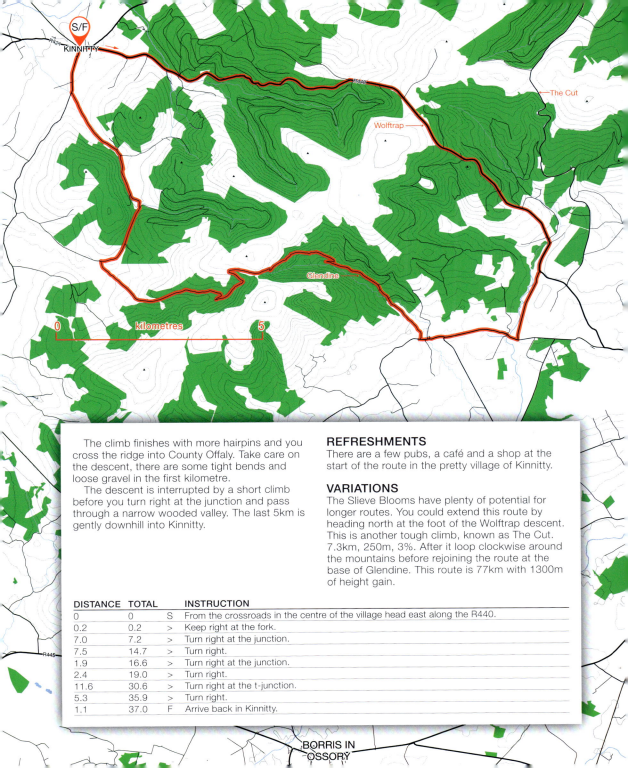

S/F
KINNITTY

The Cut

Wolftrap

Glendine

0   kilometres   5

The climb finishes with more hairpins and you cross the ridge into County Offaly. Take care on the descent, there are some tight bends and loose gravel in the first kilometre.

The descent is interrupted by a short climb before you turn right at the junction and pass through a narrow wooded valley. The last 5km is gently downhill into Kinnitty.

REFRESHMENTS

There are a few pubs, a café and a shop at the start of the route in the pretty village of Kinnitty.

VARIATIONS

The Slieve Blooms have plenty of potential for longer routes. You could extend this route by heading north at the foot of the Wolftrap descent. This is another tough climb, known as The Cut. 7.3km, 250m, 3%. After it loop clockwise around the mountains before rejoining the route at the base of Glendine. This route is 77km with 1300m of height gain.

DISTANCE	TOTAL		INSTRUCTION
0	0	S	From the crossroads in the centre of the village head east along the R440.
0.2	0.2	>	Keep right at the fork.
7.0	7.2	>	Turn right at the junction.
7.5	14.7	>	Turn right.
1.9	16.6	>	Turn right at the junction.
2.4	19.0	>	Turn right.
11.6	30.6	>	Turn right at the t-junction.
5.3	35.9	>	Turn right.
1.1	37.0	F	Arrive back in Kinnitty.

BORRIS IN OSSORY

The start of the Thunder descent on the Blue Trail on the Laois side

SLIEVE BLOOMS TRAIL CENTRES

County Offaly/Laois
MTB

52km
1090m

An extensive network of mountain bike trails spread across both sides of the mountains.

The forested valleys of the Slieve Blooms, which mark the border between Laois and Offaly, are home to two systems of purpose-built mountain bike trails that weave around the hills offering all-weather riding for riders of all levels.

There are two trailheads, one on the eastern (Laois) side and the other on the western (Offaly) side of the mountains.

The trails weave complicated routes, crossing themselves often and with numerous shortcuts and variations, but fortunately they are very clearly signposted.

The profile and distance and height gain numbers above relate to the route that combines the trails on both sides of the mountains.

KINNITTY

The pretty village of Kinnitty (*53.0978, -7.7213*) is the start/finish point for two trails, the 9.6km Kinnitty Blue (180m height gain) and the 26km Red (500m height gain). Both trails head east out of the village along the R421 before turning right at the GAA club and following a multi-use trail into the forest. They then climb, mostly on the forest road, to the highpoint of the blue. The red continues climbing, while the blue winds its way back down to the river.

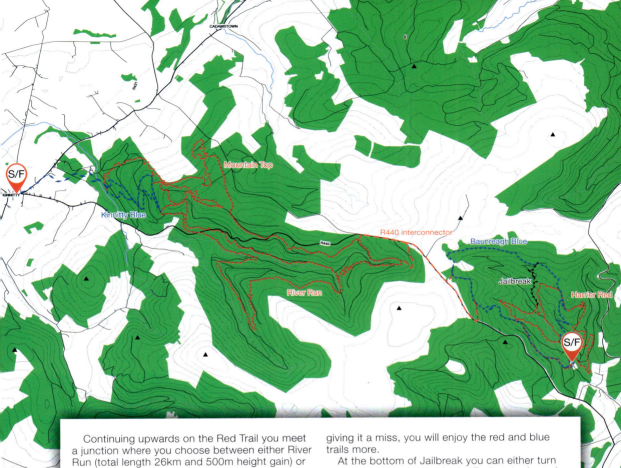

Continuing upwards on the Red Trail you meet a junction where you choose between either River Run (total length 26km and 500m height gain) or Mountain Top (total length 31km and 590m height gain).

BAUNREAGH

Baunreagh carpark (*53.0676, -7.5619*) is the trailhead for the three trails on the eastern (Laois) side of the mountains.

The 10.1km Baunreagh Blue (200m height gain) climbs the southern side of the Baunreagh Valley before descending the north side.

The 8.9km Harrier Red (190m height gain) starts along the Blue before dropping down to the Delour River and climbing steeply on forest roads up the northern slopes. It then makes a long, flowing descent back to the carpark.

Approximately 6.5km along Baunreagh Blue (*53.0851, -7.5722*) a black trail called Jailbreak drops steeply down to the river. It's definitely a level up from the other trails and if you aren't an experience mountain biker than you are better off

giving it a miss, you will enjoy the red and blue trails more.

At the bottom of Jailbreak you can either turn left to immediately join Harrier Red at the foot of the climb up the northern slopes or do an optional 3km red loop first.

Starting along Baunreagh Blue, then doing Jailbreak and finishing along Harrier Red gives a 16.5km route with 390m of height gain.

REFRESHMENTS

The village of Kinnitty (*53.0978, -7.7213*) has two pubs and a café, Peavoys. It would make an ideal base for a weekend exploring the trails.

On the east side of the hills Mountrath (*53.0011, -7.4742*) is the nearest village and it has a number of cafés.

VARIATIONS

Combining the longest trails on both side of the mountains gives an epic 52km route with 1090m of height gain. The two trail systems are connected via a short (signposted) stretch along the R440.

A grassy section of the Royal Canal

THE ROYAL–GRAND CANAL
County Dublin/Kildare/Meath/Offaly
GRAVEL

111 km
300 m

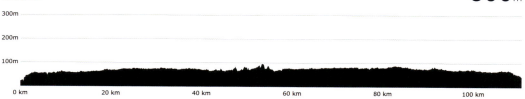

A largely off-road route that follows canal towpaths in a loop west of Dublin.

This route leaves the outskirts of Dublin following the Royal Canal west before heading south on quiet roads to meet the Grand Canal and following it back to the start. As the route is very flat it can be done in either direction but it's described in a clockwise direction to take advantage of the prevailing wind in the second half.

Over 80% of the route is on towpaths which are a mix of tarmac, gravel and grass. The surface of the Royal is significantly better than the Grand and in the near future it will be entirely paved.

Smooth tyres will work well if the ground is reasonably hard-packed and dry but they will struggle for grip after wet weather when a tyre with a more pronounced thread is required. See page 32 for more information about cycling the canals.

Even though the canal is generally quiet watch out for other users, particularly when passing under bridges and ring a bell before overtaking.

See sportireland.ie/outdoors for detailed maps of the Royal Canal Way and the Grand Canal Way.

From Lucan village (*53.3564, -6.4499*) head north crossing the River Liffey. Climb gently uphill, on a cycle path initially, to a bridge and turn left onto the Royal Canal Way.

The route alongside the canal is obvious and well signposted. As you leave the suburbs the towpath becomes quieter and the surface gets rougher. After just over 40km leave the Royal Canal and head

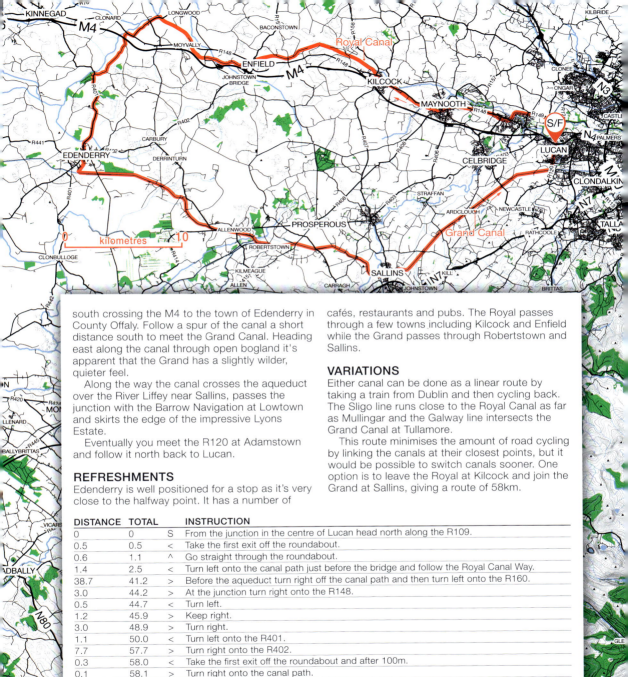

south crossing the M4 to the town of Edenderry in County Offaly. Follow a spur of the canal a short distance south to meet the Grand Canal. Heading east along the canal through open bogland it's apparent that the Grand has a slightly wilder, quieter feel.

Along the way the canal crosses the aqueduct over the River Liffey near Sallins, passes the junction with the Barrow Navigation at Lowtown and skirts the edge of the impressive Lyons Estate.

Eventually you meet the R120 at Adamstown and follow it north back to Lucan.

REFRESHMENTS
Edenderry is well positioned for a stop as it's very close to the halfway point. It has a number of

cafés, restaurants and pubs. The Royal passes through a few towns including Kilcock and Enfield while the Grand passes through Robertstown and Sallins.

VARIATIONS
Either canal can be done as a linear route by taking a train from Dublin and then cycling back. The Sligo line runs close to the Royal Canal as far as Mullingar and the Galway line intersects the Grand Canal at Tullamore.

This route minimises the amount of road cycling by linking the canals at their closest points, but it would be possible to switch canals sooner. One option is to leave the Royal at Kilcock and join the Grand at Sallins, giving a route of 58km.

DISTANCE	TOTAL		INSTRUCTION
0	0	S	From the junction in the centre of Lucan head north along the R109.
0.5	0.5	<	Take the first exit off the roundabout.
0.6	1.1	^	Go straight through the roundabout.
1.4	2.5	<	Turn left onto the canal path just before the bridge and follow the Royal Canal Way.
38.7	41.2	>	Before the aqueduct turn right off the canal path and then turn left onto the R160.
3.0	44.2	>	At the junction turn right onto the R148.
0.5	44.7	<	Turn left.
1.2	45.9	>	Keep right.
3.0	48.9	>	Turn right.
1.1	50.0	<	Turn left onto the R401.
7.7	57.7	>	Turn right onto the R402.
0.3	58.0	<	Take the first exit off the roundabout and after 100m.
0.1	58.1	>	Turn right onto the canal path.
1.6	59.7	<	Turn left onto the Grand Canal Way.
48.2	107.9	<	Turn left onto the R120.
3.0	110.9	F	Arrive back at the start in the centre of Lucan.

A few kilometres south of Ballytiglea Bridge Ballytiglea Bridge on the Barrow

THE GRAND CANAL–BARROW

County Dublin/Kildare/Laois/Carlow/Kilkenny
GRAVEL

168km
600m

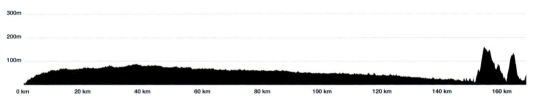

This linear route follows the Grand Canal and the Barrow Navigation from the centre of Dublin to Thomastown in Kilkenny.

F it cyclists could complete this route in a long day, but most people will need two or three days. Even through the route is very flat it can be tiring as some of the towpath is slow going.

The route finishes in the village of Thomastown where you can return to Dublin by bus or train. See page 34 for information about taking a bike on public transport.

Navigation for the most part is straightforward, it's just a matter of following the towpath. Detailed maps of both the Grand Canal Way and the Barrow Way can be downloaded from sportireland.ie/outdoors.

The towpath is a mix of tarmac, gravel, mud and long grass. Heavy rain will turn the grassy sections into thick mud so a reasonably wide tyre with a good thread is advised, particularly outside of a dry spell.

From Heuston Station (53.3461, -6.2920) head west along the R148 before taking the R811 south through Kilmainham to the Grand Canal. Follow the Grand Canal Way west for over 40km until, shortly after Robertstown, you turn onto the Barrow Way at Fenton's Bridge. For the next 100km you follow the towpath that runs alongside the Barrow Navigation and the River Barrow, the second longest river in Ireland.

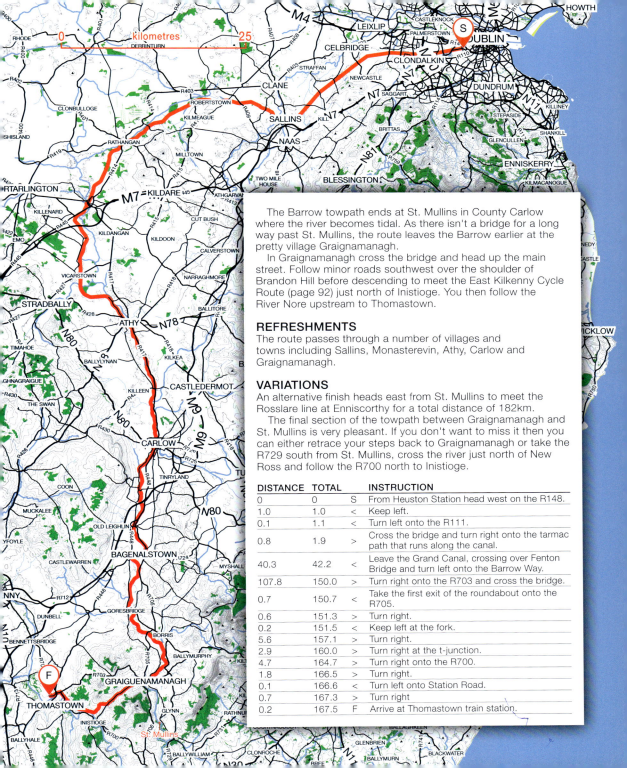

The Barrow towpath ends at St. Mullins in County Carlow where the river becomes tidal. As there isn't a bridge for a long way past St. Mullins, the route leaves the Barrow earlier at the pretty village Graignamanagh.

In Graignamanagh cross the bridge and head up the main street. Follow minor roads southwest over the shoulder of Brandon Hill before descending to meet the East Kilkenny Cycle Route (page 92) just north of Inistioge. You then follow the River Nore upstream to Thomastown.

REFRESHMENTS

The route passes through a number of villages and towns including Sallins, Monasterevin, Athy, Carlow and Graignamanagh.

VARIATIONS

An alternative finish heads east from St. Mullins to meet the Rosslare line at Enniscorthy for a total distance of 182km.

The final section of the towpath between Graignamanagh and St. Mullins is very pleasant. If you don't want to miss it then you can either retrace your steps back to Graignamanagh or take the R729 south from St. Mullins, cross the river just north of New Ross and follow the R700 north to Inistioge.

DISTANCE	TOTAL		INSTRUCTION
0	0	S	From Heuston Station head west on the R148.
1.0	1.0	<	Keep left.
0.1	1.1	<	Turn left onto the R111.
0.8	1.9	>	Cross the bridge and turn right onto the tarmac path that runs along the canal.
40.3	42.2	<	Leave the Grand Canal, crossing over Fenton Bridge and turn left onto the Barrow Way.
107.8	150.0	>	Turn right onto the R703 and cross the bridge.
0.7	150.7	<	Take the first exit of the roundabout onto the R705.
0.6	151.3	>	Turn right.
0.2	151.5	<	Keep left at the fork.
5.6	157.1	>	Turn right.
2.9	160.0	>	Turn right at the t-junction.
4.7	164.7	>	Turn right onto the R700.
1.8	166.5	>	Turn right.
0.1	166.6	<	Turn left onto Station Road.
0.7	167.3	>	Turn right
0.2	167.5	F	Arrive at Thomastown train station.

Heading south on the Nass Branch

GRAND CANAL FEEDER LOOP

County Kildare
GRAVEL

48km
100m

A very flat loop that links a number of canal towpaths.

This routes takes advantage of the quiet grassy paths that run alongside four waterways: the Naas Branch, the Milltown Feeder, the Barrow Line and the Grand Canal to form a route that is over 50% off-road.

Anything but any out-and-out road bike will manage this route though narrow tyres might struggle for grip during a wet spell. The route is described in a clockwise direction, but could just as easily be done anti-clockwise.

From Sallins train station (53.2466, -6.6647) the route heads south joining the Naas Branch of the Grand Canal. Follow a tarmac road to Naas Harbour, initially on the right-hand side before switching to

the left side. You then follow the Naas Historical Trail through the outskirts of the town. After a short distance heading west on the R445 you turn left onto Jigginstown Green. Turn left just before Limerick Bridge and continue along the left-hand side of the grassy canal path. At Connaught Bridge you swap over to the right and follow the path, which can be rough in places, along a very enjoyable 5km stretch to Corbally Harbour.

Back on the road for a while you cross the M9 and then the River Liffey heading northeast through Newbridge before joining the Milltown Feeder of the Grand Canal.

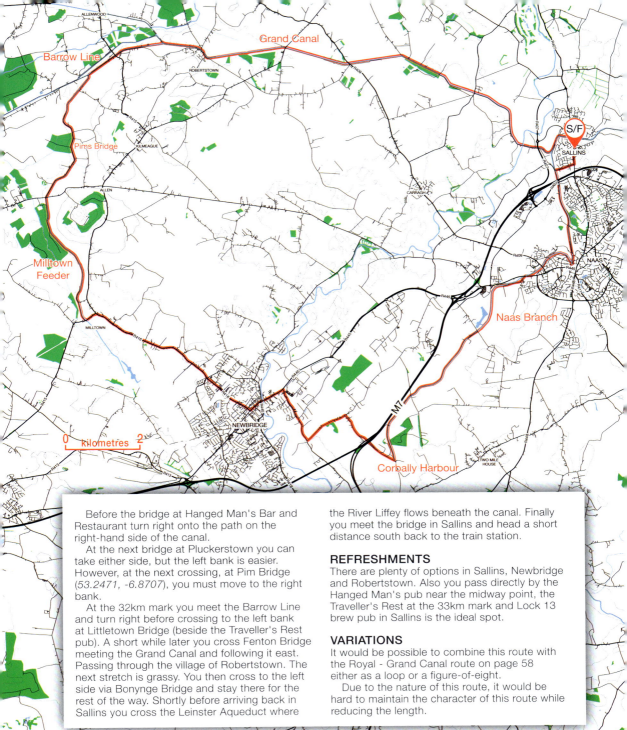

Grand Canal

Barrow Line

Pims Bridge

Milltown
Feeder

Naas Branch

Corbally Harbour

0 kilometres 2

Before the bridge at Hanged Man's Bar and Restaurant turn right onto the path on the right-hand side of the canal.

At the next bridge at Pluckerstown you can take either side, but the left bank is easier. However, at the next crossing, at Pim Bridge (53.2471, -6.8707), you must move to the right bank.

At the 32km mark you meet the Barrow Line and turn right before crossing to the left bank at Littletown Bridge (beside the Traveller's Rest pub). A short while later you cross Fenton Bridge meeting the Grand Canal and following it east. Passing through the village of Robertstown. The next stretch is grassy. You then cross to the left side via Bonynge Bridge and stay there for the rest of the way. Shortly before arriving back in Sallins you cross the Leinster Aqueduct where

the River Liffey flows beneath the canal. Finally you meet the bridge in Sallins and head a short distance south back to the train station.

REFRESHMENTS

There are plenty of options in Sallins, Newbridge and Robertstown. Also you pass directly by the Hanged Man's pub near the midway point, the Traveller's Rest at the 33km mark and Lock 13 brew pub in Sallins is the ideal spot.

VARIATIONS

It would be possible to combine this route with the Royal - Grand Canal route on page 58 either as a loop or a figure-of-eight.

Due to the nature of this route, it would be hard to maintain the character of this route while reducing the length.

The Upper Glen road in the southeast corner of the park

PHOENIX PARK
County Dublin
ROAD

10km
100m

300m
200m
100m

0 km   2 km   4 km   6 km   8 km   10 km

A gentle lap around Europe's largest urban park.

The Phoenix Park is the largest enclosed public park in a European capital city. It is home to a number of important government buildings including the President's official residence, Ordnance Survey Ireland and Garda Headquarters, as well as Dublin Zoo and a herd of over 500 wild fallow deer. The 700 hectare park consists of meadow, woodland and grass. For more information see phoenixpark.ie.

The described route is really just a suggestion, there is a huge network of tracks and paths to be explored and it's impossible to get too lost.

From the park's main entrance (*53.3482, -6.2964*) follow the bike path northwest on Chesterfield

Avenue and turn left at the roundabout onto Wellington Road, passing the monument erected to the Duke of Wellington.

Follow the road west along the southern edge of the park passing the Magazine Fort. Originally built as a gunpowder store it was in use up until the middle of the last century. After a series of sweeping bends you pass Saint Mary's Hospital.

The road gradually turns north passing the Furry Glen and Ordnance Survey Ireland before crossing Chesterfield Avenue onto North Road. You then follow the cycle path along the northern edge of the park past the Visitor Centre and Dublin Zoo before

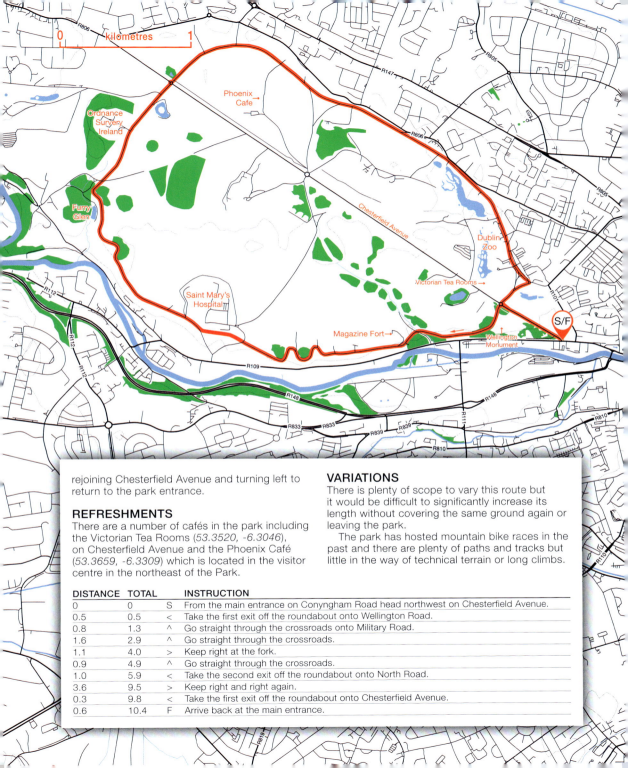

rejoining Chesterfield Avenue and turning left to
return to the park entrance.

REFRESHMENTS

There are a number of cafés in the park including
the Victorian Tea Rooms (53.3520, -6.3046),
on Chesterfield Avenue and the Phoenix Café
(53.3659, -6.3309) which is located in the visitor
centre in the northeast of the Park.

VARIATIONS

There is plenty of scope to vary this route but
it would be difficult to significantly increase its
length without covering the same ground again or
leaving the park.

The park has hosted mountain bike races in the
past and there are plenty of paths and tracks but
little in the way of technical terrain or long climbs.

DISTANCE	TOTAL		INSTRUCTION
0	0	S	From the main entrance on Conyngham Road head northwest on Chesterfield Avenue.
0.5	0.5	<	Take the first exit off the roundabout onto Wellington Road.
0.8	1.3	^	Go straight through the crossroads onto Military Road.
1.6	2.9	^	Go straight through the crossroads.
1.1	4.0	>	Keep right at the fork.
0.9	4.9	^	Go straight through the crossroads.
1.0	5.9	<	Take the second exit off the roundabout onto North Road.
3.6	9.5	>	Keep right and right again.
0.3	9.8	<	Take the first exit off the roundabout onto Chesterfield Avenue.
0.6	10.4	F	Arrive back at the main entrance.

Coliemore Harbour just outside Dalkey Village

DUBLIN BAY
County Dublin
ROAD

37 km
500 m

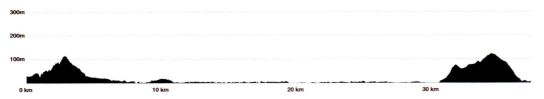

300m
200m
100m

0 km   10 km   20 km   30 km

A flat spin along Dublin Bay with an optional lap of Killiney Hill and climb over the Ben of Howth.

Work is ongoing on a continuous cycle path that will run along Dublin Bay between Sandycove in the south and Sutton in the north. Large sections are already in place and this route follows them when possible. Many of these paths are shared with walkers so exercise caution and use a bell. If you want to cycle at high speed then you may be better off sticking to the roads.

This cycle works well in either direction but is described from south to north, starting and finishing at DART stations. The DART is a handy way to return to your starting point, bicycles are allowed on

board from 10.00 to 16.00 and after 19.00 during the week and at all times on weekends.

The route has plenty of twists and turns, but it's actually quite straightforward, if you keep the sea to your right you can't go too far wrong. Detailed directions haven't been included as there isn't space and they would only confuse.

From Dalkey DART station (*53.2760, -6.1035*) head east along Sorrento Road (R119) before turning right onto Vico Road and climbing across the slopes of Killiney Hill. As you gain height Dalkey Island and the curving shore line that runs south to

Bray Head is revealed. The road then turns inland and drops back down into Dalkey.

Turn left and follow the Metals, a former railway track that was used to transport stone from Dalkey Quarry to Dun Laoghaire Harbour, now a handy traffic-free shortcut.

At People's Park in Dun Laoighaire turn left onto the main road before turning right and following a quiet road through the harbour. This links up with a path that runs along the coast to Seapoint. Follow the road to Blackrock DART station where another path leads through the park.

Back on the road in Booterstown continue north, crossing the tracks at Sandymount and following the road through Ringsend before crossing the River Liffey via the East Link toll bridge.

Heading north turn left onto East Wall Road and then right onto Alfie Byrne Road. After 150m turn right onto the cycle path, which runs along the coast to the edge of Sutton.

At the crossroads in Sutton turn right following the coast until the road turns inland and starts to climb. A steep pull leads back to the main road and after a few more short climbs you arrive at the Summit. It's worth turning right here and climbing the short distance to the viewing point to take in the view across the Bay.

Back on the main road a steep descent leads into Howth Village and the nearby DART station.

REFRESHMENTS
There are dozens of quality places along the route to eat or get a coffee.

VARIATIONS
Omitting the two climbs leaves an easy cycle with practically no climbing. As the route follows the DART line pretty closely you could cycle part of the route and return by train.

Afterburner on the east slopes of Fairy Castle

TICKNOCK TRAIL CENTRE
County Dublin
MTB

11 km
330 m

500m
400m
300m
200m
100m

0 km   2 km   4 km   6 km   8 km   10 km

A short loop around Three Rock Mountain which is only a stone's throw from the Dublin suburbs.

Ticknock Trail Centre is small, with only one relatively short trail, but it's very popular thanks to its proximity to the city. The trail is well signposted and easy to follow. Note that it should only be ridden in an anti-clockwise direction as indicated by the arrows.

There is plenty of parking in the forest but it can get busy on weekends and summer evenings. The gate to the forest is locked after dark, the closing time is on the sign at the entrance.

Even though the singletrack is for cyclists only there are some sections of gravel road that are shared with walkers so stay alert and control your speed.

With a number of rocky, technical sections the trail isn't ideal for beginners, nearby Ballinastoe (page 78) in Wicklow is a better option.

From the carpark (53.2536, -6.2466) head uphill on the tarmac road before turning right onto a short section of singletrack that drops down to the start of the main climb. It's a steady slog, initially across open hillside before the trail enters the forest and weaves up through the trees. Eventually it flattens out and a fast and flowing descent leads back to the tarmac road just below the top of Three Rock.

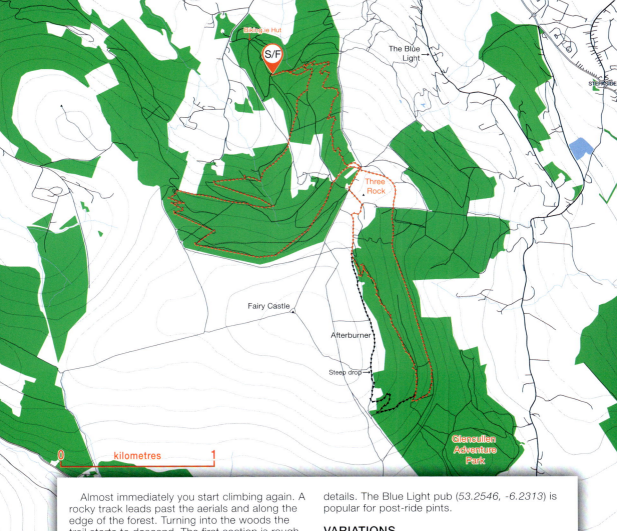

Almost immediately you start climbing again. A rocky track leads past the aerials and along the edge of the forest. Turning into the woods the trail starts to descend. The first section is rough and technical with some really nice berms. It then leaves the trees and becomes faster and more open with a series of easy drops just before the gravel road.

This gravel road leads back to the granite tors at the top of Three Rock where it's well worth stopping to take in the view over Dublin Bay. The long final descent is tricky and deserves to be treated with respect. The trail finishes just beside the gate at the carpark.

REFRESHMENTS
Bike hire and repairs as well as coffee and snacks available from the small building (*53.2557, -6.2491*) in the lower carpark, see biking.ie for

details. The Blue Light pub (*53.2546, -6.2313*) is popular for post-ride pints.

VARIATIONS
The slopes of Ticknock are riddled with unofficial trails but they are hard to make sense of unless you get shown around by a local.

There is one variation of the loop near Two Rock that continues along the edge of the forest before rejoining the main loop. Even though it's graded as harder than the Red Loop there is only really one trickier section, the steep drop at *53.2356, -6.2374*.

Just to the south of the trail is the Glencullen Adventure Park (*53.2231, -6.2252*), a private mountain bike park with about a dozen trails of various difficulties. See thegap.ie for more information.

Heading south with Bray Head in the background

BELMONT AND BRAY HEAD
County Wicklow
MTB

11 km
210 m

Combines the trails in Belmont Demesne with a loop around Bray Head.

This short figure-of-eight route links the purpose-built trails in Belmont with the natural tracks and paths on Bray Head. The route isn't technical so it could be done on either a mountain or gravel bike, however the trails in Belmont are probably more enjoyable on a mountain bike.

Beside the trailhead in Belmont Demesne (53.1621, -6.0996) is Fatbike Adventure (fatbikeadventures.ie) who offer bike hire, sales and servicing as well as guided tours. There is also a pump track beside the carpark which is a good place to warm up before tackling any of the three trails (which must be followed in a clockwise).

The 4.3km Green Trail is a straightforward route that climbs the lower slopes of the Little Sugarloaf before descending on farm tracks, it then climbs steeply though the woods before a gentle descent leads back to the start. Note, it's a shared trail so give way to walkers.

There are two blue trails, the first, Ground Control is a 1.2km loop that is suitable for beginners. It starts with a winding descent with lots of berms. You then climb back to the start via a number of steep switchbacks. The second, Sweet Wood, is a 2km linear trail that connects with the Green Trail.

The 3.3km red trail, Live Wire, is more challenging extension of Ground Control. It weaves its way through beautiful beech forest and has a few short optional sections with steeper descents and climbs.

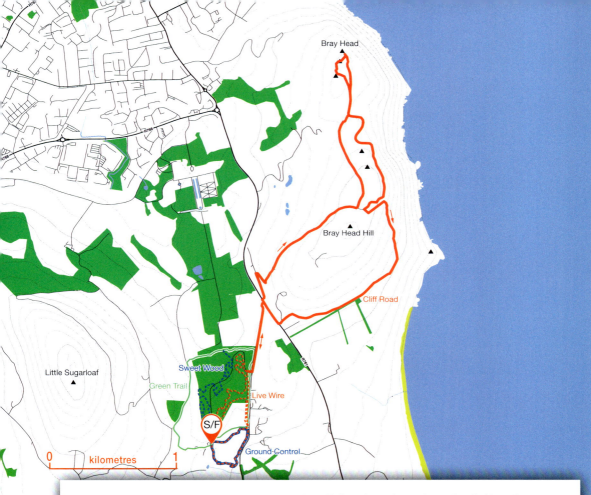

Bray Head

Bray Head Hill

Cliff Road

Little Sugarloaf

Sweet Wood

Green Trail

Live Wire

S/F

Ground Control

0   kilometres   1

Extending Live Wire to include a circuit around Bray Head offers a really nice variety of terrain and some great views. Note that Bray Head is popular with walkers so control your speed.

Follow the Live Wire for 850m and, just as it starts to descend, turn right onto the gravel road that runs through the Demesne. Climb up this and turn left onto the public road.

At the junction with the R761 cross the road and turn right up Ballynamuddagh Road. After 250m turn right onto a gravel track, this climbs up the open hillside with great views into the Wicklow Mountains. As the track flattens and the sea comes into view look out for a grassy track on the left. Follow this gently downhill for 850m until you meet a large track. Continue north climbing a little to the cross on top of Bray Head.

From the cross either retrace your steps or make a short loop around the quartzite dome.

Follow the main track south, climbing almost to the point where you left it earlier. Just before this look out on the left for a gate, go through this. Shoulder your bike and descend the rocky steps and the narrow path that runs beside the wall. As the angle eases hop back on your bike and drop down through the gorse to a gate. Go through this and climb gently up the tarmac lane. At the R761 turn right and then left to retrace your steps back to Belmont and continue along Live Wire.

REFRESHMENTS
There is a café and restaurant beside the carpark in Belmont (parking costs €3 per day).

VARIATIONS
It might be possible to include a circuit on the rocky singletrack that traverses the lower slopes of the Great Sugar Loaf.

Crossing Valleymount Bridge

BLESSINGTON RESERVOIR

County Wicklow

ROAD

36km
340m

This loop around the reservoir offers rolling terrain and great views of the Wicklow Mountains.

Despite the fact that this route doesn't have any long climbs the constantly rolling terrain takes its toll on the legs. It is best done in an anti-clockwise direction as this offers the best view of the reservoir, which generates electricity and supplies drinking water to Dublin.

Currently the 6.5km Blessington Greenway connects the town with Russborough House but there are plans to extend it all the way around the lake.

The route, which is reasonably well signposted as the Lake Drive, starts from the Duke of Downshire monument (*53.1709, -6.5324*) on the Main Street of Blessington.

Head south from the village joining the greenway at the Avon Rí adventure centre. Follow the gravel path along the lakeshore, interrupted with a short stretch along the N81, until the R758 where you turn left and cross the bridge. The greenway continues on the other side to the road to Russborough House.

After climbing over the side of Boystown Hill cross another bridge over to Valleymount. Turn left off the N758 and head north along the lakeshore.

Pass through Ballyknockan over a number of rolling hills until Lacken where the road flattens out. Shortly after crossing the bridge over the River Liffey turn left and follow the west bank of the reservoir back into Blessington.

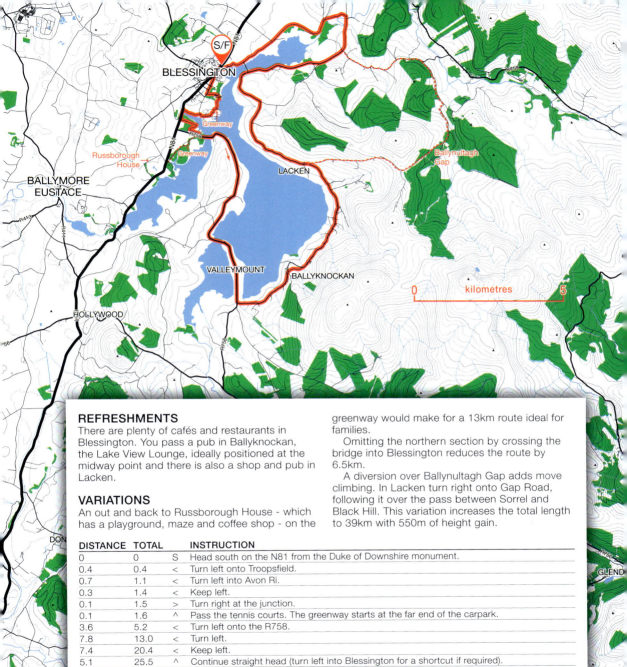

REFRESHMENTS

There are plenty of cafés and restaurants in Blessington. You pass a pub in Ballyknockan, the Lake View Lounge, ideally positioned at the midway point and there is also a shop and pub in Lacken.

VARIATIONS

An out and back to Russborough House - which has a playground, maze and coffee shop - on the greenway would make for a 13km route ideal for families.

Omitting the northern section by crossing the bridge into Blessington reduces the route by 6.5km.

A diversion over Ballynultagh Gap adds move climbing. In Lacken turn right onto Gap Road, following it over the pass between Sorrel and Black Hill. This variation increases the total length to 39km with 550m of height gain.

DISTANCE	TOTAL		INSTRUCTION
0	0	S	Head south on the N81 from the Duke of Downshire monument.
0.4	0.4	<	Turn left onto Troopsfield.
0.7	1.1	<	Turn left into Avon Ri.
0.3	1.4	<	Keep left.
0.1	1.5	>	Turn right at the junction.
0.1	1.6	^	Pass the tennis courts. The greenway starts at the far end of the carpark.
3.6	5.2	<	Turn left onto the R758.
7.8	13.0	<	Turn left.
7.4	20.4	<	Keep left.
5.1	25.5	^	Continue straight head (turn left into Blessington for a shortcut if required).
4.7	30.2	<	Just after the bridge turn left.
0.9	31.1	<	Keep left.
4.5	35.6	>	Turn right onto the N81.
0.1	35.7	F	Arrive back at the Duke of Downshire monument.

Just before the top of the climb past the Lough Bray lakes

WEST WICKLOW
County Wicklow
ROAD

37 km
860 m

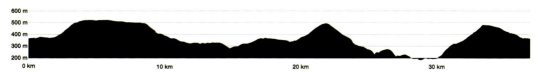

A cycle through some of the quieter parts of West Wicklow.

This route is effectively a clockwise circuit of Kippure, the highest point in Dublin. There are a number of testing climbs, but in return you get to experience a good mix of remote countryside and quiet roads.

From the start in Glencree (*53.1991, -6.2932*) follow the Military Road climbing past Lower and Upper Lough Bray to a bleak plateau.

From the crossroads at Sally Gap turn right and descend past the beautiful Scots pine of the Coronation Plantation. Watch out for sheep!

Shortly after the Kippure Estate turn right onto a boreen, climbing again. After descending past the Kilbride Army Base another tough climb leads to a great view over the city. A lightning fast descent on a great surface leads to the R114 which you follow around a few sweeping bends before turning right into Bohernabreena. You then climb gently past the reservoir to the head of the valley.

Just after a small cluster of granite cottages turn right and start up Hill Road, a beast of a climb. The first, and steepest section is 11%, before it eases back to a mere 7%. The climbing ends at the junction where you turn right onto the Military Road and follow it down into Glencree.

REFRESHMENTS
There isn't anywhere to stop on the route but there is a café at the start of the route in the Centre for Peace and Reconciliation in Glencree.

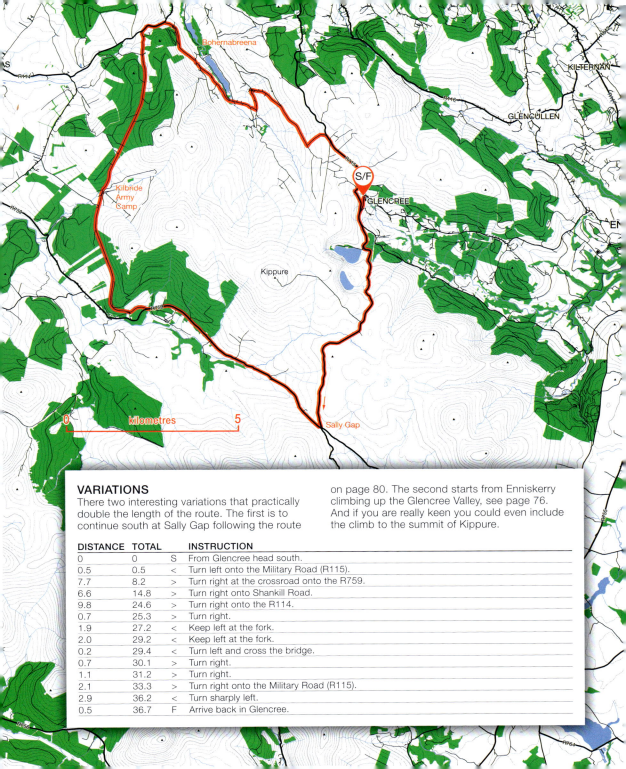

Bohernabreena

KILTERNAN

GLENCULLEN

R116

Kilbride
Army
Camp

S/F

GLENCREE

Kippure

R759

0   kilometres   5

Sally Gap

VARIATIONS

There two interesting variations that practically double the length of the route. The first is to continue south at Sally Gap following the route on page 80. The second starts from Enniskerry climbing up the Glencree Valley, see page 76. And if you are really keen you could even include the climb to the summit of Kippure.

DISTANCE	TOTAL		INSTRUCTION
0	0	S	From Glencree head south.
0.5	0.5	<	Turn left onto the Military Road (R115).
7.7	8.2	>	Turn right at the crossroad onto the R759.
6.6	14.8	>	Turn right onto Shankill Road.
9.8	24.6	>	Turn right onto the R114.
0.7	25.3	>	Turn right.
1.9	27.2	<	Keep left at the fork.
2.0	29.2	<	Keep left at the fork.
0.2	29.4	<	Turn left and cross the bridge.
0.7	30.1	>	Turn right.
1.1	31.2	>	Turn right.
2.1	33.3	>	Turn right onto the Military Road (R115).
2.9	36.2	<	Turn sharply left.
0.5	36.7	F	Arrive back in Glencree.

The descent from the mast

KIPPURE
County Wicklow
ROAD

38km
960m

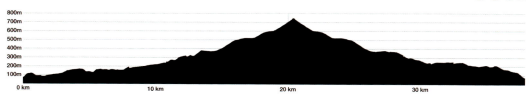

The climb up Kippure is the second longest continuous climb in the country.

The summit of Kippure, with its distinctive mast, is the highest point in Dublin and one of the highest points in the country with a surfaced road. This route climbs to the summit from the picturesque village of Enniskerry.

The route is described in a clockwise direction so that you climb the quieter roads on the south side of Glencree valley and descend the busier main road.

From the clock tower in the centre of Enniskerry (53.1926,-6.1699) follow the R760 south, climbing steeply out of the village. At the junction with Waterfall Road turn right descending to the entrance to Powerscourt Waterfall (the highest waterfall in Ireland). The steep pull just past the entrance marks the start of the climbing. The summit of Kippure lies 615m above, the average gradient is 4% but it's steeper near the top.

After the entrance to Crone Woods the roads becomes quieter. A steeper section at the head of the valley leads to the Military Road where you turn left. A brief flat stretch offers an opportunity to catch your breath before the climb past Lower and Upper Lough Bray to open bogland. There is another brief respite before the right turn onto the service road that leads to the summit.

The climb starts reasonably gently and it's only after crossing the stream that it starts to bite. The final section averages 9%.

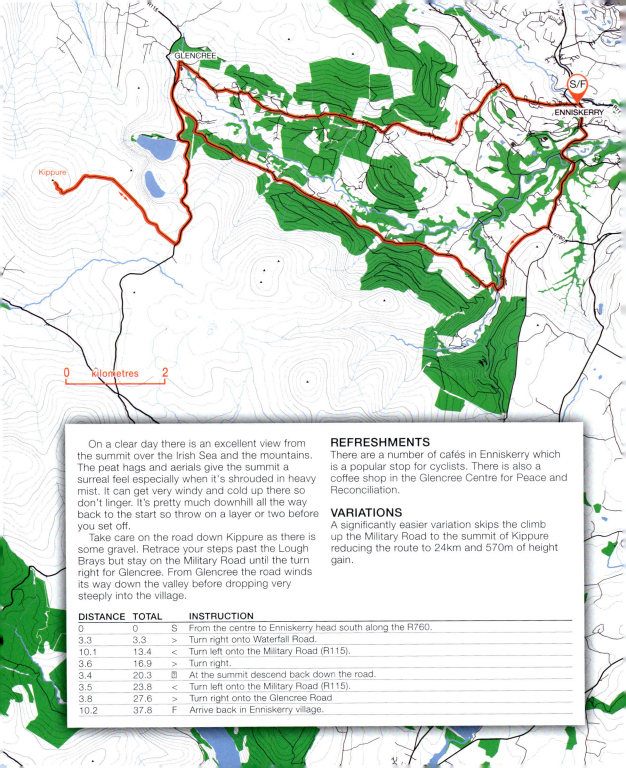

On a clear day there is an excellent view from the summit over the Irish Sea and the mountains. The peat hags and aerials give the summit a surreal feel especially when it's shrouded in heavy mist. It can get very windy and cold up there so don't linger. It's pretty much downhill all the way back to the start so throw on a layer or two before you set off.

Take care on the road down Kippure as there is some gravel. Retrace your steps past the Lough Brays but stay on the Military Road until the turn right for Glencree. From Glencree the road winds its way down the valley before dropping very steeply into the village.

REFRESHMENTS

There are a number of cafés in Enniskerry which is a popular stop for cyclists. There is also a coffee shop in the Glencree Centre for Peace and Reconciliation.

VARIATIONS

A significantly easier variation skips the climb up the Military Road to the summit of Kippure reducing the route to 24km and 570m of height gain.

DISTANCE	TOTAL		INSTRUCTION
0	0	S	From the centre to Enniskerry head south along the R760.
3.3	3.3	>	Turn right onto Waterfall Road.
10.1	13.4	<	Turn left onto the Military Road (R115).
3.6	16.9	>	Turn right.
3.4	20.3	⊡	At the summit descend back down the road.
3.5	23.8	<	Turn left onto the Military Road (R115).
3.8	27.6	>	Turn right onto the Glencree Road
10.2	37.8	F	Arrive back in Enniskerry village.

Fancy, part of the Red Trail, with Luggala in the background

BALLINASTOE TRAIL CENTRE

County Wicklow
MTB

11.2 km
280 m

A great selection of trails for more experienced riders.

In early 2023 a number of new trails opened in Ballinastoe Wood, prior to that it was home to single 16km red trail. These recent additions have dramatically increased the variety and difficulty of trails available.

The trail centre (53.1074, -6.2170) now has one blue trail, a red trail with a number of variations and four sections of black trail. The red trails seem to be a little more challenging than equivalent trails in most other centres. All the trails are well maintained with a fast-draining gravel base that is rideable throughout the year.

BLUE TRAIL

The 4.5km Blue Trail (110m height gain) climbs up Easy Rider and Cool Runnings before descending Double Trouble, House Bound and Flatliner.

RED TRAILS

The Red Trail climbs north from the carpark on a forest road. After a short distance Home Run, which leads back to the trailhead, branches out to the right. After a long, steady climb the trail continues upwards on singletrack, Zipper, before descending to a forest road (Waypoint 3). Here there are two options, Dark Loam and then Holts (6.9km, 190m

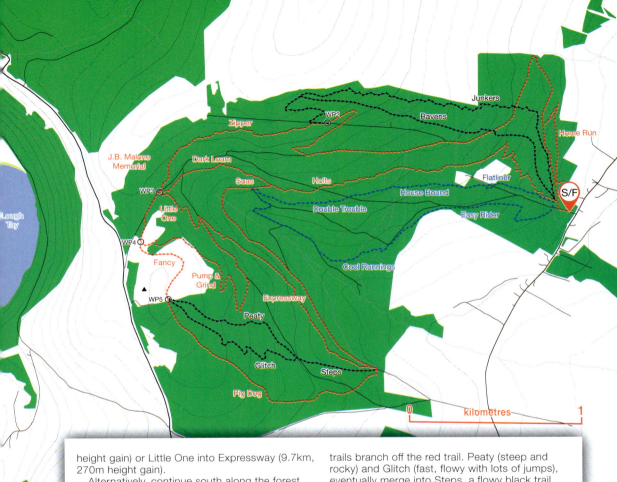

height gain) or Little One into Expressway (9.7km, 270m height gain).

Alternatively, continue south along the forest road and turn left onto the singletrack where, after short distance, you meet Waypoint 4. Here you have a choice between Pump & Grind into Expressway (11.1km, 290m height gain) or Fancy into Pig Dog (11.2km, 280m of height gain).

The latter three options all lead down to a forest road in the southeast corner which you climb back up to join Holts.

BLACK TRAILS

At the highpoint of the climb on Zipper (Waypoint 2) a black trail branches off to the right and climbs for a short distance. As it starts to descend it divides into two black trails. Junkers (more flowy) and Ravens (more technical) both lead back down to the carpark, giving a loop of 5.5km with 220m of height gain.

There are also two black variations around the back of the red trail. At Waypoint 5 two black

trails branch off the red trail. Peaty (steep and rocky) and Glitch (fast, flowy with lots of jumps), eventually merge into Steps, a flowy black trail, before rejoining the red trail at the forest road.

REFRESHMENTS

There is a hut at the trailhead that sells coffee and snacks as well as offering bike hire, repair and bike washing facilities (see biking.ie for more information). The nearby village of Roundwood (53.0646, -6.2244) has a good café and a number of decent pubs and takeaways.

VARIATIONS

Just to the north is Djouce Woods (53.1552, -6.1878) which has a huge number of unofficial trails, many of which are extremely difficult. The first time visitor will struggle to find their way around, the Strava Heatmap (labs.strava.com/heatmap) gives some sense of where the most popular trails are.

Passing Lough Tay

ROUNDWOOD AND SALLY GAP
County Wicklow
ROAD

41 km
730 m

This route, although relatively short, packs in plenty of climbing and some of the best scenery the county has to offer.

There are a number of possible routes to Sally Gap, the desolate crossroads at the heart of the Wicklow Mountains. This route is one of the best and if the views don't take your breath away then the climbs certainly will.

The route starts in the village of Roundwood, the highest in Ireland apparently. There is plenty of parking on the left just before the Roundwood Inn.

From the village (*53.0644, -6.2246*) head north following the signs for Sally Gap. After turning left at the crossroads the road starts to climb and the fields and hedgerows are replaced by open hillside and pine forest.

Near the top the road briefly relents before one last brutally steep section leads to possibly the best view in Wicklow. From the road the steep slopes fall away down to the dark, peaty water of Lough Tay offering an almost bird's eye view of the Luggala Estate.

Ahead the road stretches up to Sally Gap, where you turn left onto the Military Road which, for the next 20km, weaves through some of the most desolate and beautiful landscape in the country.

At Glenmacnass Waterfall the road drops steeply to the valley floor and it's an easy, slightly downhill run into the village of Laragh. Here you briefly follow the main road north before turning left onto the back

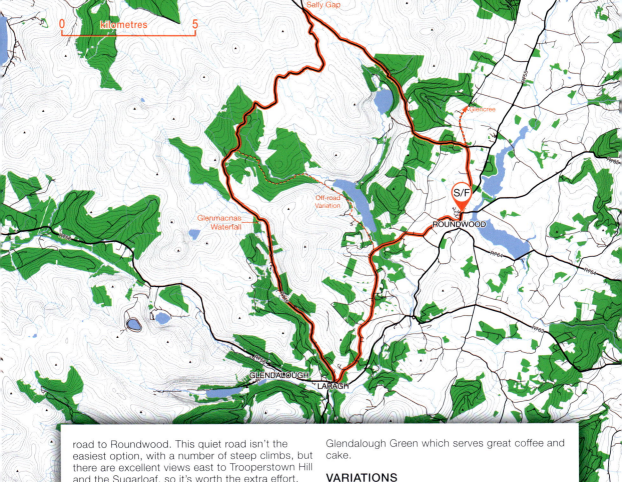

road to Roundwood. This quiet road isn't the easiest option, with a number of steep climbs, but there are excellent views east to Trooperstown Hill and the Sugarloaf, so it's worth the extra effort.

The bridge over the Avonmore River signals the start of the final climb of the day, a steep slog through beautiful oak woodland. Then it's downhill the rest of the way into Roundwood.

REFRESHMENTS

Roundwood has a number of pubs and cafés. The only other stop on the route is in Laragh at

Glendalough Green which serves great coffee and cake.

VARIATIONS

One way to extend this route would be to continue north rather than turning left towards Lough Tay. You would then drop into the Glencree valley, following the Kippure route (page 76) to the point where it turns onto the road up to Kippure. You would continue south along the Military Road and rejoin the described route at Sally Gap.

DISTANCE	TOTAL		INSTRUCTION
0	0	S	From Roundwood head north on the R755.
0.7	0.7	<	Keep left at the fork.
2.2	2.9	<	Turn left at the junction.
8.8	11.7	<	Turn left at the crossroads.
19.5	31.2	<	Keep left, pass the coffee shop and join the R755.
0.1	31.3	<	Turn left.
5.8	37.1	>	Keep right at the fork.
1.4	38.5	>	Keep right.
2.4	40.9	F	Arrive back in Roundwood village.

Just past the bridge at the mouth of the Kilcoole Estuary

WICKLOW COAST
County Wicklow
GRAVEL

32km
170m

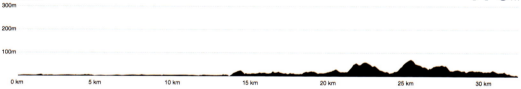

Combines technical riding on a coastal path with quiet roads and laneways.

This is a route with two very distinct halves. The first half, between Kilcoole and Wicklow Town, follows the coastal path that runs alongside the train tracks. And despite it being dead flat there are a number of challenging sections of deep sand that require plenty of power, however they are brief and most of this stretch is engaging riding on narrow paths. The second half is easier going following cycle paths, quiet roads and a few really nice rough laneways.

The loop starts and finishes in the carpark (53.1062, -6.0413) beside the train station in Kilcoole. It's best done in a clockwise direction so that you tackle the power-sapping sand with fresh legs.

From the carpark cross the tracks and head south, the next 13km follow sandy paths and tracks through the grass/dunes that back the beach.

Initially the going is reasonable, with only an occasional patch of deep sand. Further on there are a few longer sandy sections, some of which you might find easier to walk. Shortly after Five Mile Point there is a 350m stretch where the best option is to cycle on the top of the low wall, after this the going becomes easier and the last 4km into Wicklow Town are on a firm track.

From the carpark you turn right on the R999 and follow the cycle path west. Pass through Rathnew, turning right onto the R761 just after the Aldi. Look out for a narrow lane on the left-hand side 650m

82

S/F

KILCOOLE

NEWTOWNMOUNTKENNEDY

N11

N11A

R774

R765

R766

R772

NEWCASTLE

Six Mile Point

Chapel
Lane

Five Mile Point

Killoughter
Lane

R773

ROUNDWOOD

R764

R764

R763

ASHFORD

R772

RATHNEW

R999

WICKLOW

RATHDRUM

0   kilometres   2

past the crossroads. This climbs steeply and is rough in places, watch out for farm machinery. Just before it meets the road splash through the ford and turn right, then left back onto the R761. After 250m turn left onto a gravel track, Church Lane, which climbs to the route's high point of 65m.

At the t-junction, just past the church, turn left and after 100m turn right onto Leabeg Lane. This leads very pleasantly back to the R761 which you follow north for 2.5km back to Kilcoole. Turn right in the village onto Sea Road, the smooth tarmac leads back to the start.

REFRESHMENTS
The rough midpoint of the route is at Wicklow Town which has plenty of good options. There are also a number of places to stop in Kilcoole village.

VARIATIONS
It would be possible to shorten the route by leaving the coast at Killoughter Lane (*53.0254, -6.0496*), this reduces the route to 22.5km with 140m height gain. The two diversions off the R761 could be skipped, but that would be a pity as they are really enjoyable.

The descent down to the Green Road

DERRYBAWN
County Wicklow
GRAVEL

20km
760m

This off-road route has plenty of hard climbing on gravel tracks with excellent views over Glendalough.

The forested hills south of Glendalough host a network of rough gravel tracks and this routes weaves a loop around them. Despite its short length there is a lot of height gain with one long sustained climb and a number of shorter ones.

The route can be done on a gravel bike or hybrid with reasonably wide tyres but a mountain bike wouldn't be out of place either.

Note that off-road cycling is only permitted on the gravel roads in Wicklow National Park. This route shares ground with a number of signposted trails so control your speed and watch out for walkers, particularly on the descents.

The route starts and finishes in Laragh. Parking can be scarce in the village, particularly on weekends, so arrive early.

From Laragh (*53.0089, -6.2957*) head south on the R755 before turning right into the Woollen Mills. Passing through the archway on the left of the building leads to a rough track called the Green Road that links Laragh and the lakes of Glendalough.

Follow the Green Road past the Monastic Village and the Lower Lake. This section can be very busy with tourists, so take it slowly and be patient.

Shortly before the National Park information office a track leads steeply up to the left, marked by a pink

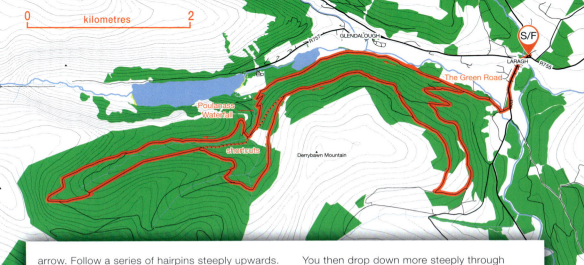

arrow. Follow a series of hairpins steeply upwards. If you want to check out Poulanass Waterfall then take the (unrideable) path to the right of the stream.

At the top of the climb turn right, cross the two bridges and follow the blue arrows. Climb steadily up the track, passing the point where the red trail turns right, until the angle eases near the head of the valley.

After you pass beneath the cliffs of Prezen Rock the track starts to descend back down the valley. After a fast straight descent turn uphill and follow the red arrows east across the open slopes of Derrybawn Mountain. You then meet the orange trail and continue east over a series of short climbs. Make sure to stop at the bench and take in the excellent views over Glendalough and down the Avonmore valley to the Irish Sea.

You then drop down more steeply through beautiful oak forest, passing through a number of gates, before rejoining the Green Road and retracing your steps to Laragh.

REFRESHMENTS

Glendalough Green in Laragh serves excellent coffee and cakes and is popular with cyclists.

VARIATIONS

There are a number of shorter variations. You could return back down by Poulanass Waterfall after completing the western section of the route or you could skip the western section entirely by following the Wicklow Way from the junction at the top of Poulanass to join the eastern half of the route.

DISTANCE	TOTAL		INSTRUCTION
0	0	S	From Glendalough Green head southwest and cross the bridge.
0.1	0.1	<	Turn left onto the R755.
0.6	0.7	>	Turn right for the Woollen Mills.
0.2	0.9	^	Go through the archway on the left hand side of the building and follow the rough track.
3.2	4.1	<	Turn left up steep track, marked by pink arrow.
0.8	4.9	>	Turn right and cross two bridges.
0.2	5.1	^	Continue straight ahead at the crossroads, following the blue arrows.
1.7	6.8	>	Keep right at the fork.
1.8	8.6	>	Turn right.
1.5	10.1	>	Turn right.
0.5	10.6	<	Keep left at the fork, following the red arrows.
1.9	12.5	>	Turn right, following the orange arrows.
1.5	14.0	>	Keep right.
2.0	16.0	<	Keep left.
1.3	17.3	>	Turn right and go through the gate.
1.1	18.4	>	Turn right onto the Green Road.
0.7	19.1	<	Turn left onto the R755.
0.8	19.9	F	Arrive back in Laragh.

The middle section of the Wicklow Gap climb

LUGNAQUILLA
County Wicklow
ROAD

72km
1570m

A tough circuit of Wicklow's highest mountain that takes in many of Wicklow's classic climbs.

This route is a real test of the legs and would be a great training ride for the Wicklow 200 with which it shares some ground. It starts with a long climb before plenty of rolling ground in the middle section and then finishes with two more tough climbs in quick succession.

The route is best done anti-clockwise to get the biggest climb finished early and to take advantage of the prevailing wind on the last two climbs.

From Laragh (53.0084, -6.2974) head west along the R756. The first few kilometres before the turn for Glendalough are flat and a good warm up for the 6.7km climb over Wicklow Gap. It's a steady 5%

gradient along a somewhat busy road which was taken by the Tour de France when it visited Ireland in 1998. The turn for the hydroelectric station at Turlough Hill marks the finish and it's a fast descent with some sweeping bends down the other side.

Turning left off the main road onto a small boreen leads through a narrow valley. Turn left at the junction and head south through the village of Donard into the Glen of Imaal. Here the terrain is rolling but the hills get bigger as you head further south. Swinging east you meet the start of the Military Road (page 88) in Aghavannagh and start the second big climb over Slieve Mann (3.2km

7.8%). After a fast descent into Glenmalure you immediately start the last climb (3.0km 7.8%) of the day. Known as the Shay Elliot after the memorial stone at the top in honour of Elliot, the first Irish cyclist to make a mark as a professional rider in Europe. From the top a winding descent leads back into Laragh.

REFRESHMENTS

There is a shop and pub in Donard and Glenmalure Lodge at the crossroads in Glenmalure serves food and drink. There is also a café, restaurant and pub in Laragh.

VARIATIONS

There isn't any scope for shortcuts however there are shorter routes nearby such as the 41km Roundwood and Sally Gap route (see page 80).

This route has plenty of climbing but if you really want to challenge yourself then include the climb to the reservoir at Turlough Hill. From Glendalough to the reservoir is just under 10km gaining 550 meters with an average gradient of 5.5% making it one of the longest climbs in the country.

DISTANCE	TOTAL		INSTRUCTION
0	0	S	From Laragh head west on the R756.
1.6	1.6	>	Keep right at the fork.
20.5	22.1	<	Turn left (signposted "St. Kevin's Way").
3.2	25.3	<	Turn left at the junction.
2.2	27.5	<	Keep left at the fork.
5.0	32.5	<	Turn left at the t-junction.
4.2	36.7	>	Turn right.
2.1	38.8	^	Go straight through the crossroads.
0.7	39.5	<	Keep left at the fork.
4.3	43.8	<	Turn left.
5.3	49.1	<	Turn left at the crossroads.
13.9	63.0	^	Go straight through the crossroads.
7.6	70.6	<	Turn left onto the R755.
1.4	72.0	F	Arrive back in Laragh.

Near the top of the climb to the Shay Elliot memorial

THE MILITARY ROAD
County Wicklow
ROAD

79km
1670m

This linear route follows the Military Road through the heart of the Wicklow Mountains tackling a number of tough climbs along the way.

The Military Road was constructed by the British Army in the early 1800s to help them suppress the Irish rebels. This linear route starts in Rathdrum which is easily accessed by train from Connolly Station in Dublin (see sportireland.ie/outdoors for details).

The route is described from south to north so that those travelling by train aren't under time pressure. Also the prevailing wind should be in your favour and the hard climbing is tackled early in the day.

From the train station in Rathdrum (52.9304, -6.2261) head west climbing from the start on quiet roads over the shoulder of Coolgarrow Mountain.

You then descend by a slightly convoluted route to the very start of the Military Road at an unassuming junction. A short distance later cross the River Ow for the second time and arrive in the townland of Aghavannagh.

Shortly after the old barracks you start the second of the day's four climbs over the shoulder of Slieve Mann which has an 8% average gradient over 250m of height gain. You then drop into Glenmalure and immediately start the second climb to the Shay Elliot memorial. Elliot was the first Irish cyclist to make a mark as a professional rider in Europe and won stages in all three Grand Tours. The climb is of

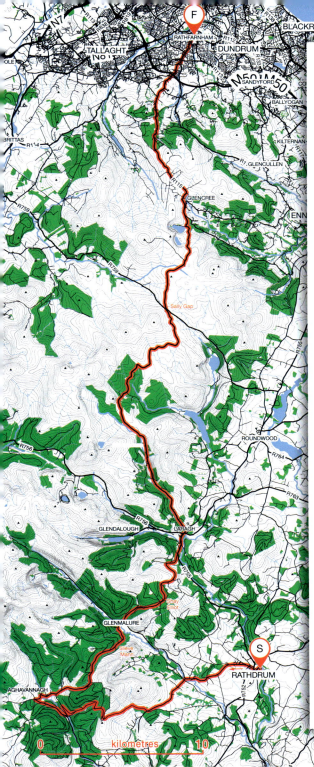

almost identical difficulty to the previous one and from the memorial stone that marks the top it's a fast descent into Laragh.

The final climb of the day up Glenmacnass valley is steady and the gradient is gentle, but it's long, nearly 20km. There is one steep section (6%) from the valley floor to the top of the waterfall.

The cluster of signposts at Sally Gap signal the end of the day's climbing. After descending past the Lough Brays there is a brief climb to the Featherbeds, the last patch of wilderness before the steep descent into the suburbs. A short distance after crossing the motorway the Military Road finishes at the Yellowhouse pub in Rathfarnham.

REFRESHMENTS

Glenmalure Inn offers food and drink and there are a number of cafés, restaurant and a shop in Laragh, which is close to the halfway mark. There is also a coffee shop just off the route in the Centre for Peace and Reconciliation in Glencree.

VARIATIONS

An easier variation also starts in Rathdrum but heads directly to meet the Military Road in Laragh via the R755. This route is 53km with 790m of height gain.

DISTANCE	TOTAL		INSTRUCTION
0	0	S	Head north from the train station and turn left onto the R752.
0.5	0.5	>	Turn right onto Main Street.
0.3	0.8	<	Turn left onto Brewery Lane.
0.5	1.3	<	Keep left.
1.1	2.4	<	Keep left.
3.2	5.6	<	Turn left over the bridge.
3.4	9.0	>	Turn right.
7.6	16.6	<	Sharp left turn.
0.8	17.4	>	Turn right and cross the bridge.
0.2	17.6	>	Keep right.
0.1	17.7	>	Keep right.
0.7	18.4	>	Keep right.
1.4	19.8	>	Turn right onto the Military Road.
9.4	29.2	^	Go straight through the crossroads.
7.6	36.8	<	Turn left onto the R755.
1.4	38.2	>	Turn right at the t-junction.
0.1	38.3	<	Turn left and then left again on the R115.
19.6	57.9	^	Go straight through the crossroads.
18.0	75.9	<	Second exit off the roundabout.
0.8	76.7	>	Turn right.
0.4	77.1	<	Turn left.
0.1	77.2	<	Second exit off the roundabout.
1.9	79.1	F	Arrive at the end of the Military Road at the Yellowhouse.

The final climb to the summit of Mount Leinster

MOUNT LEINSTER
County Carlow/Wexford
ROAD

43km
1090m

A hard route featuring one of the longest road climbs in the country.

While not all that long this route packs a serious punch with 665m of height gain in one continuous climb. It's best done in a clockwise direction so you are well warmed up before you start climbing. However if you really want to maximise the suffering then do it anti-clockwise as the climb from Bunclody to the top of Mount Leinster, with 750m of height gain, is the longest in Ireland.

From the Main Street of Bunclody (*52.6550, -6.6514*) head west and turn left before St. Mary's Church following the quiet road out of the town. The Blackstairs Mountains appear on your right and Mount Leinster is easily recognised by the RTE transmitter on its summit.

The route passes through rolling farmland avoiding the R746 and R702 where possible on quiet side roads, some of which are a little rough. If you are in

a hurry or want a smooth ride then stick to the R746 and R702.

In the village of Kiltealy turn right and climb over Scullogue Gap taking a shortcut along a back road. After re-joining the R702 turn right at the stone and follow the road downhill across the lower slopes of Knockroe.

Soon the road starts to climb and it's uphill all the way to Nine Stones and onwards to the top of Mount Leinster. The gradient isn't too bad, it's steeper at the start but it eases back. After 5km and 300m of height gain you arrive at the carpark at Nine Stones.

From the carpark it's 2.5km to the summit with an average gradient of 13%. To do this without stopping takes serious fitness, most mortals will run out of gears and end up walking, but it's worth the slog for the amazing 360° views from the top.

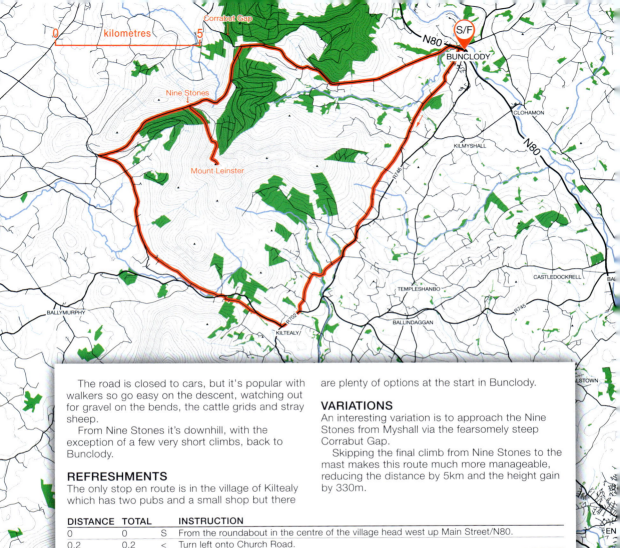

The road is closed to cars, but it's popular with walkers so go easy on the descent, watching out for gravel on the bends, the cattle grids and stray sheep.

From Nine Stones it's downhill, with the exception of a few very short climbs, back to Bunclody.

REFRESHMENTS

The only stop en route is in the village of Kiltealy which has two pubs and a small shop but there are plenty of options at the start in Bunclody.

VARIATIONS

An interesting variation is to approach the Nine Stones from Myshall via the fearsomely steep Corrabut Gap.

Skipping the final climb from Nine Stones to the mast makes this route much more manageable, reducing the distance by 5km and the height gain by 330m.

DISTANCE	TOTAL		INSTRUCTION
0	0	S	From the roundabout in the centre of the village head west up Main Street/N80.
0.2	0.2	<	Turn left onto Church Road.
7.8	8.0	>	Turn right onto the R746.
1.0	9.0	>	Turn right.
2.8	11.8	>	Turn right onto the R702.
0.8	12.6	>	Turn right staying on the R702.
1.1	13.7	>	Turn left off the R702.
1.3	15.0	<	Turn left onto the R702.
0.2	15.2	>	Turn right.
7.2	22.4	>	Turn sharply right.
3.7	26.1	>	Turn right onto the road up to the mast.
2.7	28.8	^	Summit of Mount Leinster, back down you go.
2.6	31.4	>	Turn right.
3.3	34.7	>	Turn right at the junction.
8.2	42.9	>	Turn right onto the N80.
0.4	43.3	F	Arrive back at the roundabout.

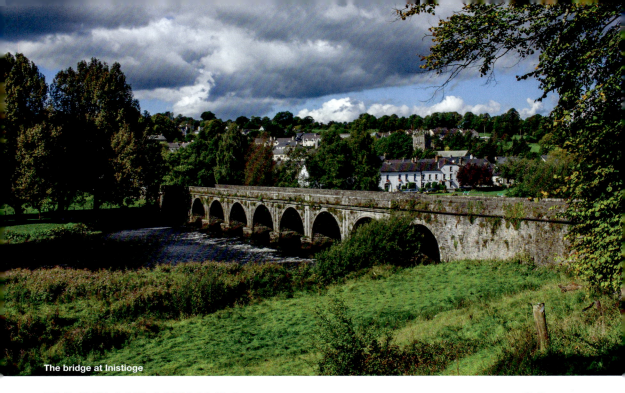

The bridge at Inistioge

EAST KILKENNY
County Kilkenny
ROAD

63km
750m

A loop through the Kilkenny countryside following the course of two of Ireland's largest rivers the Barrow and the Nore.

This route follows the East Kilkenny Cycle route which is one of four Trail Kilkenny (trailkilkenny.ie) cycling routes. It is described in a clockwise direction but is just as good in the other. The route is well signposted in both directions (route number 2) so turn by turn directions aren't required. There aren't any long climbs on the route but there are plenty of shorter steep ones.

From the village of Bennettsbridge, which has parking (52.5925, -7.1831) opposite the shrine on the Gowran road, head northeast on quiet flat roads to Gowran. After a short steep climb out of the

village veer east following the R702 to Goresbridge. Ahead in the distance are the Blackstairs Mountains.

In Goresbridge turn right and climb gently to the highest point of the route before dropping down to Graiguenamanagh. Leaving the pretty village you climb over the shoulder of Brandon Hill. As you gain height above the valley floor there are good views of the remains of the monastery at St. Mullins nestling among the trees.

Leaving the busy R705 the route drops down to meet the River Nore in Inistioge. From the edge of the village follow the road along the eastern bank of the river. A good climb with a steep initial section

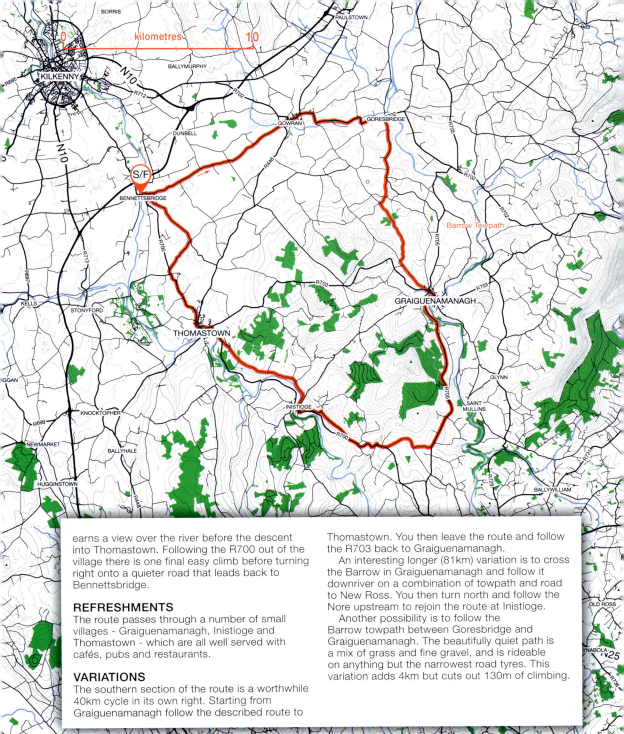

earns a view over the river before the descent into Thomastown. Following the R700 out of the village there is one final easy climb before turning right onto a quieter road that leads back to Bennettsbridge.

REFRESHMENTS
The route passes through a number of small villages - Graiguenamanagh, Inistioge and Thomastown - which are all well served with cafés, pubs and restaurants.

VARIATIONS
The southern section of the route is a worthwhile 40km cycle in its own right. Starting from Graiguenamanagh follow the described route to Thomastown. You then leave the route and follow the R703 back to Graiguenamanagh.

An interesting longer (81km) variation is to cross the Barrow in Graiguenamanagh and follow it downriver on a combination of towpath and road to New Ross. You then turn north and follow the Nore upstream to rejoin the route at Inistioge.

Another possibility is to follow the Barrow towpath between Goresbridge and Graiguenamanagh. The beautifully quiet path is a mix of grass and fine gravel, and is rideable on anything but the narrowest road tyres. This variation adds 4km but cuts out 130m of climbing.

SOUTH

The Gap of Dunloe, Kerry, see page 124

FAMILY CYCLING IN THE SOUTH

All of the following route are traffic-free and reasonably short.

CLARE

1 O'BRIENSBRIDGE *52.7528, -8.4988*
A wonderful path runs alongside the River Shannon from O'Briensbridge to Parteen Weir where you can either retrace your steps (1.75km each way) or continue along the gravel track in an anti-clockwise direction (3.5km).

LIMERICK

2 LIMERICK RIVERBANK *52.6761, -8.5836*
This 3.25km multi-use trail runs along the River Shannon linking the University of Limerick with the city centre. There are a number of other cycling trails in the city.

3 CURRAGHCHASE FOREST PARK *52.6182, -8.8802*
This woodland estate has 8km of multi-use trails including the 2.4km Curragh and 3.6km Glenisca trails. There are two children's playgrounds as well as picnic and barbecue facilities.

4 BALLYHOURA TRAIL CENTRE *52.3189, -8.5067*
This mountain bike trail centre has a number of trails for all levels including the 6km Green Trail and a short skills loop that are ideal for beginners. See page 104 for more information.

KERRY

5 TRALEE CANAL *52.2611, -9.7487*
A towpath runs for 2.5km alongside the canal that connects Tralee Bay with the town. As the path runs close to the water's edge this cycle isn't suitable for very young children.

6 GLANTEENASSIG *52.2053, -10.0486*
This forest park is hidden in the mountains on the north side of the Dingle Peninsula. A gravel road loops around the park for 8km. Pay attention as the gravel track is also used by cars.

7 INCH BEACH *52.1424, -9.9830*
The vast sandy spit that stretches out from the southern shore of the Dingle Peninsula is ideal for cycling. The sand is hard-packed and there is a huge amount of space. There may be cars parked on the beach but it's always possible to find a quieter area.

8 MUCKROSS LAKE *52.0186, -9.5009*
The 10km loop around the middle of the three Killarney lakes is ideal for kids. It's all off-road with the exception of one short section of busy road that can be avoided. There is plenty to see in the park and lots of other paths and tracks to explore. See page 122 for a detailed description of this route.

CORK

9 GOUGANE BARRA FOREST PARK *51.8306, -9.3328*
This forest park is nestled deep in the spectacular Sheehy Mountains. A 2.7km gravel road loops through the park, it's suitable for children but as it's shared with cars care must be taken.

10 CARRIGALINE TO CROSSHAVEN GREENWAY *51.8110, -8.3714*
This 5km cycle path runs along the southern shore of the Owenabue River connecting Carrigaline and Crosshaven.

11 DONERAILE PARK *52.2220, -8.5816*
The 160 hectare landscaped park near Mallow has an extensive network of paths running through its manicured grounds. A map board in the carpark details the various trails and loops. There is a playground beside the carpark and a café in the courtyard of Doneraile House.

WATERFORD

12 WATERFORD GREENWAY *52.0932, -7.6220*
The hugely popular greenway is ideal for kids of all ages. The initial 20km stretch between Dungarvan and Kilmacthomas is the most interesting with a long tunnel and a number of impressive viaducts. See page 98 for more information.

Ballyvoyle Viaduct

WATERFORD GREENWAY
County Waterford
ROAD

41 km

550 m

The Greenway has been very popular with families and leisure cyclists since it opened in the spring of 2017.

The Waterford Greenway follows the course of the disused Waterford to Mallow railway crossing eleven bridges, three viaducts and passing through one long tunnel on its 41km journey between Dungarvan and Waterford City.

The greenway is very family-friendly with only the most gradual inclines that are barely noticeable. It has been very popular since it opened, and it can get very busy particularly during school holidays and at weekends.

As many of the users are small children or people who haven't been on a bike for years you have to be very alert, a bell is essential for overtaking safely. It

isn't suitable for cyclists who are looking for a hard workout unless you choose a time when it's very quiet.

The surface is generally good, mostly tarmac but there are a few sections of gravel.

If you are planning to cycle the greenway in one direction then it's probably best to take advantage of the prevailing wind by starting in Dungarvan and heading northeast to Waterford City.

From the free carpark near the N25 in Dungarvan (*52.0932, -7.6220*) the route crosses the Colligan River and heads east through the outskirts of the town. After 7km it turns inland and crosses the

Ballyvoyle Viaduct. The original stone viaduct was constructed in 1878, and after it was blown up during the Civil War in 1922 it was replaced with the steep truss structure.

A short distance later you come to the 400m Durrow (Ballyvoyle) tunnel, one of the most memorable features of the greenway. Either side of the tunnel the steep walls are covered in a thick layer of ferns and mosses giving an almost tropical feel.

The next point of interest is the seven arch Durrow Viaduct built in 1878. Just before you arrive in the village of Kilmacthomas you cross the very impressive curved eight arch viaduct that spans the River Mahon.

The next 10km are a slightly monotonous stretch but there are some good views of the Comeragh Mountains. In Kilmeaden, you cycle alongside the tracks of the narrow gauge Suir Valley Railway and meet the banks of River Suir which leads to the edge of the city. Crossing the N25 you cycle through the wooded campus of the Waterford Institute of Technology to the finish at the large carpark (52.2546, -7.1804).

REFRESHMENTS

The greenway passes through or very close by a number of villages and they all have plenty of places to eat and drink. Two convenient places to stop for a break are Coach House Coffee (52.2018, -7.4063) on the eastern side of Kilmacthomas and the café housed in a disused train carriage on the platform at Kilmeaden Station (52.2467, -7.2471).

VARIATIONS

There are plenty of bike hire companies along the route, who also provide a shuttle service if you are planning to do the route in one direction only. If you have limited time then the most interesting part of the route is the 20km stretch between Dungarvan and Kilmacthomas.

If you want to cycle the entire greenway and return via a different route then the 73km signposted Coastal Route, that runs from Passage East (just east of Waterford City) along the Copper Coast to Dungarvan is a good option.

Three quarters of the way up Powers the Pot

NORTH COMERAGHS
County Waterford/Tipperary
ROAD

72km
720m

This route combines a climb through the Nire Valley with an easy stretch along the Suir Blueway.

It was on the steep climbs of the Comeraghs that Sean Kelly, a native of Carrick-on-Suir who reigned as the world's number one cyclist for five consecutive years, laid the foundations for his amazing career. This route takes in one of these climbs, up the Nire Valley, and then follows the newly constructed Blueway up the River Suir from Carrick-on-Suir to Clonmel.

From the Old Bridge in Clonmel (*52.3506, -7.7168*) head south on the R671 warming up on rolling ground with good views across to the Knockmealdown Mountains.

Shortly before the village of Ballymacarbry the road starts to climb gently but it's only when you cross the bridge over the Nire that you start into the meat of the climb up the Nire Valley. The gradient is fairly steady and never gets too steep. As you gain height you are surrounded by heather hillside and with the top of the climb in sight the angle eases.

Just before the cattle grid turn right and then left at the junction. This road (known as Power's the Pot) leads down to the R678 which you follow through Rathgormack to the R676. Turn left and follow the road into Carrick-on-Suir. Make sure your

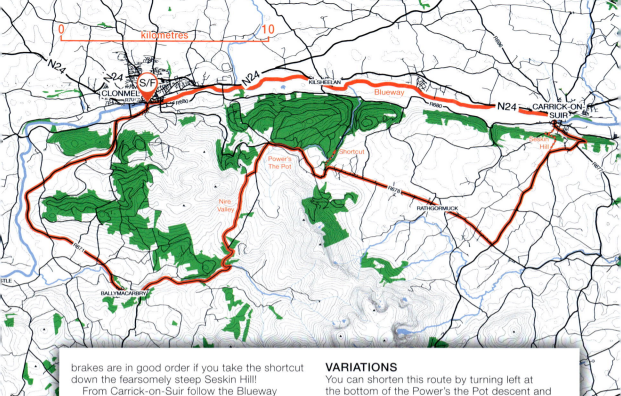

brakes are in good order if you take the shortcut down the fearsomely steep Seskin Hill!

From Carrick-on-Suir follow the Blueway upstream along the northern bank of the Suir on a good tarmac surface. A very flat and peaceful 20km leads back to Clonmel.

REFRESHMENTS
There is a café in Rathgormack shortly after the halfway mark and plenty of options in Carrick-on-Suir.

VARIATIONS
You can shorten this route by turning left at the bottom of the Power's the Pot descent and continuing down to Kilsheelan where you meet the Blueway and follow it to Clonmel. This route is 49km with 640m height gain.

The nearby town of Dungarvan is a cycle hub with two long signposted routes that loop around the Comeraghs, the 160km Kelly Comeragh Challenge and the 105km Kelly Legacy. See page 27 for more information.

DISTANCE	TOTAL		INSTRUCTION
0	0	S	From the Old Bridge across the Suir head south.
0.2	0.2	>	Turn right onto the R671
0.9	1.1	<	Take the first exit off the roundabout onto the R665.
0.7	1.8	<	Turn left onto the R671.
14.4	16.2	<	Turn left.
5.2	21.4	<	Keep left at the fork and cross the bridge.
1.6	23.0	<	Turn left.
4.0	27.0	>	Turn right.
0.5	27.5	<	Turn left.
1.5	29.0	>	Turn right onto the R678.
13.0	42.0	<	Turn left onto the R676.
9.2	51.2	^	Continue straight ahead (the R676 veers right).
0.2	51.4	^	Go straight at the crossroads and walk across the bridge (it's one way).
0.1	51.5	<	Turn left.
0.3	51.8	^	At the bend enter the park and follow the path alongside the river upstream.
20.0	71.8	^	Continue straight on the R884.
0.5	72.3	F	Arrive back at the Old Bridge.

The Vee

THE KNOCKMEALDOWNS
County Tipperary/Waterford
ROAD

47km
670m

400m
300m
200m
100m

0 km   10 km   20 km   30 km   40 km

A tour through the eastern part of the Knockmealdown Mountains.

The shapely peaks of the Knockmealdowns loom over the surrounding fertile pasture of the Golden Vale and the Galtee Mountains. Though relatively modest in height there are some tough climbs. This route loops around the eastern section of the mountains taking on two long but steady climbs.

From the small village of Newcastle (*52.2725, -7.8108*) head west following the course of the River Tar which runs beside the road as far as Goatenbridge. The first 10km to Clogheen are flat and serve as an easy warm up.

After turning left onto the R668 on the outskirts of Clogheen the climbing starts immediately. This climb

is known as the Vee after the sharp hairpin bend that lies midway up the climb. It has a consistent gradient of 3% so if you pace yourself well it passes without too much pain.

As you leave the village you pass through forests of Scot's pines and an overabundance of rhododendron. This invasive species has run riot, choking out all other plant-life, however it produces a spectacularly colourful bloom of pink flowers every year in late May/early June.

After the Vee itself you leave the trees for the open hillside. Climbing up the valley past Bay Lough you reach the top where there are two stone shelters and a cross. The shelter nearest the road is a handy

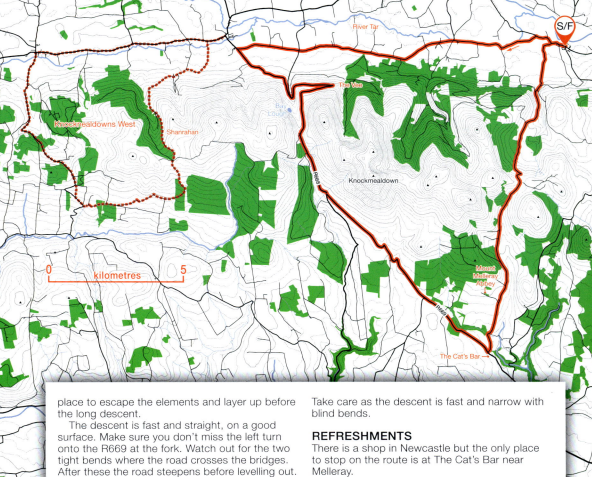

place to escape the elements and layer up before the long descent.

The descent is fast and straight, on a good surface. Make sure you don't miss the left turn onto the R669 at the fork. Watch out for the two tight bends where the road crosses the bridges. After these the road steepens before levelling out.

Just before the The Cat's Bar turn left and descend briefly before crossing the bridge and starting the 6.1km climb. The average gradient is 4% but it steepens near the top.

As you gain height you pass near the Mount Melleray Abbey and as the valley narrows the grassy fields are replaced by forestry and heather hillside.

At the top the road crosses the border back into Waterford and descends back to Newcastle.

Take care as the descent is fast and narrow with blind bends.

REFRESHMENTS
There is a shop in Newcastle but the only place to stop on the route is at The Cat's Bar near Melleray.

VARIATIONS
There is another route around the western Knockmealdowns that could either be combined with the described route to create a figure of eight or done as a route in itself. The 27km loop (with 540m of height gain) starts from Clogheen with a tough climb (7% for 5.5km) over Shanrahan. You then descend rough roads before heading north into Ballyporeen and following the R665 back to Clogheen.

DISTANCE	TOTAL		INSTRUCTION
0	0	S	From the crossroads in the centre of Newcastle head west.
0.5	0.5	>	Keep right.
12.4	12.9	<	Turn left onto the R668.
10.5	23.4	<	Turn left at the fork onto the R669.
9.1	32.5	<	Turn left.
13.5	46.0	>	Turn right.
0.6	46.6	F	Arrive back in Newcastle.

The Greenwood Route

BALLYHOURA TRAIL CENTRE
County Limerick/Cork
MTB

51 km
930 m

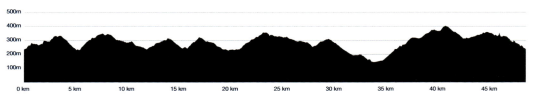

An extensive network of singletrack on the forested slopes of the Ballyhoura Mountains.

The relatively low-lying Ballyhoura Mountains, which straddle the border between Limerick and Cork, are home to one of the largest mountain bike trail centres in the country. The network of signposted trails follow a mixture of forest roads and tight singletrack with sections of boardwalk, berms and rock gardens.

The one-way trail system consists of five trails that are arranged so that each trails links with the next one. Each loop is slightly more difficult than the last, featuring more technical riding and longer, steeper climbs and descents.

The trail system was updated and revised just before this edition went to print in August 2023.

The trails have hosted a number of international mountain bike races including the World Single Speed Championships and the European Marathon Championships.

The carpark (*52.3189, -8.5067*) is open daily between 08.00 and 22.00 and it costs €5 to park (card only). There is a bike wash, toilet and shower. Trailriders (trailriders.ie) offer on-site bike hire and repair.

GREENWOOD ROUTE 7km 240m
This relatively short blue trail is ideal for those new to mountain biking and is marked with blue circles.

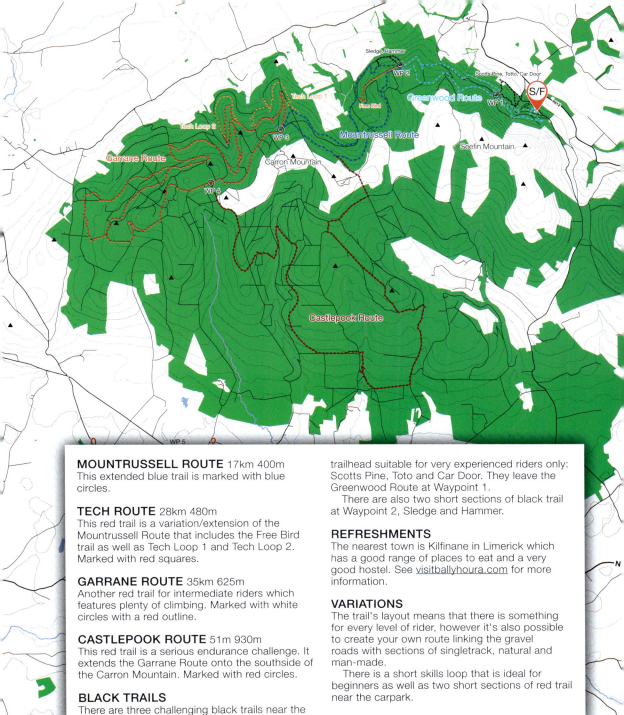

MOUNTRUSSELL ROUTE 17km 400m
This extended blue trail is marked with blue circles.

TECH ROUTE 28km 480m
This red trail is a variation/extension of the Mountrussell Route that includes the Free Bird trail as well as Tech Loop 1 and Tech Loop 2. Marked with red squares.

GARRANE ROUTE 35km 625m
Another red trail for intermediate riders which features plenty of climbing. Marked with white circles with a red outline.

CASTLEPOOK ROUTE 51m 930m
This red trail is a serious endurance challenge. It extends the Garrane Route onto the southside of the Carron Mountain. Marked with red circles.

BLACK TRAILS
There are three challenging black trails near the trailhead suitable for very experienced riders only: Scotts Pine, Toto and Car Door. They leave the Greenwood Route at Waypoint 1.

There are also two short sections of black trail at Waypoint 2, Sledge and Hammer.

REFRESHMENTS
The nearest town is Kilfinane in Limerick which has a good range of places to eat and a very good hostel. See visitballyhoura.com for more information.

VARIATIONS
The trail's layout means that there is something for every level of rider, however it's also possible to create your own route linking the gravel roads with sections of singletrack, natural and man-made.

There is a short skills loop that is ideal for beginners as well as two short sections of red trail near the carpark.

The final climb towards Boggeragh Wind Farm

BOGGERAGH MOUNTAINS

County Cork
ROAD/GRAVEL

42km
800m

A very hilly loop on a mix of backroads, boreens and gravel tracks.

The Boggeragh Mountains are a group of low-lying hills that lie between Mallow and Millstreet in mid-west Cork. The rounded slopes are covered in a mix of forestry, bog and wind farms.

The majority of this route is on paved roads, some are pretty rough, but there is an 8km stretch of gravel. The gravel section isn't too bad and could be manageable on all but the most delicate of road bikes.

This route is probably marginally better if done in a clockwise as this means the first half features the more gentle climbing.

Start from the small village of Lyre (*52.0818, -8.8577*) where there is parking outside the derelict hall. Heading southeast for 2km, a fast descent leads to the R759 where you turn right, pass Nadd Pub and start climbing gently. After 1.8km you turn left onto a quiet boreen. You follow this south for 4.5km, climbing gradually with the exception of one short steep ramp. Look out for the milk churn stand, leftover from the days when dairy farmers left their milk out for collection by truck or cart.

You then turn right onto a straight gravel road, The gravel is quite fine and there isn't any ruts or potholes so the going is good. After 2km of gentle climbing the track drops down to the R759.

106

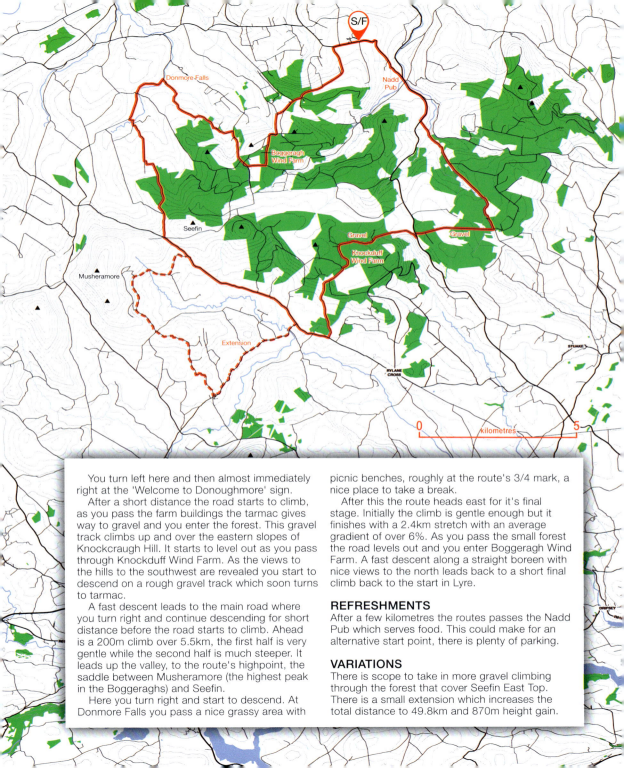

You turn left here and then almost immediately right at the 'Welcome to Donoughmore' sign.

After a short distance the road starts to climb, as you pass the farm buildings the tarmac gives way to gravel and you enter the forest. This gravel track climbs up and over the eastern slopes of Knockcraugh Hill. It starts to level out as you pass through Knockduff Wind Farm. As the views to the hills to the southwest are revealed you start to descend on a rough gravel track which soon turns to tarmac.

A fast descent leads to the main road where you turn right and continue descending for short distance before the road starts to climb. Ahead is a 200m climb over 5.5km, the first half is very gentle while the second half is much steeper. It leads up the valley, to the route's highpoint, the saddle between Musheramore (the highest peak in the Boggeraghs) and Seefin.

Here you turn right and start to descend. At Donmore Falls you pass a nice grassy area with picnic benches, roughly at the route's 3/4 mark, a nice place to take a break.

After this the route heads east for it's final stage. Initially the climb is gentle enough but it finishes with a 2.4km stretch with an average gradient of over 6%. As you pass the small forest the road levels out and you enter Boggeragh Wind Farm. A fast descent along a straight boreen with nice views to the north leads back to a short final climb back to the start in Lyre.

REFRESHMENTS
After a few kilometres the routes passes the Nadd Pub which serves food. This could make for an alternative start point, there is plenty of parking.

VARIATIONS
There is scope to take in more gravel climbing through the forest that cover Seefin East Top. There is a small extension which increases the total distance to 49.8km and 870m height gain.

Crossing the northwest slopes of Knocknamaddree

MIZEN HEAD
County Cork
ROAD

54km
870m

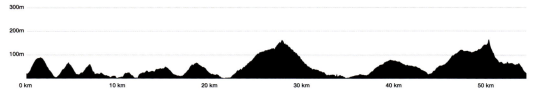

A hilly loop around Ireland's most southwesterly headland.

This quiet route explores the hills and coast near Mizen Head. It doesn't have any really hard climbing but the first half is packed with short rolling hills and the second half has two longish but fairly gentle climbs. The route is best done in a clockwise direction to take advantage of the prevailing wind on the exposed north coast.

From the carpark overlooking the sea in Schull (*51.5269, -9.5439*) climb steeply up the Main Street before turning left onto a quiet back road which has good views to the lighthouse on Fastnet Rock a few miles offshore. After a few short but steep climbs you regain the R592 and follow it west along the coast, passing through Ballyrisode Wood.

The climb out of Goleen marks the end of the rolling terrain and after descending to the coast you turn inland and start to climb. It never gets too steep, with an average gradient of 2.6%. Initially you climb between the fields before crossing the ridge onto the headland's more rugged northern slopes. After crossing over the shoulder of Knocknamaddree there are great views across Dunmanus Bay to the Sheep's Head.

A long descent leads back to sea level where you pass some interesting sea cliffs and arches. The route then rejoins the R591 and follows it northeast for a few kilometres before turning inland and climbing gently over the shoulder of Mount

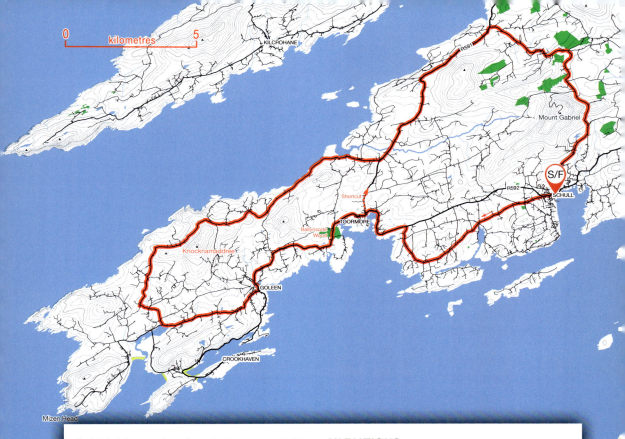

Gabriel. After passing through the narrow cleft in the hillside at the top of the climb a fast descent followed by a few flat kilometres leads back into Schull.

REFRESHMENTS

There are number of cafés, restaurants and pubs in Schull. On the route the only place to get something to eat or drink is the village of Goleen which has a café and a shop.

VARIATIONS

The obvious extension is to continue to Mizen Head at the very tip of the headland. From the Mizen Head visitor centre (*51.4515, -9.8111*) it's a short walk to the spectacularly positioned bridge to the lighthouse. This adds another 10km to the route.

You could shorten the route by following it as far Toormore and taking the R591 to meet the second half of the route. This shortcut reduces the route to 31km with 500m of height gain.

DISTANCE	TOTAL		INSTRUCTION
0	0	S	Head west up the Main Street in Schull.
0.5	0.5	<	Turn left.
7.3	7.8	<	Turn left on the R592.
9.3	17.1	>	Turn right.
4.3	21.4	>	Turn right.
9.2	30.6	<	Keep left at the fork and keep right at the next one.
5.4	36.0	<	Turn left onto the R591.
7.5	43.5	>	Turn right.
3.6	47.1	>	Turn right at the crossroads.
4.0	51.1	>	Keep right at the fork.
3.0	54.1	F	Arrive back at the Main Street of Schull.

Climbing the western shoulder of Caher Mountain

SHEEP'S HEAD
County Cork
ROAD

68km
1190m

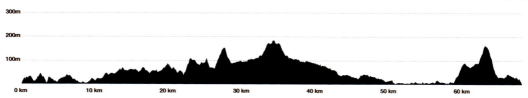

A lumpy route around the coast of the smallest and quietest of the Cork/Kerry peninsulas.

This route follows the signposted Sheep's Head Cycle Route in a loop around the coast, visiting the spectacularly positioned lighthouse at the very tip of the peninsula before climbing over the rocky spine of the headland via the Goat's Path.

It is best done in an anti-clockwise direction so that you have the prevailing wind at your back later in the day.

From the cemetery (*51.6771, -9.4717*) on the west side of Bantry briefly head south on the N71 before turning right onto the coast road that runs west along the barren northern coast. Initially the road stays close to the shore before gradually gaining height and offering better views across Bantry Bay to Beara.

After the turn for Catherine's Pass (a possible shortcut) the road becomes little more than a gravel track. It follows the contours of the hill before turning inland and climbing steeply over the western shoulder of Caher Mountain. You then descend to a junction where you turn right and climb to the carpark at the end of the road. From here it's a 2km (each way) walk to the lighthouse.

Retracing your steps descend along the more populated southern coast passing through Kilcrohane and Ahakista. Just before Durrus turn inland climbing the winding Goat's Path over the

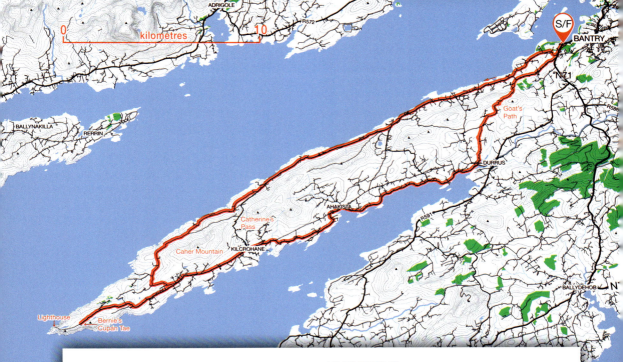

hills. You then drop steeply down the other side on a narrow, winding road. Watch out as some of the bends are very tight and there is plenty of gravel. A few flat kilometres lead back to the N71 and your starting point.

REFRESHMENTS

There is a good café and restaurant in Kilcrohane, not far past the halfway point, called The Old Creamery. At the end of the road to the lighthouse is Bernie's Cupán Tae known as 'the tea shop at the end of the world'.

VARIATIONS

Skipping the out and back section to the lighthouse reduces the distance by 12km and the height gain by 260m, but it would be shame to miss out on the views from the end of the headland.

A better way to shorten the route is to start from Kilcrohane and climb north over Catherine's Pass before following the route anti-clockwise around the headland. This variation is 16km with 400m of height gain.

DISTANCE	TOTAL		INSTRUCTION
0	0	S	From the cemetery head south along the N71.
0.7	0.7	>	Turn right.
17.5	18.2	>	Turn right.
1.6	19.8	>	Keep right.
6.6	26.4	<	Turn left.
0.6	27.0	<	Turn left.
1.3	28.3	>	Turn right.
5.8	34.1	↶	At carpark at the end of the road turn around and retrace your steps.
5.8	39.9	^	Continue straight on.
18.4	58.3	<	Turn left.
2.2	60.5	>	Keep right.
0.6	61.1	>	Keep right.
3.2	64.3	>	Keep right.
0.2	64.5	>	Turn right at the junction.
2.5	67.0	<	Turn left on the N71.
0.8	67.8	F	Arrive back at the cemetery.

Passing through the tunnel on the climb up Borlin Valley

PRIEST'S LEAP AND BORLIN

County Cork/Kerry
ROAD

55km
1170m

A tough route taking on two of the hardest mountain passes in the country.

This is a really great but challenging route with a remote feel. Priest's Leap is a brutal climb, and while Borlin doesn't feel as bad you still need to keep plenty of energy in reserve for it.

There isn't much traffic on either of the passes and the views are excellent. This route is best done in a clockwise direction to get the hardest climb out of the way early.

From the small carpark (*51.7435, -9.4567*) near Coomhola bridge head north towards the bridge and turn left at the junction. The next turn right leads straight into the first climb of the day, Priest's Leap. It's one of the hardest in the country with 440m of height gain over 5.3km and an average gradient of 8.2%. But those number don't tell the whole story, the gradient isn't consistent, steeper ramps alternate with slightly gentler sections making it very hard to get into any sort of rhythm.

A third of the way up the climb you leave the fields and enter the open uplands. This point is marked by a sign that warns rather ominously "Narrow, steep mountain pass road ahead. Not the main route". So you can't say you weren't warned!

A final very steep section leads to the top of the pass and over the border into County Kerry where there are great views north to the mountains of Iveragh.

The descent requires care, some of it is very steep and there is plenty of gravel in the median so keep control of your speed.

In a matter of a few minutes you are back in the lowlands and it's a gentle run down the valley towards Kenmare.

After just over 20km turn right and follow a boreen with good views of the Roughty Valley. Near the edge of Kilgarvan village turn right and start the climb up Borlin Valley.

It's a long and steady climb with an average gradient of 3% over 12.6km but thankfully a fair bit easier than Priest's Leap. The road winds its way across the wooded hillside passing through a rock tunnel before emerging onto more open ground for the final steeper stretch.

At the top you cross back into Country Cork and a long descent down the valley leads back to the start.

REFRESHMENTS

The only facilities on the route are at the Kilgarvan Motor Museum which is open between Tuesdays and Saturdays from April to October. Alternatively you could divert the short distance to the village of Kilgarvan which has a shop and a few pubs or to the town of Kenmare which adds about 5km.

VARIATIONS

One interesting variation would be to substitute either of the two climbs with one of the Beara passes, Caha or Healy (page 119).

DISTANCE	TOTAL		INSTRUCTION
0	0	S	From the parking area head north and turn left at the junction.
0.1	0.1	>	Turn right.
20.1	20.2	>	Turn right at the junction.
8.0	28.2	>	Turn right at the junction.
27.0	55.2	>	Turn right at the junction, cross the bridge and turn left.
0.1	55.3	F	Arrive back at the start.

Looking up the Ouvane River valley

GOUGANE BARRA
County Cork
ROAD

31 km
550 m

A lumpy circuit through the Shedy Mountains following backroads and rough boreens.

This route follows sections of two signposted cycling routes: the Cork City to Gougane Barra and the Beara-Breifne Way. Both are missing signposts in places and neither are well documented online so you are better off following the directions here.

This route is probably best done in an anti-clockwise direction so that you tackle the only busy section, along the R584, going downhill.

From the start in the village of Ballingeary (*51.8460, -9.2391*) you briefly head south on the R584 until after the bridge over the River Lee where you turn left and follow a quiet road downstream along the banks of the Lee and Lough Allua. After

5km the bridge over Sruhaunphadern Stream signals the start of the first, and biggest, climb. As you gain height the views improve and as you leave the conifer plantation the road starts to descend steeply.

The small bridge over the Ouvane River marks the start of the next climb. Over its 3.1km there are two steep sections, the last comes just before you meet the R584. Turn right and descend the busy road that cuts through the rocky slopes of the Pass of Keimaneigh. After 2.6km turn left and climb gently to the shore of Gougane Barra Lake with its famous island 6th church - St. Finbarr's Oratory.

From the lake you head east continuing up winding boreens over the shoulder of Coomataggart

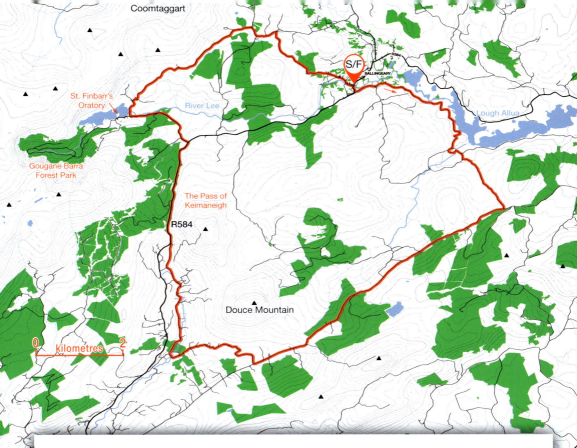

mountain before dropping down the other side back into Ballingeary.

REFRESHMENTS

This is a pretty remote route, the only place to get refreshments along the way is the café in Gougane Barra, overlooking the oratory. There are a few pubs and a shop at the start/finish in Ballingeary.

VARIATIONS

It would be possible to stay on the R584, saving 5km, rather than heading to Gougane Barra, but it would be a shame to miss the final section with its wonderful views.

Adding the figure of nine loop around the lush Gougane Barra Forest Park adds 6km and 100m of height gain.

This route could also be extended to include the formidable climbs over Borlin Valley (see page 112) and the Top of Coom which would give a challenging 76km route with 1210m of height gain.

DISTANCE	TOTAL		INSTRUCTION
0	0	S	Head south on the R584 from Ballingeary village.
0.2	0.2	<	Turn left.
4.06	4.26	<	Turn left.
0.41	4.67	>	Turn right
0.14	4.81	<	Turn left.
2.67	6.48	>	Turn right at the t-junction.
7.22	13.7	>	Turn right just before the small bridge.
2.8	16.5	>	Turn right just after the small bridge.
3.1	19.6	>	Turn right onto the R584.
2.5	22.1	<	Turn left, signposted Gougane Barra.
1.8	23.9	>	Turn right.
4.2	28.1	>	Keep right then turn right.
0.2	28.3	<	Keep left.
0.5	28.8	>	Turn right.
2.5	31.3	F	Arrive back at the start.

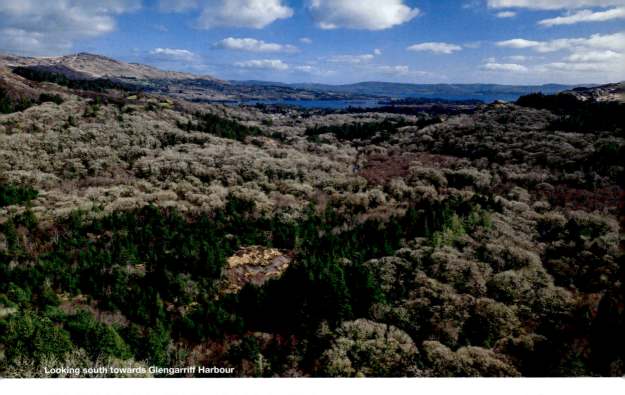

Looking south towards Glengarriff Harbour

GLENGARRIFF WOODS
County Cork
ROAD

11 km
210 m

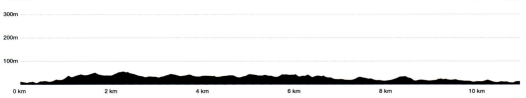

An easy route through beautiful woodland.

The 300 hectare forest, which was once part of Lord Bantry's estate, lies nestled in a sheltered pocket of the Caha Mountains. It was handed over to the State in 1955 and is now a nature reserve home to a mix of oak, birch, holly and rowan.

It would be easy to spend a day exploring the beautiful forest and the signposted walks (note that cycling isn't permitted on footpaths in the reserve).

The route is flat with the exception of one short climb near the start and a few other gentle inclines. The roads within the park are very quiet so this route is suitable for families but be on the lookout for the occasional car. The route is described in a clockwise direction starting from the village but it can be done in either direction.

From Glengarriff (*51.7500, -9.5523*) head south along the R572 before turning right onto a quiet road that climbs briefly before levelling out and passing a series of rounded domes of Old Red Sandstone.

You re-enter the woods and a short distance later pass on the left the (signposted) path up to Lady Bantry's Lookout. It's a short walk to the viewpoint which offers a panoramic view of the Caha Mountains and Bantry Bay.

The well surfaced tarmac road continues west through beautiful mossy oak forest. Occasionally the trees part and you can look out over the

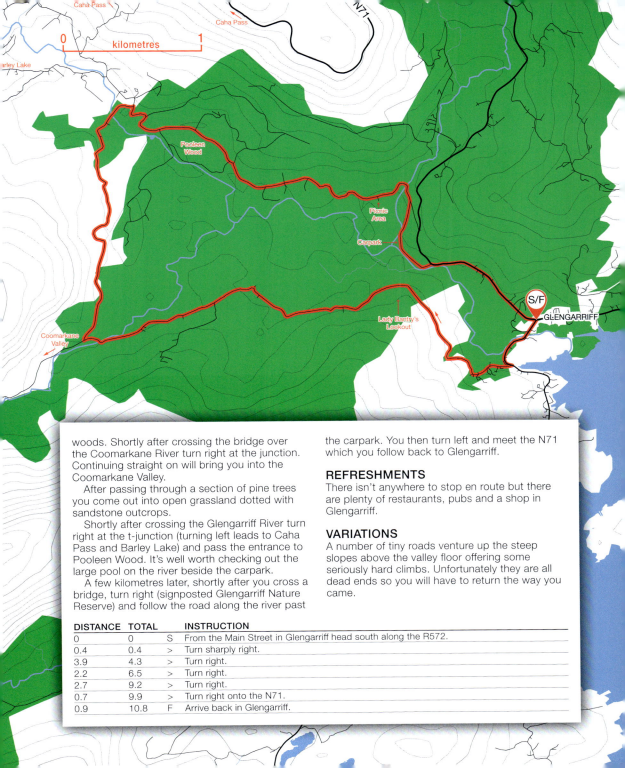

woods. Shortly after crossing the bridge over the Coomarkane River turn right at the junction. Continuing straight on will bring you into the Coomarkane Valley.

After passing through a section of pine trees you come out into open grassland dotted with sandstone outcrops.

Shortly after crossing the Glengarriff River turn right at the t-junction (turning left leads to Caha Pass and Barley Lake) and pass the entrance to Pooleen Wood. It's well worth checking out the large pool on the river beside the carpark.

A few kilometres later, shortly after you cross a bridge, turn right (signposted Glengarriff Nature Reserve) and follow the road along the river past the carpark. You then turn left and meet the N71 which you follow back to Glengarriff.

REFRESHMENTS
There isn't anywhere to stop en route but there are plenty of restaurants, pubs and a shop in Glengarriff.

VARIATIONS
A number of tiny roads venture up the steep slopes above the valley floor offering some seriously hard climbs. Unfortunately they are all dead ends so you will have to return the way you came.

DISTANCE	TOTAL		INSTRUCTION
0	0	S	From the Main Street in Glengarriff head south along the R572.
0.4	0.4	>	Turn sharply right.
3.9	4.3	>	Turn right.
2.2	6.5	>	Turn right.
2.7	9.2	>	Turn right.
0.7	9.9	>	Turn right onto the N71.
0.9	10.8	F	Arrive back in Glengarriff.

Climbing up the southside of Healy Pass

HEALY AND CAHA PASS

County Cork/Kerry

ROAD

69 km

1410 m

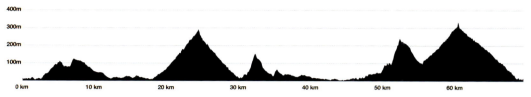

A testing route that takes in both of the Beara Peninsula's classic climbs.

There are plenty of hard climbs in Counties Cork and Kerry and this route takes on two of the very best. The first climb, up the winding Healy Pass, is probably the closest thing in Ireland to an alpine pass. The second climb, over Caha Pass, is a little busier but this route avoids as much of the main road as possible by approaching via a quiet side valley.

The route is best done in a clockwise direction so that you are well warmed up before the start of the climbing.

From Glengarriff (*51.7500, -9.5523*) head southwest along the R572 taking in good views over Bantry Bay and inland to the distinctive conical shape of Sugarloaf Mountain. The road is good and there is a hard shoulder most of the way. You tackle a few short steep climbs near Seal Harbour before a gentle downhill run to the edge of Adrigole village.

Turn right onto the R574 and start the climb over Healy Pass. The gradient stays at a consistent 5% as it winds up the pass around a dozen or so hairpin bends.

From the top there is an amazing view north over Glanmore Lake and the mountains of the Iveragh Peninsula. The descent is fast and open on a good surface.

Passing through the crossroads at Lauragh you tackle a short but steep (8%) climb over the shoulder of Knockatee mountain before descending back to sea level.

You meet the R571 and follow the coast for 10km before turning right. The quiet road rises and falls as it climbs up the Gortnabinny valley. Ahead steep slopes appear to block all passage and, as you pass Dromoughty Lake, the climbing really begins. It's a 2.6km climb at an average gradient of 7%, with some much steeper sections, up the narrow boreen to the top of the pass.

A quick descent leads to the busy N71 which you follow through the three tunnels to the top of Caha Pass. The 5km climb has a very consistent 4% gradient so it's just a matter of spinning the legs and taking in the view.

Emerging from the last tunnel into County Cork all that's left is a pleasant descent down the valley to Glengarriff.

See the map on page 113.

REFRESHMENTS

At the start of the route in Glengarriff there are a number of pubs and restaurants as well as a shop. There is also a shop just off the route in Adrigole. You pass the Smokey Pickle Café in Lauragh and a small shop in Tuosist.

VARIATIONS

There isn't any scope for a shorter route that takes in both passes. This route is effectively a shorter version of the Ring of Beara (page 120) which is a good alternative if you are looking for something longer.

Between Glengarriff and Adrigole you could follow the quieter backroads taken by the Beara Way Cycle Route. On the descent of Caha Pass you could divert through Glengarriff Wood rather than follow the N71.

DISTANCE	TOTAL		INSTRUCTION
0	0	S	From Glengarriff head southwest on the R572.
17.6	17.6	>	Turn right onto the R574.
12.8	30.4	∧	At the junction with the R571 go straight ahead.
4.6	35.0	∧	Continue straight through the crossroads.
0.2	35.2	∧	Continue straight through the crossroads.
1.3	36.5	>	Turn right at the junction.
0.6	37.1	<	Turn left onto the R571.
8.8	45.9	>	Turn right.
0.6	46.5	>	Turn right at the crossroads.
1.9	48.4	<	Keep left at the fork.
2.1	50.6	<	Turn left.
3.9	54.5	<	Turn left.
0.7	55.2	>	Turn right onto the N71.
14.0	69.2	F	Arrive back in Glengarriff.

A few kilometres north of Allihies village

THE RING OF BEARA
County Cork/Kerry
ROAD

139km
2120m

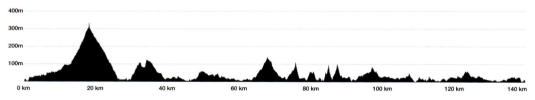

400m							
300m							
200m							
100m							

0 km   20 km   40 km   60 km   80 km   100 km   120 km   140 km

A hard loop around the Beara Peninsula that starts with a long climb over Caha Pass.

This route follows the coast road around Beara and while there is only one long climb, Caha Pass, there is still plenty of height gain thanks to the numerous shorter climbs. The road can be a little busy in places but it isn't too bad.

The route starts in Kenmare and travels clockwise to get the longest climb out of the way early and take advantage of a tailwind on the exposed second half when the legs are fading.

From Kenmare (*51.8787, -9.5817*) head south on the N71. The first few flat kilometres warm the legs up for the climb up Caha Pass. About 10km up the valley the angle steepens and it's a steady 5% for the last 5km of the climb. The road can be quite busy but the surface is excellent and there is a hard shoulder most of the way.

A long tunnel, the last of three, signals the end of the climb. A fast descent leads to Glengarriff where you turn right. With the exception of one short sharp climb, it's a gentle run west along the coast through Adrigole and Castletownbere.

A few kilometres after Castletownbere the road climbs for 4km over Gour Pass with an average gradient of 3%. From the top there are great views over Bere Island and Bantry Bay.

After descending back to sea level turn north and tackle another short climb through a narrow gap in the hills. From the top you can see the distinctive

brightly painted houses of Allihies against the backdrop of the gnarled hillside.

After a short descent to Ballydonegan Strand you climb a little to Allihies. From the village the road follows an intricate route through the rocky hills. A series of short climbs lead over the narrow pass between Knocknagallaun and Eagle Hill. You then descend to the coast and follow the road northeast with great views across the bay to Iveragh. The final 50km is pretty flat and you pass through the villages of Eyeries, Ardgroom and Lauragh before arriving back in Kenmare.

REFRESHMENTS
The route passes through a number of towns and villages so there are plenty of places to refuel and rehydrate. The Copper Café in Allihies, near the halfway mark, is a good place to stop.

VARIATIONS
The described route keeps to the main roads but there is an alternative, the Beara Way Cycle Route, that avoids them where possible. It's well signposted with brown signs marked with a pink flower. Roughly half of the time it follows the Ring however it makes a number of interesting diversions that, time permitting, are worth considering. It's marked as the dashed line on the map above.

DISTANCE	TOTAL		INSTRUCTION
0	0	S	From the Main Street in Kenmare head south along the N71.
0.1	0.1	<	Take the first exit off the roundabout.
26.7	26.8	>	Turn right onto the R572.
48.3	75.1	^	Continue straight onto to the R575.
19.0	94.1	<	Turn left onto the R571.
18.0	112.1	<	Turn left onto the R573.
11.0	123.1	<	Turn left onto the R571.
14.8	137.9	<	Turn left onto the R71.
1.0	138.9	>	Take the second exit off the roundabout.
0.1	139.0	F	Arrive back at the Main Street of Kenmare.

Brickeen Bridge

MUCKROSS LAKE
County Kerry
ROAD

10km
130m

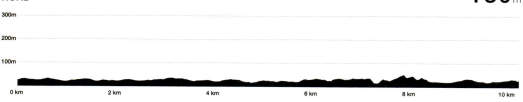

A flat traffic-free loop around the Middle Lake, ideal for families.

This route through the beautiful ancient oak forest of Killarney National Park has some amazing views over the lakes and surrounding mountains. It is very flat and the vast majority of it follows traffic-free paths and tracks. In spite of the route's short length there is so much to see that you could easily spend a day meandering along it, soaking up the spectacular setting.

The National Park requests that cyclists follow the route around the lake in an anti-clockwise direction. The route is popular with walkers so give way and use a bell.

From the main carpark (*52.0186, -9.5009*) at Muckross House head west past the house before turning right onto a tarmac road. You then turn left at the fork following signs for Dinis Cottage along a track that leads west across the narrow finger of land that separates Muckross Lake from Lough Leane. Along the way you pass a number of tiny sandy beaches that overlook the small limestone islands found in this part of the lake.

The distinctive high arch of Brickeen Bridge, which spans the narrow channel that connects the two lakes, leads to the first of two small islands.

The second island is home to Dinis Cottage Tea Rooms. Just past the cottage, after the bridge, a narrow path leads right through the trees to the Meeting of the Waters, the point where the water

from the three lakes mingle. It's an idyllic spot and well worth a look.

Back on the track another 1.5km leads to the N71 where you turn left onto the busy road. It's quite narrow and winding so extreme caution is required. It's possible to avoid this section by crossing into Torc Woods where a footpath runs parallel to the road. Cycling isn't permitted so you should, in theory at least, walk your bike along it.

Opposite Torc Waterfall carpark turn left and follow the road through the trees. It's well worth the five minute walk to check out the beautiful waterfall. The road leads through forest and open grassland, which offer great views, to the front

lawn of Muckross House. Follow the track around the house back to the carpark.

REFRESHMENTS
There is a large café in the Muckross Visitor Centre. The Dinis Cottage Tea Rooms near the midway point serve tea and coffee.

VARIATIONS
You could extend the loop to take in more of the National Park by starting from the centre of Killarney and looping around the Ross Demesne before heading south on bike lanes to Muckross.

DISTANCE	TOTAL		INSTRUCTION
0	0	S	From the carpark head west passing Muckross House.
0.2	0.2	>	Turn right.
0.3	0.5	<	Turn left at the fork (signposted "Dinis Cottage").
6.3	6.8	<	Turn left onto the N71.
1.6	8.4	<	Turn left opposite the carpark and follow the signs for Muckross House.
1.7	10.1	F	Arrive back at Muckross House.

Passing the Turnpike Rocks in the Gap of Dunloe

KILLARNEY LAKES
County Kerry
ROAD

55km
820m

This circuit of the lakes cuts through the Macgillycuddy's Reeks and is packed with scenery.

From the tourist town of Killarney this route climbs through the Gap of Dunloe into the Black Valley before climbing up to Moll's Gap and descending back to Killarney along the N71. From start to finish the views are astounding and on a nice day you could spend hours enjoying them.

From the roundabout beside the Lidl (*52.0689, -9.5172*) head west on the N72. It's possible to avoid much of this road by following the Fossa Way, a traffic-free cycling and walking track.

Turning off the N72 the road starts to climb towards the Gap of Dunloe, the steep sided valley that cuts through the Macgillycuddy's Reeks. Just after Kate Kearney's cottage the road steepens. Be

very careful on this road as it's narrow and can get very busy with cars, walkers and horse-drawn carts.

After climbing past a number of small lakes, a series of tight hairpin bends leads to the top of the pass where there is a great view down into the Black Valley. After a quick descent into the valley you climb alongside a stream into another valley. On the hillside to the left you will be able to make out the Moll's Gap road but to get there continue further up the valley before turning left and climbing steeply. A short stretch on the R569 leads to Moll's Gap, named after Moll Kissane who ran a shebeen there, selling booze to the workers who built the Kenmare to Killarney road in the 1820s. Nowadays it's home

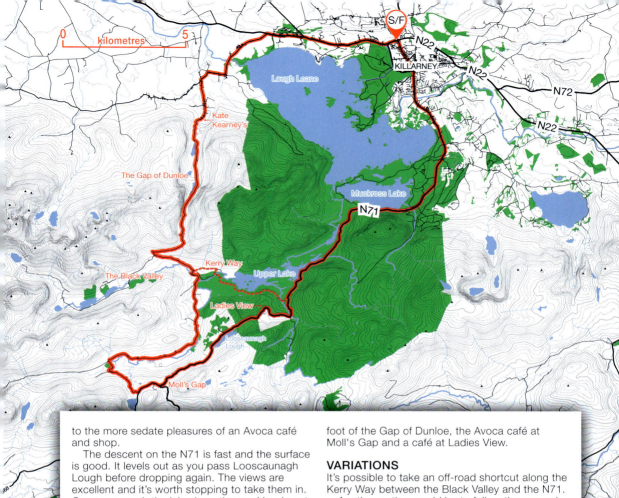

to the more sedate pleasures of an Avoca café and shop.

The descent on the N71 is fast and the surface is good. It levels out as you pass Looscaunagh Lough before dropping again. The views are excellent and it's worth stopping to take them in. Once you reach the lakeshore the road levels out and it's a fast run back into Killarney.

REFRESHMENTS

Along the route you pass Kate Kearney's at the foot of the Gap of Dunloe, the Avoca café at Moll's Gap and a café at Ladies View.

VARIATIONS

It's possible to take an off-road shortcut along the Kerry Way between the Black Valley and the N71.

Another option would be to follow the second half of the Muckross Lakes route (page 122) through the National Park on quiet paths instead of the busy N71.

DISTANCE	TOTAL		INSTRUCTION
0	0	S	From the roundabout head west on the N72.
0.4	0.4	<	Take the third exit off the roundabout onto the N72.
5.0	5.4	<	Turn left.
3.8	9.2	<	Turn left.
9.7	18.9	<	Turn left.
1.6	20.5	>	Keep right.
7.6	28.1	>	Turn right.
2.6	30.7	<	Turn left onto the R568.
0.9	31.6	<	Turn left onto the N71.
23.4	54.0	>	Take the second exit off the roundabout onto Main Street.
0.5	54.5	<	Turn left onto the R876.
0.9	55.4	F	Arrive back at the roundabout where you started.

Descending to Glenbeigh

THE RING OF KERRY

County Kerry

ROAD

170km
1680m

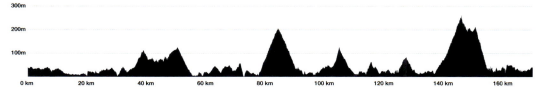

A scenic but challenging loop around the world famous Ring of Kerry.

Every July the Iveragh Peninsula's coast road is thronged with cyclists taking part in the most popular Irish sportive, the Ring of Kerry. During the sportive there is generally very little other traffic, however the rest of the year the roads can be busy, particularly during the summer months.

The route is challenging with two climbs of note, Coomakista Pass just outside of Waterville and Moll's Gap which is the sting in the tail as you tackle it late in the day.

Cars are advised to drive clockwise around the Ring while tour buses travel anti-clockwise. The sportive goes anti-clockwise which means that you face the prevailing wind early and the biggest climb very late in the day.

From Killarney (*52.0690, -9.5170*) the route follows the busy N72 west to the town of Killorglin, famous for hosting the Puck Fair every year. Heading southwest on the N70 the road follows the coast with spectacular views across the bay to the Dingle Peninsula.

There is another steep pull as the road turns inland before descending into Cahersiveen. Heading southeast rolling hills lead through Waterville to the first of the big climbs, Coomakista, which has an average gradient of 3%. It's worth pausing at the top to take in the view over Derrynane and the Beara Peninsula before the fast descent back to sea level.

Leaving the coast the road climbs over Dereenauliff. It then descends into Sneem and gently rolling terrain leads to the outskirts of Kenmare.

You then turn left onto the N71 and start the 9km climb to Moll's Gap. The gradient averages 3% but it steepens near the finish. At the top you are rewarded with a magnificent view of the Macgillycuddy's Reeks.

From Moll's Gap it's downhill to Killarney. Take care on the fast, winding descent as it can get very busy with tour buses who have to swing very wide on some of the tighter bends. Shortly after Ladies View you reach the lake and it's an easy run into the finish.

The route is marked as the red line on the map on page 129.

REFRESHMENTS

You pass through a number of villages and towns along the route. Waterville, which is just before the halfway mark (with most of the climbing to come), is a good place to stop for a break.

VARIATIONS

Unless you are particularly set on following the route of the sportive there are better options, such as the Tour of Iveragh (page 128), that avoid most of the busy roads.

Another good alternative is the signposted variation of the Ring known as the Ring of Kerry Cycle Route, which follows backroads when possible. It is marked by brown signs with a bike and a crown in white. See the red dashed line on the map on page 129.

DISTANCE	TOTAL		INSTRUCTION
0	0	S	From the roundabout head west on the N72.
0.4	0.4	<	Take the third exit off the roundabout onto the N72.
19.2	19.6	<	Turn left onto the N70.
0.3	19.9	^	Continue straight on.
0.2	20.1	<	Take the first exit off the roundabout following the N70
116.1	136.2	<	Turn left onto the N71.
31.4	167.6	>	Take the second exit off the roundabout onto Main Street.
0.6	168.2	<	Turn left onto the N71.
0.9	169.1	F	Arrive back at the roundabout in Killarney.

Castlequinn bridge just north of Cahersiveen

TOUR OF IVERAGH
County Kerry
ROAD

207 km
2780 m

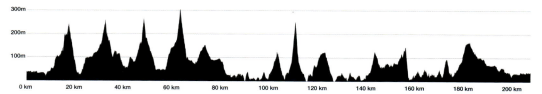

A long and quiet loop through the mountains and along the coast of the Iveragh Peninsula.

This is an amazing route, maybe the best in the book. It combines a number of epic mountain passes with spectacular coastal scenery and quiet backroads. It's a very worthwhile alternative to the Ring of Kerry as it takes in many of the highlights of Iveragh that aren't on the Ring such as: the Gap of Dunloe, the Black Valley, Ballaghbeama Gap, Ballaghisheen Pass, Coomanaspic and Valentia Island.

This route could be done, by the fittest riders, in a day, but with so much to see it's probably best spread over a few days. If you plan to do it over two days then Waterville, near the midpoint, is a good place to stay. Over three days Glencar and Cahersiveen are the best options.

This route is best done in a clockwise direction to take advantage of the prevailing wind on the exposed section along the northern coast. This also means you are fresh for the harder climbs.

From Killarney (52.0690, -9.5170) follow the busy N72 west around Lough Leane. The Fossa Way cycle path offers a quieter option. Turn off the main road and climb through the spectacular Gap of Dunloe before descending into the remote Black Valley.

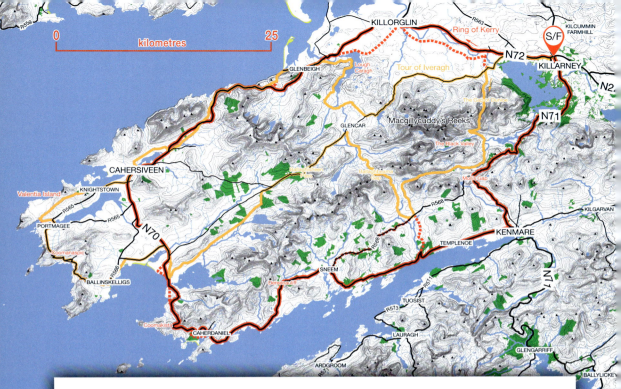

You then follow the Owenreagh River upstream into a broad flat valley. At head of the valley the road climbs over a pass, the gradient average 4% but it gets a little steeper near the top.

You then follow a roundabout route passing Lough Brin to Ballaghbeama Gap. The 4km climb averages 5% and is steeper near the top. Descend the narrow pass and turn left before Glencar. A few easy kilometres leads to Ballaghisheen Pass, the hardest climb on the route. The 1.6km climb is steep, with an average gradient of 9%, but there are great views northeast towards the Macgillycuddy's Reeks from the top.

A fast descent leads back into the lowlands. Follow the main road west before turning left onto a back road that leads into Waterville. Elevated above the main road it offers better views and minimal traffic.

From Waterville the route heads north, initially on the busy N70 before heading west through Ballinskelligs. You then climb over a low pass, and descend to St Finian's Bay before starting up the fearsome Coomanaspic. The climbs starts off gently enough but the last 1.5km of switchbacks are brutal with an average gradient of 11%.

A fast descent leads to Portmagee where you cross the bridge onto Valentia Island. Follow the quiet road across the island to Knightstown and make the short ferry crossing to the mainland. The ferry operates daily from April 1st to the end of September, and runs continuously from 08:30 to 22:30 every day of the week.

Pass through Cahersiveen and cross the bridge over the inlet. You then head northeast following a quiet road that runs parallel to the N70 before dropping down towards Kells. Here you join the N70 and make fast progress before turning left and climbing briefly to a spectacular view over Rossbeigh beach. Descend into the village of Glenbeigh where you rejoin the N70 for a few kilometres. Turn right onto a quiet road passing Lough Caragh and through Lickeen Wood. Then turn left and follow the road around the northern side of the Reeks to the N70 and final few kilometres back into Killarney.

REFRESHMENTS

Knightstown and Waterville, near the halfway point, are good places to stop but there are plenty of other options along the route.

VARIATIONS

This route shares ground with two shorter routes, Killarney Lakes (page 124) and the Ring of the Reeks (page 130).

Descending the north side of Ballaghbeama Gap

THE RING OF THE REEKS
County Kerry
ROAD

68km
1000m

A circuit around Ireland's highest mountains, the Macgillycuddy's Reeks.

This route follow quiet roads through Ireland's most impressive mountain range tackling three challenging climbs along the way. The route travels clockwise to get the busier roads out of the way early.

From the Climber's Inn in Glencar (*51.9944, -9.8576*) head northeast along the main road climbing slightly. At the shore of Lough Acoose the road starts to descend gently as it makes its way around the eastern and then the northern slopes of the mountains.

The right turn into the Gap of Dunloe signals the start of the first climb. Shortly after Kate Kearney's Cottage the view opens up and you enter the Gap

proper. The road can get busy during the summer with horses-drawn carts and other traffic so take it very carefully.

The setting is spectacular, only the narrowest space exists between the mountains and the road, as it winds upwards with the steep rocky slopes rearing up on both sides. The climb has an average gradient of 3% but there are a few steep ramps, the worst of which is at Turnpike Rocks, the big boulders either side of the road. After a steep section of hairpins you arrive at the top of the Gap and look down into the Black Valley. A fast descent leads to the valley floor.

REFRESHMENTS

The Climber's Inn at the start of the route offers food and accommodation. You also pass Kate Kearney's in the Gap of Dunloe.

VARIATIONS

This route forms part of the Tour of Iveragh (page 128) and it could be easily extended to take in more of that route.

There isn't any scope for shortcuts on this route but the Killarney Lakes route (page 124) is a good alternative if you are looking for a shorter option.

Climbing up the other side of the valley, follow the Owenreagh River up into a broad flat valley. The road climbs over the pass, averaging 4% but is a little steeper near the top. Ahead is Ballaghbeama Gap but you must follow a circuitous route down and up the valley before getting to grips with it.

The 4km climb through the spectacular Ballaghbeama Gap has an average gradient of 5%, steepening near the finish where the hillsides converge. The descent down the narrow winding road leads into a wide valley and it's only a few more easy kilometres back into Glencar.

DISTANCE	TOTAL		INSTRUCTION
0	0	S	From the Climber's Inn head northeast along the main road.
8.1	8.1	>	Keep right at the fork.
1.0	9.1	>	Keep right at the fork (signposted "Killarney").
10.8	19.9	>	Turn right (signposted "Gap of Dunloe").
9.6	29.5	<	Turn left.
1.7	31.2	>	Keep right.
18.4	49.6	>	Turn right onto the R568.
0.5	50.1	>	Turn right.
1.9	52.0	>	Turn right (signposted "Ballaghbeama").
11.8	63.8	<	Turn left at the t-junction.
2.9	66.7	>	Turn right.
1.6	68.3	F	Arrive back at the Climber's Inn.

Just north of Slea Head

SLEA HEAD
County Kerry
ROAD

43km
580m

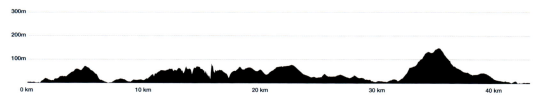

300m
200m
100m

0 km   10 km   20 km   30 km   40 km

This circuit around Slea Head at the tip of the Dingle Peninsula follows one of the most scenic roads in the country.

The R559, aka the Slea Head Drive, which loops around Slea Head from Dingle Town, is a very popular drive and rightly so - it's spectacular. It's a gentle route, and is ideal for cycling as there are so many points to stop and take in the view.

Rather than follow the R559 throughout this route takes quiet backroads where possible. Obviously you could also just follow the R559.

This route should definitely be done clockwise so that you are cycling towards the best views and on the sea side of the road.

From the Tourist Information Office (*52.1392, -10.2744*) beside the harbour in Dingle Town follow the R559 west. Shortly after crossing the bridge take the right fork onto a quieter road that leads into Ventry. In Ventry rejoin the R559 and follow it west as it makes its way between the slopes of Mount Eagle and the sea. The coastline gradually becomes more dramatic as you travel west, culminating in the rounding of Slea Head when the view across Coumeenoole Beach and the Blasket Islands is revealed.

The road continues through Dunquin to another excellent viewing point where you can look north

over Sybil Head, the Three Sisters and Mount Brandon.

Loosing a bit of height the road runs gently downhill through the village of Ballyferriter. A short distance past the village at the Dingle Peninsula Hotel continue straight on where the R559 turns left. You then climb the lower slopes of Lateeve Hill and cross the R559 before the road drops down a series of tight bends. This quiet road leads down to the R559 and onwards into Dingle.

REFRESHMENTS
There is no end of places to eat and drink in Dingle Town and there is also plenty of options along the route in Ventry, Dunquin and Ballyferriter.

VARIATIONS
There is a shorter variation (34km 560m) that climbs over Mám Clasach, the pass between Mount Eagle and Cruach Mhárthain. In Dunquin take the right turn (signposted "Mám Clasach") off the R559 and follow the steep (6% average gradient) road over the pass. A quick descent leads to Ventry where you retrace your steps back to Dingle.

DISTANCE	TOTAL		INSTRUCTION
0	0	S	From the Tourist Information Office at the seafront head west along the R559.
0.9	0.9	<	Take the first exit off the roundabout and cross the bridge.
0.8	1.7	>	Turn right.
4.4	6.1	>	Turn right onto the R559.
25.6	31.7	^	Continue straight on where the R559 turns left.
2.0	33.7	^	Continue straight through the crossroad.
1.1	34.8	>	Turn right.
1.6	36.4	<	Keep left.
1.0	37.4	>	Turn right.
3.2	40.6	>	Turn right onto the R559.
1.0	41.6	<	Turn left.
0.3	41.9	<	Take the third exit off the roundabout.
1.0	42.9	F	Arrive back at the seafront in Dingle.

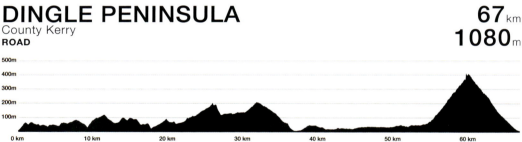

Climbing the north side of Conor Pass

DINGLE PENINSULA
County Kerry
ROAD

67 km
1080 m

A circuit of the Dingle peninsula taking in the classic climb over Conor Pass.

This route visits both coasts of the peninsula crossing the ridge of mountains that run west to east across Dingle twice. The first climb between Annascaul and Camp is straightforward while the second, over Conor Pass, is simply spectacular, the views go a long way towards taking the sting out of what is a tough climb.

The route is best done in an anti-clockwise direction so that you climb up the more interesting side of Conor Pass.

From the bottom of Main Street in Dingle Town (*52.1409, -10.2671*) the route heads east on quiet inland roads, avoiding the busy N86 apart from one brief stretch, into Annascaul.

From Annascaul take the N86 northeast. After a short distance turn left onto a quieter road and climb steadily up the valley enjoying the view of Annascaul Lake. Rejoining the N86 for the final, slightly steeper, stretch over the top of the pass where the view north over Tralee Bay is revealed.

It's a fast fairly straight descent down the other side. Just after the long sweeping right bend turn left onto a quieter road and continue down to sea level. Follow the very flat R560 west for 16km before the road starts to rise signalling the beginning of the Conor Pass climb. It's a 5km climb to the top, gaining 340m at a steady 7% gradient on a good surface. And from the start there are great views

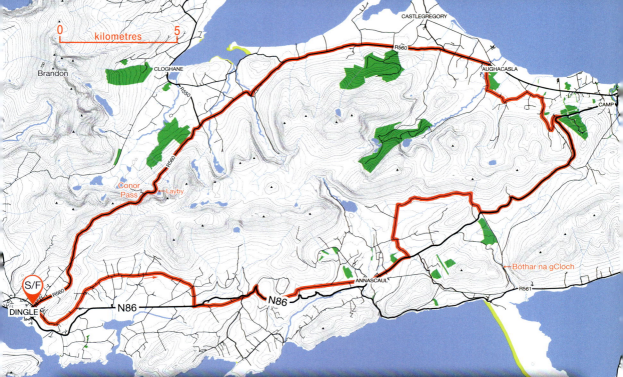

of the Brandon Mountains. As you gain height the surroundings become rockier and the road begins to weave following the contours of the mountainside.

The last 1.5km from the layby to the top are the most spectacular as the road narrows and the ground drops away steeply on one side while rising over the road on the other.

And then all of sudden it's over and all that remains is the fast descent, on an excellent surface, back to Dingle Town.

REFRESHMENTS

You pass the South Pole Inn in Annascaul, which was once the home of legendary Antarctic explorer Tom Crean. Both Castlegregory and Camp, which are only a short diversion from the route, also offer food and drink.

VARIATIONS

A possible variation is to follow the R561 east along the coast from Annascaul to tackle the fearsome climb known as Bóthar na gCloch. The 3km climb has an average gradient of 9%. You can then descend into Camp and follow the N86 to rejoin the original route.

DISTANCE	TOTAL		INSTRUCTION
0	0	S	From Main Street head southwest along John Street.
2.4	2.4	<	Keep left at the fork.
5.8	8.2	>	Keep right at the fork.
0.9	9.1	<	Turn left onto the N86.
0.2	9.3	>	Turn right onto the narrow road.
2.1	11.4	>	Turn right onto the N86
2.0	13.4	<	Turn left.
0.1	13.5	>	Turn right at the fork.
1.0	14.5	^	Go straight through the offset crossroads.
1.4	15.9	>	Keep right at the fork.
1.7	17.6	>	Turn right and then immediately left onto the N86.
2.0	19.6	<	Turn left.
1.1	20.7	<	Turn left at the t-junction.
5.5	26.2	<	Turn left at the fork.
0.6	26.8	<	Turn left onto the N86.
7.3	34.1	<	Turn sharply left.
0.6	34.7	>	Keep right at the fork.
2.0	36.7	<	Turn left at the t-junction.
0.6	37.3	<	Turn left.
2.2	39.5	>	Turn right at the t-junction.
1.2	40.7	<	Turn left onto the R560.
25.8	66.5	F	Arrive back at Main Street.

The east end of the Barnagh Tunnel

LIMERICK GREENWAY
County Limerick/Kerry
ROAD

49km
220m

This multi-use route passes through the rolling Limerick countryside, connecting the market towns of Rathkeale, Newcastle West, Abbeyfeale and Listowel.

The Limerick Greenway runs between Rathkeale in County Limerick and Listowel in County Kerry following the course of the former Limerick to Tralee railway line which closed to passengers in 1963.

There are plans to extend the greenway westwards to connect with the Tralee to Fenit Harbour Greenway and eastwards to Limerick City. For more information see limerick.ie/greenway.

The greenway has a smooth tarmac surface and the gradient is generally very gentle so it doesn't take much effort to zip along, therefore it's vital to

control your speed and watch our for walkers and less experienced cyclists. A bell is very useful.

A shuttle bus operates on weekends in June and then daily during July and August. There are two return trips each day between Rathkeale, Newcastle West and Abbeyfeale. See limerickgreenwaybikehire.ie for details.

The eastern end of the greenway starts in Rathkeale Station (*52.5250, -8.9445*), heading southwest for 9km to Ardagh, passing under a number of stone bridges along the way. Ardagh was where the famous 8th century chalice was found in 1868.

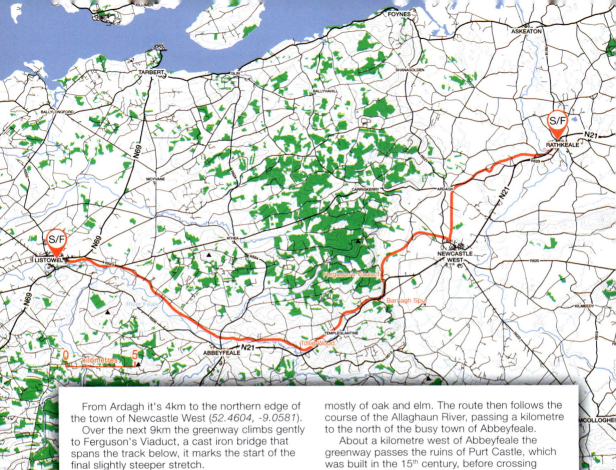

From Ardagh it's 4km to the northern edge of the town of Newcastle West (52.4604, -9.0581).

Over the next 9km the greenway climbs gently to Ferguson's Viaduct, a cast iron bridge that spans the track below, it marks the start of the final slightly steeper stretch.

As the route briefly runs alongside the busy N21 it passes the highpoint of the greenway.

A short distance into the descent look out for the brightly painted underpass on the left. This marks the start of a kilometre long spur of the greenway that passes a number of interesting sights. The first of which is the Barnagh Station, shortly after the station the surroundings rise above the greenway until it is hemmed in by vegetated vertical walls and it passes through the 115m long Barnagh Tunnel.

Further on again the spur passes the entrance to the Barnagh Greenway Hub (52.4195, -9.1333), which has a café, playground and crazy golf, before ending at the viewing point beside the N21 that offers great views over the rich grasslands of the Golden Vale.

Back on the main route, over the next 13km the greenway descends gently down to Abbeyfeale. Along the way it passes through Tullig Wood, a 750m stretch of native woodland consisting

mostly of oak and elm. The route then follows the course of the Allaghaun River, passing a kilometre to the north of the busy town of Abbeyfeale.

About a kilometre west of Abbeyfeale the greenway passes the ruins of Purt Castle, which was built in the 15th century, before crossing the border into County Kerry and following the River Feale downstream for 12km into Listowel (52.4479, -9.4698).

REFRESHMENTS

There are plenty of places to eat in the towns and villages on or very near the greenway including: Rathkeale, Ardagh, Newcastle West, Barnagh, Templeglantine, Abbeyfeale and Listowel.

VARIATIONS

Obviously if you don't have enough time to tackle the full length any section of the greenway could be done as an out-and-back. The shuttle could also be used to cycle one section and return by bus.

The nearby forested hills of the Sliabh Luchra region may offer potential for extensions of the greenway on boreens and gravel roads.

The bridge across the Mulkane River

SILVERMINES
County Tipperary
ROAD/GRAVEL

31 km
400 m

A rolling route following rough boreens around this quiet mountain range.

This route loops around the lower slopes of Keeper Hill, which at 694m, is the highest summit in the Slivermine Mountains. It's described in an anti-clockwise direction so that the climbs are more gradual and the steep sections are tackled in descent.

This route follows quiet roads, with a few rough sections, notably the boreen at the 3km mark and the climb up the south side of Knockane.

The first third of the route follows signs for Sarsfield's Ride, a heritage route that commemorates a famous cavalry ride to intercept and destroy a siege train that was on its way to Limerick in 1690.

The route starts in the neat little village of Killoscully, just outside Ryan's Bar (*52.7687, -8.3272*). You briefly head north before turning right onto a small boreen. After a short descent it climbs into the hills, briefly becoming rough before you turn right and drop down to the road that runs south from Killoscully. After a few flat kilometres you turn left and start the gradual climb up the Doonane valley, passing through the pretty village of Toor.

The climb is interrupted by a brief descent through a wooded valley, after which you turn left and continue upwards.

At the 19km mark you turn left onto a rough road that leads north over the shoulder of Knockane. The

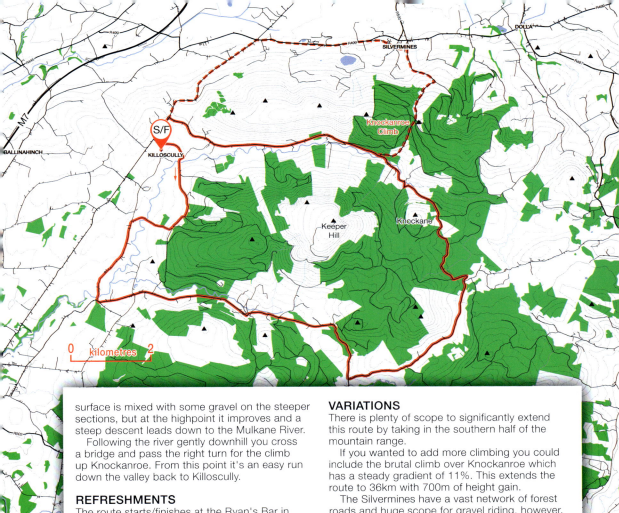

surface is mixed with some gravel on the steeper sections, but at the highpoint it improves and a steep descent leads down to the Mulkane River.

Following the river gently downhill you cross a bridge and pass the right turn for the climb up Knockanroe. From this point it's an easy run down the valley back to Killoscully.

REFRESHMENTS

The route starts/finishes at the Ryan's Bar in Killoscully. Just under 5km southwest of the route is the village of Newport which has a few cafés and shops. The town of Silvermines is a similar distance to the north.

VARIATIONS

There is plenty of scope to significantly extend this route by taking in the southern half of the mountain range.

If you wanted to add more climbing you could include the brutal climb over Knockanroe which has a steady gradient of 11%. This extends the route to 36km with 700m of height gain.

The Silvermines have a vast network of forest roads and huge scope for gravel riding, however, due to access restrictions it isn't possible to document them here.

DISTANCE	TOTAL		INSTRUCTION
0	0	S	Head north from the start at Ryan's Bar in Killoscully.
0.15	0.15	>	Turn right onto a boreen, signposted 'Sarsfield's Ride'.
2.85	3.00	>	Turn right at crossroads.
1.2	4.2	<	Turn left, signposted 'Sarsfield's Ride'.
2.4	6.6	<	Turn left at the t-junction.
0.1	6.7	<	Turn left.
7.8	14.5	<	Turn left.
4.5	19.0	<	Turn left onto gravel road.
11.0	30.0	<	Turn left.
0.3	30.3	<	Turn left at stone marked 'Killoscully'.
0.6	30.9	F	Arrive back in Killoscully village.

Just east of Dunlicky Castle on the final stretch into Kilkee

LOOP HEAD
County Clare
ROAD

65km
570m

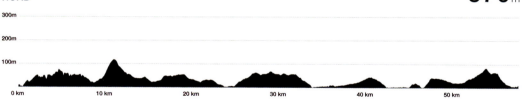

A gentle circuit around Loop Head with excellent sea views.

The narrow peninsula of Loop Head, which lies between the Atlantic coast and the gentler waters of the Shannon Estuary, is a much overlooked part of the west coast. This route follows the coastline in a loop from Kilkee on quiet, reasonably flat roads.

This route follows the Loop Head Cycleway, but as there are some missing signs turn-by-turn directions are included. It is best done in a clockwise direction so that you have the assistance of the prevailing wind on the exposed coastal section.

From the seafront in Kilkee (*52.6777, -9.6506*) head east along the N67 before turning right onto quieter roads. You pass Poulnasherry Bay on your left before turning west and following the shore of the Shannon Estuary through the villages of Carrigaholt and Kilbaha.

Just before Kilbaha you meet the R487 and follow it to the lighthouse at the very tip of Loop Head. It's well worth walking the short loop along the cliff edge for the spectacular views across the Estuary and the North Kerry coast.

Back on the bike retrace your steps along the R487 before turning left onto the coast road. The road heads northeast passing numerous opportunities to stop and take in the views of the cliffs, arches, stacks, caves and narrow chasms. Look out for the signpost for the Bridges of Ross, it's worth the short diversion to check out the last remaining sea arch.

Midway along the coast you climb over Knocknagarhoon Hill, the high point of the route, before continuing past more spectacular coastal architecture into Kilkee.

REFRESHMENTS

Kilkee offers plenty of options. The route passes The Long Dock in Carrigaholt which serves excellent seafood and there are also a number of places in Kilbaha including the café at Kilbaha Gallery.

VARIATIONS

A shorter (33km) variation taking in the most scenic part of the route follows the R487 southwest for 15km before meeting the described route and following it back along the coast.

DISTANCE	TOTAL		INSTRUCTION
0	0	S	From the roundabout on the seafront in Kilkee head west along Circular Road.
0.5	0.5	>	Turn right onto the R67.
0.6	1.1	>	Turn right.
2.5	3.6	<	Turn left.
1.8	5.4	>	Turn right.
2.3	7.7	<	Turn left.
0.5	8.2	>	Turn sharply right.
10.9	19.1	<	Turn left onto the R488.
1.9	21.0	>	Turn right.
6.7	27.7	>	Keep right.
3.6	31.3	<	Turn left onto the R487.
5.4	36.7	?	At the Loop Head Lighthouse retrace your steps back along the road.
1.6	38.3	<	Turn left.
3.3	41.6	<	Turn left.
3.9	45.5	<	Turn left onto the R487.
3.9	49.4	<	Turn left.
2.8	52.2	<	Turn left.
3.9	56.1	<	Turn left at the t-junction.
1.2	57.3	<	Turn left.
5.6	62.9	<	Turn left.
2.2	65.1	>	Turn right.
0.5	65.6	F	Arrive back at the roundabout in Kilkee.

The rough track that connects Poulnabrone Dolmen and the road to Carron

THE BURREN
County Clare
ROAD

45km
630m

300m

200m

100m

0 km   10 km   20 km   30 km   40 km

A figure of eight through the quiet limestone uplands of the Burren.

The unique topology and geology of the Burren is ideally suited to exploration by bike. There is so much to see from tiny wild flowers growing out of the limestone pavement to large neolithic forts. This route is mostly on roads with the exception of a short stretch of rough track. All but the frailest road bike will mange this track if you take it easy but it's also possible to skip it.

This figure of eight route links two separate loops both of which start and finish in Carron, the only village in the Burren uplands, at the carpark (*53.0352, -9.0768*) opposite Cassidy's Pub.

The eastern loop heads north through the village before turning right and descending briefly to a junction where you turn left. Following the road, climbing steadily, through the Clob Valley past the Burren Perfumery and the rocky shoulder of Slieve Carran. A sequence of tight bends leads down to a junction where you turn right and head south to a junction.

Here a sign marks the start of the climb up the Glann Corkscrew. The sign is equipped with an NFC (Near Field Communication) chip that will take you to a page on Strava where you can see how others have fared on the climb. The winding road is hard work with a steady 7% gradient but at the top there is a great view and it's well worth stopping to take

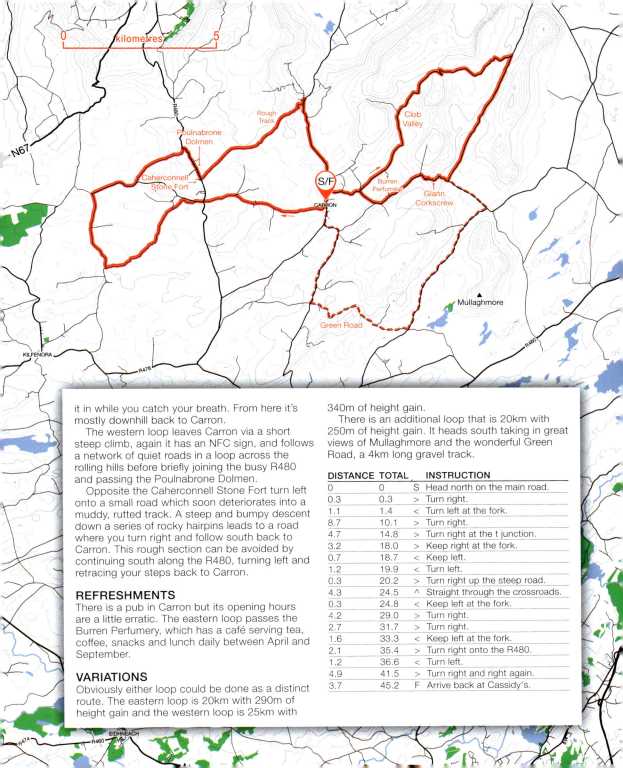

it in while you catch your breath. From here it's mostly downhill back to Carron.

The western loop leaves Carron via a short steep climb, again it has an NFC sign, and follows a network of quiet roads in a loop across the rolling hills before briefly joining the busy R480 and passing the Poulnabrone Dolmen.

Opposite the Caherconnell Stone Fort turn left onto a small road which soon deteriorates into a muddy, rutted track. A steep and bumpy descent down a series of rocky hairpins leads to a road where you turn right and follow south back to Carron. This rough section can be avoided by continuing south along the R480, turning left and retracing your steps back to Carron.

REFRESHMENTS

There is a pub in Carron but its opening hours are a little erratic. The eastern loop passes the Burren Perfumery, which has a café serving tea, coffee, snacks and lunch daily between April and September.

VARIATIONS

Obviously either loop could be done as a distinct route. The eastern loop is 20km with 290m of height gain and the western loop is 25km with

340m of height gain.

There is an additional loop that is 20km with 250m of height gain. It heads south taking in great views of Mullaghmore and the wonderful Green Road, a 4km long gravel track.

DISTANCE	TOTAL		INSTRUCTION
0	0	S	Head north on the main road.
0.3	0.3	>	Turn right.
1.1	1.4	<	Turn left at the fork.
8.7	10.1	>	Turn right.
4.7	14.8	>	Turn right at the t junction.
3.2	18.0	>	Keep right at the fork.
0.7	18.7	<	Keep left.
1.2	19.9	<	Turn left.
0.3	20.2	>	Turn right up the steep road.
4.3	24.5	^	Straight through the crossroads.
0.3	24.8	>	Keep left at the fork.
4.2	29.0	>	Turn right.
2.7	31.7	>	Turn right.
1.6	33.3	<	Keep left at the fork.
2.1	35.4	>	Turn right onto the R480.
1.2	36.6	<	Turn left.
4.9	41.5	>	Turn right and right again.
3.7	45.2	F	Arrive back at Cassidy's.

Passing Black Head Lighthouse

BLACK HEAD
County Clare
ROAD

46km
500m

A loop around the northwestern edge of the Burren.

The R477, which runs from Lisdoonvarna to Ballyvaughan, is one of the most scenic roads in the country with magnificent views over the Atlantic. However it can be busy at the weekends and during the summer so start early if you want it all to yourself.

The route is best done in a clockwise direction to take advantage of the prevailing wind on the exposed section along the coast.

From Ballyvaughan (*53.1156, -9.1493*) head south along the N67 and after a few flat kilometres climb Corkscrew Hill. The winding road gains just under 200m over 4.6km and is steepest at the hairpin bends.

At the top of the climb you emerge onto the barren Burren uplands. Follow the road southwest and downhill into the town of Lisdoonvarna.

The N67 leaves the town heading west. After a few kilometres turn right onto the R477, climbing gently before descending a series of tight swooping bends to the coast.

At the coast you meet the Burren's famous limestone pavements. A short distance later you pass a layby beside the low cliffs on the inland side of the road. This is a good place to stop to inspect the limestone pavement and peer down the vertical cliffs of Ailladie into the sea.

144

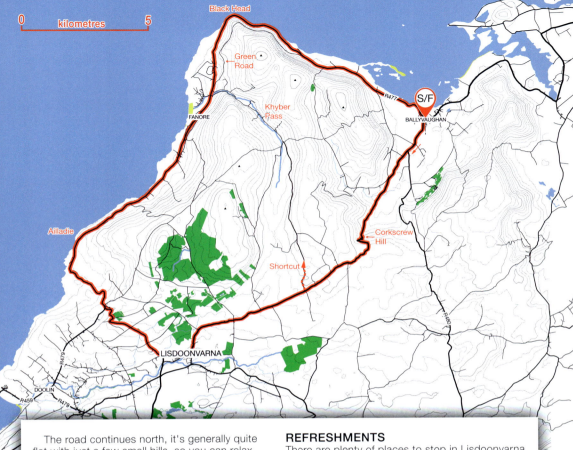

The road continues north, it's generally quite flat with just a few small hills, so you can relax and take in the views of the Aran Islands to the southwest and north across Galway Bay to the mountains of Connemara.

Shortly after Fanore the golden sands of the beach come into view and the terraced slopes of Murrooghkilly start to rise on the inland side. The terrain becomes more barren as the road curves around Black Head. After the small white lighthouse, which marks the tip of the headland, you turn east. As you head further into the bay to Ballyvaughan the limestone pavements are replaced by green fields and thickets of hazel.

REFRESHMENTS

There are plenty of places to stop in Lisdoonvarna and Ballyvaughan. There is a shop and a pub that serves food in Fanore.

VARIATIONS

There is a shortcut that reduces the route to 33km. Turn right off the N67 earlier (10.3km from Ballyvaughan) and climb gently up the wide valley before descending through the Khyber Pass to the coast road at Fanore where you join the described route.

The Green Road, which runs above the coast road around Black Head, offers excellent mountain biking and even better views. It could easily be incorporated into an off-road loop around the hills however it's not an officially sanctioned mountain bike trail.

DISTANCE	TOTAL		INSTRUCTION
0	0S	S	From the centre of Ballyvaughan head south on the N67.
17.0	17.0	>	Turn right onto the R477
28.7	45.7	F	Arrive back in Ballyvaughan.

Overlooking Lough Melvin from the Glenaniff route, Leitrim, see page 194

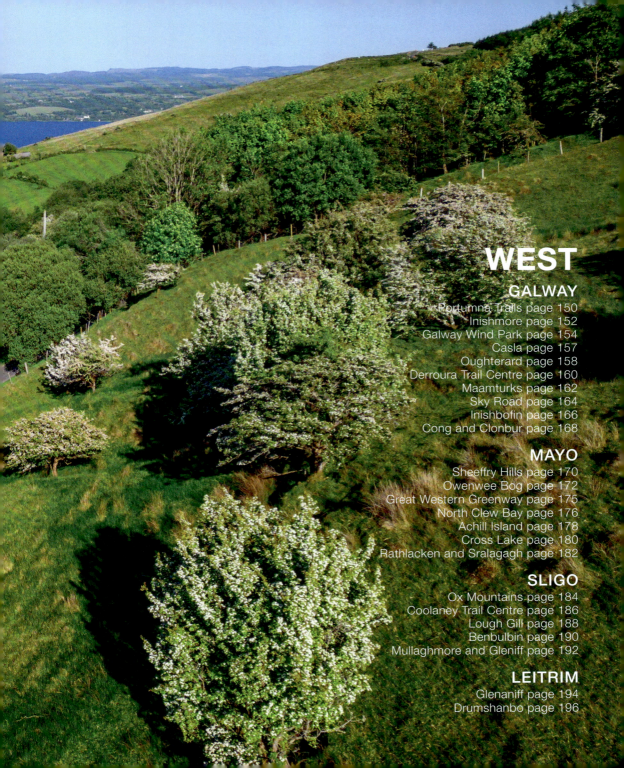

WEST

FAMILY CYCLING IN THE WEST

The following routes are all traffic-free and reasonably short so are ideal for families and younger children.

SLIGO

1 DOORLY PARK *54.2647, -8.4459*
There is a network of paths running through the woods on the southern bank of the Garavoge River on the edge of Sligo Town.

LEITRIM

2 GLENFARNE DEMESNE *54.2999, -7.9638*
A 4km multi-use trail that explores the Glenfarne Demesne on the western shore of Upper Lough Macnean.

3 DRUMLEAGUE LOCK LOOPED CYCLING TRAIL *53.9955, -8.0778*
This 5km trail is part of the Shannon Blueway. It follows the canal north from Battlebridge before crossing over the canal at Drumleague Lock for the return journey. Note this route isn't suitable for very small children due to the proximity of the canal to the path.

ROSCOMMON

4 LOUGH KEY PARK *53.9850, -8.2325*
An 8km cycling trail that loops through the woods and along the lakeshore. The trails are wide and flat and there is plenty to see en route.

MAYO

5 BELLECK WOOD *54.1292, -9.1434*
This 4.2km multi-use linear trail passes through mature woodland with splendid views of the River Moy.

6 GREAT WESTERN GREENWAY *53.7981, -9.5504*
The original Irish greenway stretches from Westport to Achill Island but it's possible to do a shorter out and back section or get a shuttle back from one of the many bike hire outfits. See page 175 for more information.

7 CLARE LAKE FOREST GREENWAY *53.7156, -9.0037*
Known as the Land of the Giants this 5km gravel loop features a number of oversized everyday objects that are sure to surprise and delight young kids.

GALWAY

8 AGHRANE FOREST *53.5357, -8.3287*
The 5.7km Castlekelly Trail is a family-friendly cycling and walking trail. It starts in Castlekelly village and explores a mix of commercial forest and beautiful parkland trees planted by the old estate.

9 MOUNTBELLEW *53.468, -8.5106*
This 2.2km bike trail leads through a diverse forest containing a wide range of exotic and native trees.

10 DERROURA TRAIL CENTRE *53.4418, -9.4502*
This mountain bike trail centre on the edge of Connemara has a short (4km) loop that is suitable for beginners. There is also a longer (16km) trail for experienced riders. See page 160 for more information.

11 PORTUMNA FOREST PARK *53.08262, -8.24099*
The 180 hectare Coillte park on the northern shore of Lough Derg has four multi-use trails ranging in length from 1.4km to 10.5km. The gentle winding trails are an ideal introduction to mountain biking.

The Bonaveen Trail near Fowlers Island

PORTUMNA TRAILS

County Galway
GRAVEL

15km
70m

300m
200m
100m

0 km   5 km   10 km   15 km

The flat winding forest trails are the ideal place to get a first taste of mountain biking.

The 450 hectare Portumna Forest Park lies on the northern shore of Lough Derg on the western edge of Galway. The park, far from being a rectilinear plantation of spruce, has a wide variety of trees (including Scots pine, oak, ash, hazel, beech and birch plus the occasional yew and juniper) and terrain, with patches of semi-native woodland, meadows, marshland and ponds. It is also home to over a dozen species of mammals including red squirrels and a herd of fallow deer.

The park offers little in the way of rocks, roots or steep hills making it an ideal place for anyone new to mountain biking. In fact a mountain bike isn't even required, a gravel or hybrid bike would be well able

for the trails. Bear in mind that all the loops should be done in an anti-clockwise direction starting from the carpark (*53.0827, -8.2413*) and that cyclists should give way to walkers when they meet.

The park has four multi-use trails. The 1.4km Forest Friendly Trail (white arrows) follows a wide tarmac path and is suitable for all, including wheelchair users and children on bikes with stabilisers.

The 2km Woodland Trail (blue arrows) is a little more adventurous but is still suitable for small kids. The loop takes in a mix of gravel, forest paths and timber boardwalk to the south of the carpark.

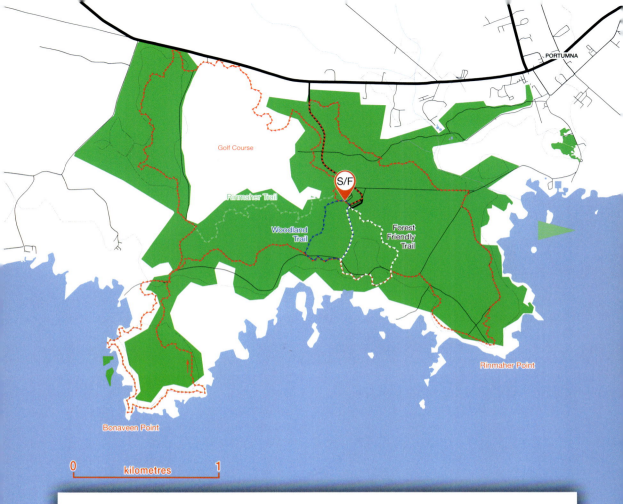

PORTUMNA

Golf Course

Rinmaher Trail

S/F

Woodland Trail

Forest Friendly Trail

Rinmaher Point

Bonaveen Point

0   kilometres   1

The two longer trails, Rinmaher and Bonaveen, mostly consist of narrow winding singletrack and the route detailed here combines the two trails into a very enjoyable 15.1km loop.

From the carpark follow the Bonaveen Trail (red arrows) north, after a kilometre the Rinmaher Trail (green arrows) joins it from the right and they continue together around the northeastern corner of the park, passing the shores of a turlough (a seasonal lake).

After 4.3km, beside the limekiln, the Rinmaher Trail (green arrows) continues straight ahead, heading back to the carpark. Stick with the Bonaveen Trail, following the red arrows, which heads south towards the shore of Lough Derg making an anti-clockwise loop around the Bonaveen headland. The trail then heads west, at the 9.7km mark you leave the Bonaveen

Trail which returns to the carpark and continue following the green arrows. After Rinmaher Point you continue until you meet the park's access road near the entrance. Follow this road south back to the carpark.

REFRESHMENTS
Portumna village is just down the road and has plenty of places to eat and drink.

VARIATIONS
The described route makes the most of the signposted trails. If you are looking for shorter, more child friendly variations then consider one of the other signposted trails.

The rough track on the northernmost section of the route

INISHMORE
County Galway
GRAVEL

28 km
300 m

A figure of eight loop around the island's network of roads, tracks and paths.

The island of Inishmore, the largest of the three Aran Islands, lies a short distance off the coast of Counties Clare and Galway. Due to the island's small size most visitors arrive on foot and explore the island by bicycle.

This is a route to enjoy at a leisurely pace. If you have never been to the island before then it's well worth diverting to visit the spectacular natural pool, Poll na bPéist (also known as the Wormhole) and the cliff-top fort of Dún Aonghasa.

Ferries sail to the island from Doolin in Clare and Rossaveal in Galway, see page 264 for more information. Bike hire is available at the pier or you can take your own bike on the ferry for a small charge, making sure to book it in advance.

The route follows minor roads and tracks some of which are quite rough so a hybrid or mountain bike is required.

From the pier (53.1194, -9.6657) in Kilronan head southwest before turning inland and climbing a steep road to one of the highest points of the island. Here there are great views east to the Burren and north to the mountains of Connemara.

The tracks levels out and as you make your way west, you pass through a patchwork of the iconic dry-stone walls that divide the land into innumerable tiny fields. As Dún Aonghasa comes into view the surface improves and the track drops steeply into the tiny village of Gort na gCapall.

From the village a series of tracks lead to the main road at Kilmurvey with its white sandy beach, the best on the island.

The route follows the main road for a short distance before turning right onto a rough track that heads towards the north shore and then west to the far end of the island. Follow the main road back into Kilmurvey.

From Kilmurvey take the low road that runs along the northern shore of the island.

Shortly before the main road turn left down a narrow lane that leads to a beach. At the far end of the beach follow a grassy path to a track near the lake. This leads back to the pier in Kilronan.

REFRESHMENTS

There is a supermarket and a number of restaurants and cafés in Kilronan and a small shop and café in Kilmurvey. There is plenty of accommodation on the island including camping, hostels, B+Bs and hotels. It's advisable to book ahead during the summer.

VARIATIONS

If you are tight on time you could just do the eastern section of the loop. This is 16km with 180m of height gain.

DISTANCE	TOTAL		INSTRUCTION
0	0	S	From the bike shop at the pier follow the main road southwest through the village.
1.0	1.0	>	Turn right onto the Back Road.
4.8	5.8	>	Keep right at fork.
0.4	6.2	<	Turn left onto the grassy track.
1.2	7.4	^	Continue straight through the junction. A left turn leads up to Dún Aonghasa.
1.8	9.2	>	Turn right onto the track.
0.1	9.3	<	Keep left at the fork.
1.5	10.8	>	Keep right following the coast road.
3.1	13.9	<	Turn left onto the main road.
5.7	19.6	<	Back in Kilmurvey keep left at the fork onto the Low Road.
5.8	25.4	<	Turn left onto the track that leads down to the beach.
0.4	25.8	>	Turn right and push your bike across the sand.
0.1	25.9	^	At the far end of the beach look out for a grassy track that leads between the stone walls.
0.3	26.2	<	Turn left at the junction.
0.7	26.9	>	Turn right.
1.0	27.9	F	Finish outside the bike hire shop.

Climbing up to the summit of Letir

GALWAY WIND PARK
County Galway
GRAVEL

41 km
550 m

An entirely off-road route that follows gravel tracks through a wild landscape

This vast area of bog, lakes and conifer plantations, which lies between the mountains of Connemara and the Galway coast, is home to Galway Wind Park. The park is one of the largest wind farms in the country with 58 towering turbines that generate enough power for every home in Galway. This route combines many of the newly-build wind farm tracks with existing forestry tracks into a 100% gravel route.

Much of this route is also taken by the Galway Gravel Grinder (galwaygravelgrinder.com), an off-road sportive that runs each summer.

On first glance this route may seem a little convoluted and obviously there are some sections where it covers the same ground twice, but ultimately it has been designed to take advantage of the abundant gravel roads and tracks. It's very rare in Ireland to find a forty plus kilometre route that's entirely on gravel.

The route starts/finishes from the carpark (*53.3829, -9.3744*) on the Oughterard to Rossaveal road (L1311). It begins by following the Lough Seecon Trail (green markers) clockwise for 4km, descending through some magical forest, with mossy boulders and lichen covered pines. Note that this trail is shared with walkers so control your speed.

You then pass Lough Seecon and a short while later you arrive at the junction with the main access

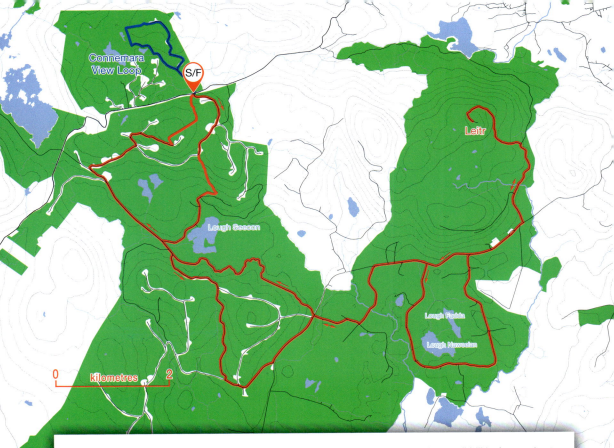

road where you turn left following the Forest Cycleway (blue markers).

After just under 10km you arrive at the point where the Forest Cycleway turns left and heads for home (*53.3462, -9.3423*), however you continue east. After another 2.5km the route turns south to do a circuit around Lough Fadda and Lough Naweelan. Once back on the main track you head east for 1.2km before turning left onto a narrower track.

At the fork you turn left and climb a rough track to the 261m summit which is topped by a telecommunications mast. This hill is unnamed on the OS map, but known locally as Letir. Soak up the excellent views of Galway Bay, the Burren, Lough Corrib and the mountains of Connemara before retracing your steps, taking care on the rocky descent.

On the return keep to the direct route, omitting the two longer southern sections. Just as the access road starts to climb you re-join the Lough Seecon Trail (green markers). Follow it clockwise, continuing on the access road, climbing for

150m to the summit of a small hill before a short descent leads back to the start/finish.

REFRESHMENTS

This is a very remote route with nothing along the way, however the nearby town of Oughterard (*53.4285, -9.3194*) offers plenty of options.

VARIATIONS

The western half of the route, which combines the Lough Seecon Trail (green markers) and Forest Cycleway (blue markers), is 19km with 320m height gain and is a worthwhile route in it's own right.

The route as described takes the longer options on the outward leg and skips them on the return, obviously they could be omitted in both directions, to give a route of 34km with 510m height gain.

The route could also be extended by including the Connemara View Loop (adds 4.2km and 70m of height gain) which makes a figure-of-nine north of the start/finish.

The bog road

CASLA
County Galway
GRAVEL

17km
110m

300m			
200m			
100m			
0 km	5 km	10 km	15 km

This short flat route follows a mix of bog roads and empty backroads.

The terrain in this corner of south Connemara is incredibly flat and a vast expanse of blanket bog stretches from the rocky coastline to the foot of the mountains to the north. This route links coast and bog in a short anti-clockwise loop starting from the small village of Casla (or Costelloe in English) in the gaeltacht (Irish speaking) region of south Connemara.

Just under half of this route is on bog roads, rough tracks really, so something a little beefier than a narrow road tyre is required.

From the Texaco garage in Casla (*53.2888, -9.5537*) head east for a few hundred metres before turning north onto the R336. This road can be busy and there isn't much of a hard shoulder so it's a relief to turn right onto the bog road.

Head north following the gravel track through the bog which is speckled with small lakes and granite boulders.

Eventually the track leads to a junction. Turn right onto the R336 and follow it for a short distance before turning left onto a quieter road.

Make your way west crossing a bridge over a small inlet of Camus Bay and turn south passing through more open bog. At the junction turn left onto the R374 and follow it back to the start.

See the map on page 159.

REFRESHMENTS
There is a shop, café and pub at the start/finish in Casla.

VARIATIONS
This route could easily be extended to explore the area known as Ceantar na Oileáin, the Islands District. This small collection of islands, which are linked by bridges and causeways, is a much overlooked part of Connemara. The flat but rocky islands have plenty of quiet boreens perfect for cycling.

DISTANCE	TOTAL		INSTRUCTION
0	0	S	From Casla head east along the R343.
0.3	0.3	<	Turn left onto the R336.
1.1	1.4	>	Turn right onto the gravel track.
0.1	1.5	<	Keep left at the fork.
6.9	8.4	>	Turn right onto the R336.
0.9	9.3	<	Turn left.
0.7	10.0	>	Keep right.
0.8	10.8	<	Keep left.
4.3	15.1	<	Turn left onto the R343.
1.9	17.0	F	Arrive back at the garage in Casla.

Heading north towards Galway Wind Farm

OUGHTERARD
County Galway
ROAD

65km
600m

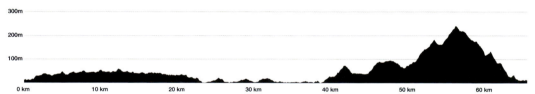

A loop of contrasts, the first two thirds are fast and flat while the last third is a long climb through remote bogland.

E ven through the first stretch of the route along the N59 is busy and may not be to everyone's taste, the rest of the route is quiet and there are great views throughout.

The route is described in an anti-clockwise direction in the hope that the prevailing wind will help on the climb. Be warned that if a strong southwesterly is blowing the first two thirds of the route will be hard going as they are very exposed.

From the large carpark (53.4277, -9.3167) on the east side of Oughterard follow the N59 west. This stretch of road can be busy with fast moving traffic. As you head west the surroundings become

wilder with open hillside and pine forest. At Maam Cross turn left and head south on the quieter R336. The road is flat with an excellent surface so it's fast going but don't forget to stop to take in the view across the mountains and bog.

At Casla (the village is a short distance right from the junction) the sea appears on the left. Follow the shore southeast for a short distance before turning left.

For the next 25km a quiet road leads through the wilds of south Connemara. With little sign of civilisation apart from the occasional cottage and the wind turbines of Galway Wind Farm you head

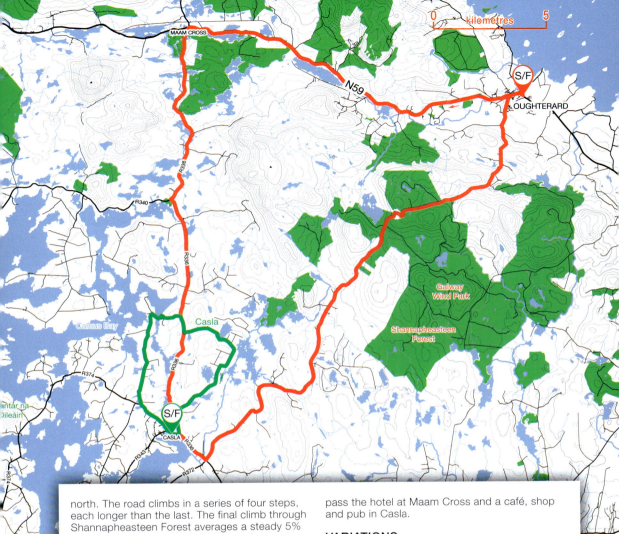

north. The road climbs in a series of four steps, each longer than the last. The final climb through Shannapheasteen Forest averages a steady 5% culminating in a series of hairpin bends.

Halfway down the fast descent Lough Corrib comes into view and it isn't long before you arrive back into Oughterard village.

REFRESHMENTS
There are plenty of options in Oughterard. You pass the hotel at Maam Cross and a café, shop and pub in Casla.

VARIATIONS
You could vary the route slightly by following a section of the Casla route (page 157). If you are looking for a challenge you could combine this route with the Maamturks route (page 162) to create a 107km figure of eight circuit of mid-Connemara.

DISTANCE	TOTAL		INSTRUCTION
0	0	S	From the carpark on the east side of Oughterard village head west along the N59.
16.6	16.6	<	Turn left onto the R336.
21.9	38.5	<	Turn left (signposted 'Uachtar Ard').
26.1	64.6	>	Turn right at the t-junction.
0.7	65.3	F	Arrive back at the start.

The final descent back to the carpark

DERROURA TRAIL CENTRE
County Galway
MTB

16km
160m

300m
200m
100m
0 km   5 km   10 km   15

This mountain bike trail offers plenty of singletrack and excellent views over Connemara.

Conveniently set just off the N59, this 16km trail offers a good workout and extensive views of the Maamturks, the Twelve Bens and Lough Corrib. The trail loops around the slopes of Knockbrack Hill in an anti-clockwise direction. The first half consists of a 6.7km climb at a steady 3% gradient.

The vast majority of the trail is singletrack and the reminder is gravel road. There aren't too many technical sections so the trails is suitable for less experienced mountain bikers.

This part of the country gets a lot of rain and some of the trail is very exposed to the elements so dress appropriately. The ground is very soft in places

and a number of sections of wooden boardwalks have been installed to prevent erosion. They can get very slippery when wet despite the rubber matting so take care.

Derroura Bike Hire (fb.com/Derrourabikehire) are based very close to the trailhead and offer bike hire.

From the carpark (53.4421, -9.4501), which is just off the N59 between Oughterard and Maam Cross, climb initially on a gravel road before turning onto singletrack. Follow a gravel road to the mast and turn sharply left onto more singletrack. Continue climbing over the shoulder of Letterfore. The climb ends on the east slopes of Keeraunnageeragh where there is a great view north over Lough Corrib.

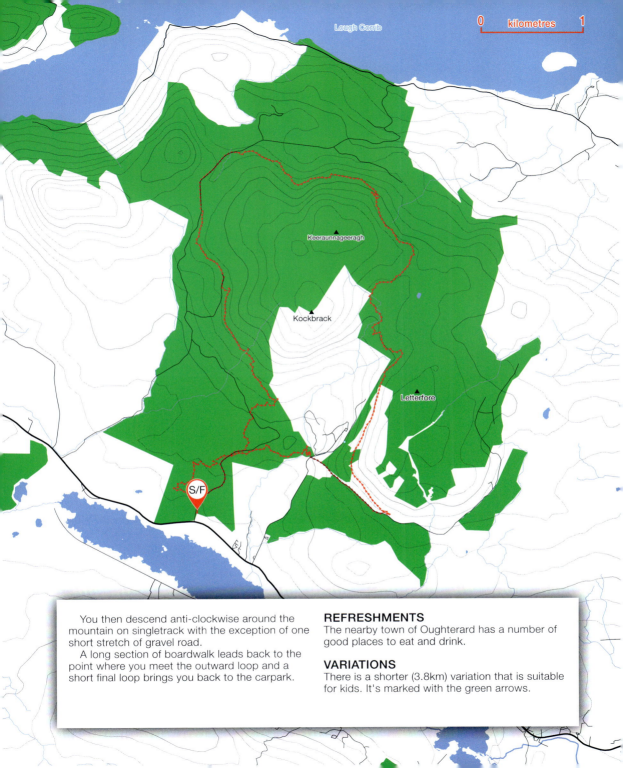

Lough Corrib

0   kilometres   1

Keeraunnageeragh ▲

Kockbrack ▲

Letterfore ▲

S/F

You then descend anti-clockwise around the mountain on singletrack with the exception of one short stretch of gravel road.

A long section of boardwalk leads back to the point where you meet the outward loop and a short final loop brings you back to the carpark.

REFRESHMENTS
The nearby town of Oughterard has a number of good places to eat and drink.

VARIATIONS
There is a shorter (3.8km) variation that is suitable for kids. It's marked with the green arrows.

Descending towards the R344 with the Twelve Bens in the background

MAAMTURKS
County Galway
ROAD

62km
660m

A very scenic loop around the mountains of Connemara.

The Maamturks Mountains are packed tightly between the Twelve Bens to the west and the Partry Mountains to the east. While this route passes through some spectacular mountain scenery the valleys that it follows never rise far above sea-level. The highest point on the route is a mere 105m which adds to the sense of the mountains looming overhead. As a result there aren't any major climbs, just a healthy number of short hills.

The initial stretch on the N59 is very busy but fortunately the rest of the route is quieter.

From Maam Cross (*53.4558, -9.5407*) head west along the N59. The road follows the course of the Galway to Clifden railway. This is in the early stages

of being developed as a greenway. Once completed it will offer a much more pleasant alternative.

After ten kilometres turn right onto quieter roads that lead through a beautiful valley. The road climbs towards the mountains before swinging left and losing some height before another short climb. As the road descends to the R344 there is a great view across Lough Inagh to the Twelve Bens.

Turn right onto the R344 and follow it to the junction with the N59 where you turn right. After two short climbs descend to the southern shore of Killary Harbour and follow the shore east to Leenane.

In the village turn onto the R336 and climb steeply up the valley. Turn right off the main road onto a very

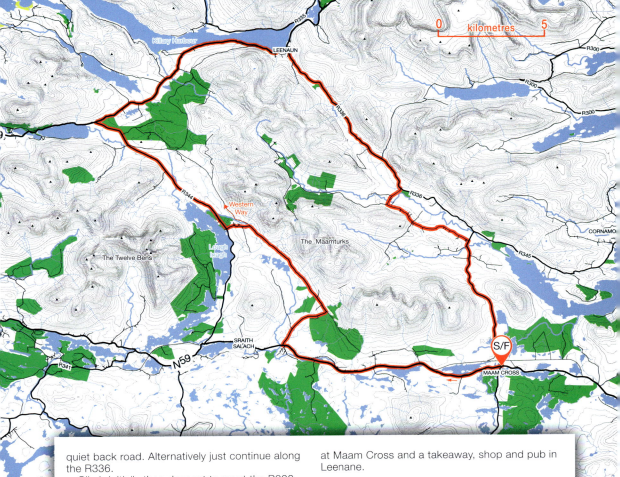

quiet back road. Alternatively just continue along the R336.

Climb initially then descent to meet the R336 at the foot of the last climb of the day past Maumwee Lough. From the lake it's just a matter of rolling down the hill into Maam Cross.

REFRESHMENTS
There is a bar and restaurant in Peacockes Hotel at Maam Cross and a takeaway, shop and pub in Leenane.

VARIATIONS
There is good potential for an interesting off-road variation of this route following sections of the Western Way, see sportireland.ie/outdoors for more information including maps.

DISTANCE	TOTAL		INSTRUCTION
0	0	S	From the crossroads at Maam Cross head west along the N59.
11.1	11.1	>	Turn right.
9.7	20.8	>	Turn right onto the R344.
8.4	29.2	>	Turn right onto the R59.
11.2	40.4	>	Turn right onto the R336.
9.2	49.6	>	Turn right (signposted 'Mámén').
1.1	50.7	<	Turn left at t-junction.
1.5	52.2	<	Keep left.
3.1	55.3	>	Turn right onto the R336.
6.9	62.2	F	Arrive back at Maam Cross.

Upper Sky Road

SKY ROAD
County Galway
ROAD

15km
280m

| 0 km | 5 km | 10 km | 15 km |

A short loop around the scenic headland just west of Clifden.

The road around the headland just west of Clifden is known as Sky Road. The extensive views over the coast of Connemara make it a popular tourist attraction.

The route is similar to Loop 1 of the Clifden cycle hub but it skips the less interesting northern section of Sky Road and avoids the busy N59.

From the centre of Clifden (*53.4883, -10.0227*) follow the road west along the bay until, just before the Boat Club, it climbs a very steep winding road up to the Sky Road. Turn left and then keep left at the fork dropping down onto Lower Sky Road. You follow this road in a loop climbing to the junction where it meets Upper Sky Road. Heading east continue up to the highpoint of the route where there are excellent views south to Ballyconneely and Roundstone Bog.

Continue east descending into Clifden. Look out for the John D'Arcy Monument on the right. It's worth a quick diversion to check out the excellent view over the town to the Twelve Bens.

REFRESHMENTS
Clifden has a wide range of places to eat and drink from small coffee shops to gourmet seafood restaurants.

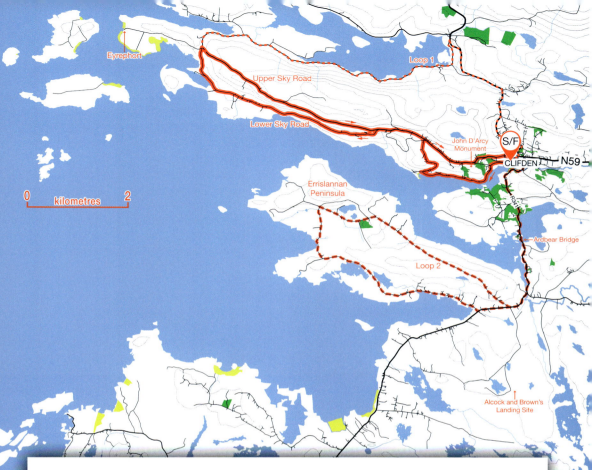

VARIATIONS

If you have time it's worth heading out to the tip of the headland to the sandy beach at Eyrephort, where there are fine views of the islands just offshore. This adds 3.2km to the route.

Clifden cycle hub has four routes, including a variation of the Sky Road route. The other three routes are all worthwhile.

The 17km Loop 2 is an interesting extension to the Sky Road route. It heads south from Clifden and loops around the Errislannan Peninsula passing close by the site of Alcock and Brown's crash landing after the first transatlantic flight. Take care on the stretch of winding, narrow road just after Ardbear bridge.

See page 25 for more information about the other routes.

DISTANCE	TOTAL		INSTRUCTION
0	0	S	From the roundabout in the centre of Clifden head west along Seaview Road.
0.1	0.1	<	Keep left at the fork.
1.9	2.0	>	Turn right (signposted 'Abbey Glen Hotel').
1.1	3.1	<	Turn left onto Upper Sky Road.
0.9	4.0	<	Turn left onto Lower Sky Road.
4.4	8.4	>	Turn right onto Upper Sky Road.
6.8	15.2	>	Turn onto Church Street.
0.1	15.3	F	Arrive back at the roundabout in the centre of Clifden.

The Green Road

INISHBOFIN
County Galway
GRAVEL

16km
180m

300m
200m
100m

0 km   5 km   10 km   15 km

A varied loop around the coast of this small island just off the Connemara coast.

Inishbofin, which is only a short ferry ride from Cleggan, offers an excellent perspective on the mountains of Galway and Mayo. This route combines sections of three signposted trails into an anti-clockwise loop around the island. It follows roads, tracks and a few sections of rough path so a gravel bike is ideal but a hybrid will manage the vast majority of the terrain.

From the pier (*53.6135, -10.2123*) follow the red arrows of the Cloonamore Trail around the eastern end of the island. Shortly after traversing Cloonamore Strand leave the road and cross open hillside before returning to the village along the High Road. Here you pick up the Middlequarter

Loop (blue arrows) and turn right following the trail inland. After crossing the hill behind the runway join the Westquarter Loop and follow the purple arrows across the narrow causeway between Lough Bó Finne and the Atlantic. Continue along the good track to the western end of the island where the track gives way to grassy commonage.

Follow the coast around the headland to the Green Road which leads past the spectacular Trá Gheal beach. The track then meets the Low Road which brings you back to the pier.

REFRESHMENTS

There are a couple of pubs and restaurants on the island. If you are planning to stay overnight there are a number of hotels and B+Bs, a campsite and a hostel. See inishbofin.com for details.

VARIATIONS

This route makes the most of the island's tracks and roads so it would be difficult to extend it without covering some of the same ground twice. If you are looking for a shorter route you could follow one of the signposted routes, the Westquarter Loop (purple arrows) is the pick of the bunch.

DISTANCE	TOTAL		INSTRUCTION
0	0	S	From the pier head east along the Low Road.
0.2	0.2	<	Turn left at the fork.
2.1	2.3	<	Turn left at the junction.
0.4	2.7	>	Turn right onto the rough track alongside the beach.
0.4	3.1	<	Turn left onto the road.
0.3	3.4	>	Turn right onto the track.
0.8	4.2	<	Turn left onto the rough path.
0.2	4.4	<	Turn left onto the track.
0.6	5.2	>	Turn right onto the road.
0.4	5.6	>	Turn right at the fork.
1.2	6.8	>	Turn right at the fork.
1.0	7.8	<	Turn left onto the path.
0.1	7.9	>	Turn right onto the track.
0.1	8.0	<	Keep left at the fork.
0.7	8.7	<	Turn left onto the track.
0.8	9.5	>	Turn right.
0.5	10.0	<	Cross the beach.
0.2	10.2	>	Turn right onto the road.
1.6	11.8	^	As the track peters out head south across the grass.
1.2	13.0	^	Follow the Green Road east.
1.5	14.5	^	Continue east along the Low Road.
1.4	15.9	F	Arrive back at the pier.

Cong Woods

CONG AND CLONBUR
County Galway/Mayo
GRAVEL

19km
170m

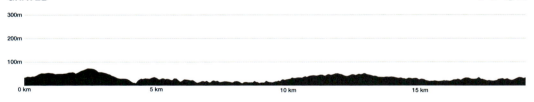

300m
200m
100m
0 km   5 km   10 km   15 km

A lovely loop through the forest between Lough Mask and Lough Corrib.

This short off-road route weaves its way around the narrow strip of forest that lies between Lough Mask and Lough Corrib. It can be done in either direction but is described anti-clockwise, as if you approach Ashford Castle from the other direction you may be charged an entrance fee.

This route, which is mostly on forest tracks and paths with the exception of the first few kilometres of road, is ideal for a hybrid or gravel bike.

From the village of Clonbur (*53.5451, -9.3653*) head south along the R345 before turning left and climbing a small hill that offers good views over Lough Corrib. You then descent to the lakeshore. At the far side of the small bay a narrow path leads

steeply uphill (you may need to push your bike up it). After 100m you meet an overgrown track and follow it east to a crossroads where you turn right. Pass through the carpark and turn left following the track along the lakeshore into the grounds of Ashford Castle. After passing the impressive five-star hotel cross the bridge over the Cong River.

Turn left after the second bridge, go through Cong Abbey and cross the footbridge into Cong Woods. Follow the green arrows of the Cong to Clonbur trail through the forest. Cross the road and continue climbing gently. Look out on your right for the Pigeonhole, the deep sinkhole is well worth a look.

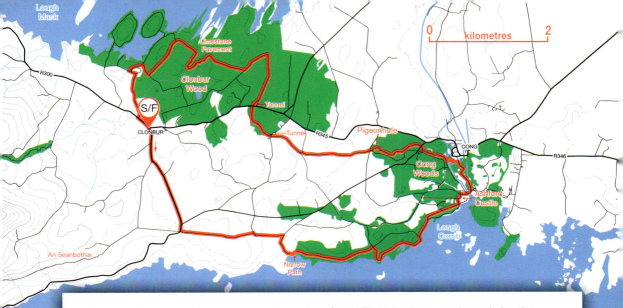

Cross another road and wind your way through the trees and under two tunnels into Clonbur Wood. Continue along the green trail past an area of limestone pavements, the largest outside of the Burren. Look out for signs for the white trail and follow it to the forest entrance. Pass the graveyard and climb the laneway to the R300 where you turn left and return to Clonbur.

REFRESHMENTS

There are plenty of places to eat and drink in Cong Village but it can get busy during the summer. Clonbur is quieter and has a couple of bars that serve food.

VARIATIONS

It's possible to extend this route to include An Seanbothar, the quiet back road that links Clonbur and Cornamona.

If you are looking for a shorter route then the woods of Clonbur and Cong offer plenty of tracks and paths to explore.

DISTANCE	TOTAL		INSTRUCTION
0	0	S	From the centre of Clonbur head south along the R345.
1.9	1.9	<	Turn left.
1.3	3.2	>	Turn right and then immediately turn left.
0.5	3.7	>	Turn right.
0.5	4.2	^	At the far end of the carpark look for a narrow path that leads up through the trees.
1.4	5.6	>	At the crossroads turn right.
1.3	6.9	>	Keep right at the fork.
0.3	7.2	<	Keep left at the fork.
0.6	7.8	<	Turn left at the crossroads and pass the front of the castle and cross the bridge.
0.4	8.2	<	After crossing the bridge keep left at the fork.
0.7	8.9	<	Just after the bridge turn left through the gate onto a path.
0.1	9.0	<	Turn left and cross the footbridge.
0.1	9.1	>	Turn right at the junction.
0.5	9.6	>	Turn right at the junction.
1.0	10.6	^	Cross the road.
3.5	14.1	<	Turn left at the junction.
0.5	14.6	>	Turn right at the junction.
2.6	17.2	>	Turn right.
0.3	17.5	<	Turn left.
0.2	17.7	<	Turn left into the graveyard.
1.0	18.7	<	Turn left onto the R300
0.2	18.9	F	Arrive back in Clonbur.

The second river crossing

SHEEFFRY HILLS
County Mayo
ROAD

52km
440m

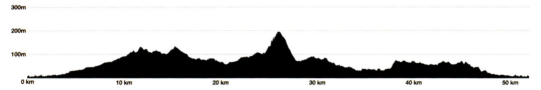

This route explores the backroads and the quiet valleys of the Sheeffry Hills.

The Sheeffry Hills are a compact, little visited range surrounded by more prominent neighbours such as Mweelrea to the west and Croagh Patrick to the north. This route passes through the range's valleys taking in some great mountain scenery while avoiding an excessive amount of climbing.

Despite the fact that the route includes two river crossing and a short stretch of rough track it's suitable for a road bike.

From the village of Louisburgh (*53.7623, -9.8100*) the route heads south on quiet roads before turning left into the wonderfully named valley of Tangincartoor. As you climb the road becomes

rougher until, shortly after passing a number of farm buildings, it ends at a small river.

The best option is to remove your shoes and socks and wade through the water. A short stretch of rocky track leads to a second ford. On the far side the road improves. Continue climbing to the junction and turn right (Loop 3 of the cycle hub goes left). Descend for 5km and turn right onto the road to Sheeffry Pass, the only substantial climb on the route.

The road cuts diagonally across the steep mountainside and while it looks intimidating the gradient is gentle and it's soon over. From the top there are great views inland towards Ben Gorm

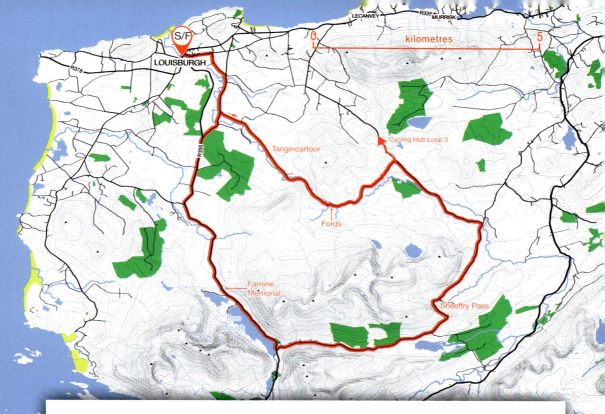

and the Partry Mountains. A fast descent past Tawnyard Lough leads down the valley to Doo Lough where you turn right onto the R335. This slightly busier road follows the eastern shore of the lake north past the Famine Memorial.

After another fairly flat 10km turn right onto a quieter road. A short distance later you rejoin the outbound route and follow it back into Louisburgh.

REFRESHMENTS

There is nowhere along the route but there are two cafés and a few pubs in Louisburgh.

VARIATIONS

The Louisburgh cycle hub (page 25) has three loops, one of which is a 26km variation of the route described here.

DISTANCE	TOTAL		INSTRUCTION
0	0	S	Head north along the Main Street.
0.1	0.1	>	Turn right onto Chapel Street.
1.2	1.3	>	Turn right.
1.3	2.6	>	Turn right at the crossroads.
1.7	4.3	<	Turn left at fork.
6.8	11.1	≈	Ford the river.
0.3	11.4	≈	Ford the river.
3.8	15.2	>	Turn right at t-junction.
5.1	20.3	>	Turn right at t-junction.
13.8	34.1	>	Turn right at t-junction onto the R335.
11.8	45.9	>	Turn right.
3.2	49.1	<	Turn left at crossroads.
1.3	50.4	<	Turn left at t-junction.
1.2	51.6	<	Turn left onto Main Street.
0.2	51.8	F	Arrive back at the start.

The Skelp

OWENWEE BOG
County Mayo
MTB

16km
270m

This short route packs in a variety of terrain from quiet roads to rough mountain tracks.

Looping around the valley south of Croagh Patrick this route offers an interesting perspective on the holy mountain as well as a great view of Clew Bay from the route's highest point.

The descent of the Skelp is very rough so a mountain bike is probably the best option, however you could manage the route on a hybrid or gravel bike if you walk down the Skelp.

This loop is best done in a clockwise direction so that you descend rather than climb the rougher northern side of the Skelp.

To get to the start of the route head south on the N59 from Westport. After 7km turn right (signposted 'OWENWEE'), at the next fork turn right, follow the road a short distance and park in the gravel layby beside the National School (*53.7539, -9.5626*).

Follow the quiet road west, turning onto a track that climbs gradually up to Owenwee Bog. The track passes bog cuttings and there are good views of the southern slopes of Croagh Patrick.

You enter the forest and turn right before rejoining the road. After a few kilometres turn left onto the track that rises diagonally across the hillside to the Skelp, the narrow gap in the hillside. The climb is gentle and surface is good so it should be rideable.

At the top the view over Clew Bay is revealed and you begin the rocky descent. Depending on

172

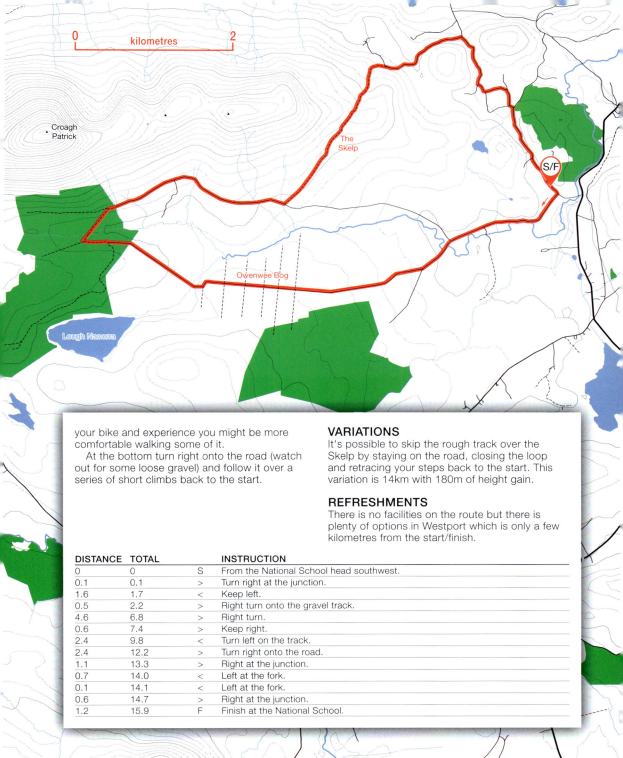

your bike and experience you might be more comfortable walking some of it.

At the bottom turn right onto the road (watch out for some loose gravel) and follow it over a series of short climbs back to the start.

VARIATIONS

It's possible to skip the rough track over the Skelp by staying on the road, closing the loop and retracing your steps back to the start. This variation is 14km with 180m of height gain.

REFRESHMENTS

There is no facilities on the route but there is plenty of options in Westport which is only a few kilometres from the start/finish.

DISTANCE	TOTAL		INSTRUCTION
0	0	S	From the National School head southwest.
0.1	0.1	>	Turn right at the junction.
1.6	1.7	<	Keep left.
0.5	2.2	>	Right turn onto the gravel track.
4.6	6.8	>	Right turn.
0.6	7.4	>	Keep right.
2.4	9.8	<	Turn left on the track.
2.4	12.2	>	Turn right onto the road.
1.1	13.3	>	Right at the junction.
0.7	14.0	<	Left at the fork.
0.1	14.1	<	Left at the fork.
0.6	14.7	>	Right at the junction.
1.2	15.9	F	Finish at the National School.

The Blue Bridge midway between Mulranny and Achill

GREAT WESTERN GREENWAY

County MAYO
ROAD

44km
260m

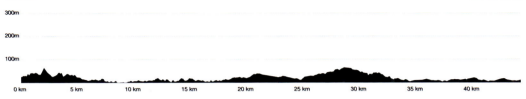

The Great Western Greenway is a traffic-free route that connects Westport to Achill Island.

The 44km Greenway follows the route of the Westport to Achill railway which closed in 1937. Since the greenway opened in 2011 it has been very popular, with 300 people walking or cycling the scenic route daily in the summer.

The route is well signposted and traffic-free so it's very safe for children. The surface is a mix of compact gravel and tarmac that is suitable for most bikes, although a very delicate road bike might be a little uncomfortable.

The greenway crosses active farmland so please respect private property and livestock and have regard for farming activities. Note that the greenway is closed to the public on the 21st of February every year.

The route can be divided into three sections:

WESTPORT TO NEWPORT 13km
The greenway starts from the shore of Clew Bay on the western edge of Westport. It then swings around the town before heading north. It's possible to save a few kilometres by meeting the greenway on the north side of the town where Golf Course Road meets the N59.

The greenway then makes its way north following the course of the N59. While this section is pleasant it's probably the least interesting part of the route.

NEWPORT TO MULRANNY 18km
From Newport the greenway continues north through gentle pasture land. Shortly after crossing the stone bridge at Burrishoole it swings west. Gradually the ground becomes a little more undulating and the route has a wilder feel with the Nephin Beg mountains rising up to the north.

As you approach Mulranny you gain height and there is a good view across Clew Bay to Croagh Patrick.

MULRANNY TO ACHILL 13km
From Mulranny the greenway descends through the trees to more open ground near Bellacragher Bay. As you head northwest you are sheltered from the wind by the mountains.

Once you turn west the distinctive triangular profile of Slievemore on Achill Island comes into view. The route then descends into the finish at the bridge over Achill Sound.

See the map on page 177.

VARIATIONS
The Rocky Mountain Way (page 176), which follows a route parallel to the greenway but higher up the hillside on old bog roads, is a good option for those who are looking for something a little more challenging.

The greenway could also be connected with the Achill Island route (page 178) to create a longer, possibly multi-day, cycle.

The National Coastal Trail is a 9.2km cycle path that connects the southern end of the greenway with Murrisk at the foot of Croagh Patrick.

The Clew Bay Trail is a 99km circuit of the bay. Starting in Westport it follows the 9km National Coastal Trail west along the southern shore of the bay past Croagh Patrick. From Murrisk a 20km road section leads to the pier at Roonagh. After the short ferry crossing to Clare Island you can do a (approximately 18km) loop around the island before boarding another ferry to cross the mouth of the bay to the southern tip of Achill Island. Heading north for 8km on quiet roads leads to the western end of the greenway which is followed for 44km back to Westport. See clewbaybiketrail.ie for details.

REFRESHMENTS
A whole industry has sprung up around feeding and watering cyclists so there is no shortage of places to refuel along or near the route.

The greenway is very popular with families some of whom only do a shorter section of the route before being picked up by one of the many companies that offer shuttle and bike hire services.

See greenway.ie for route maps and the latest information on bike hire.

Passing Lough Pol shortly after leaving the Greenway

NORTH CLEW BAY
County Mayo
GRAVEL

35km
380m

This route's mix of quiet roads and gravel tracks offers a more adventurous alternative to the Great Western Greenway.

This route combines sections of the Rocky Mountain Way - a signposted off-road cycle route, the greenway and two other signposted trails to create a 35km loop. With the exception of one stretch of rough path there isn't any technical riding and a hybrid or gravel bike will suffice.

The route is described in an anti-clockwise direction to get the climbing over and done with earlier.

From Newport (53.8844, -9.5460) follow the greenway north on a good, flat surface. Shortly after turning right off the greenway (following signs for the

Rocky Mountain Way) weave around the maze of small lakes before climbing onto the open hillside.

As you gain height the road turns into a good track, which rises and falls as it crosses the southern slopes of the Nephin Beg Range. To the south are spectacular views across Clew Bay to Croagh Patrick. Look out for the small shelter beside the track on the right (53.9217,-9.6222). It's a handy place to stop for a break in bad weather.

After nearly 15km there is a testing stretch of rough path lined with flagstones. Shortly after this you meet the greenway and turn left following it downhill towards Newport. After a short distance

turn right (marked as Zone 8) and follow the red arrows of the Glenthomas Loop along quiet lanes to the N59. Turn right off the N59 opposite the Newfield Inn. This quiet road, which is initially very rough, leads along the coast past Roigh Pier and the 16th century Rockfleet Castle which was once home to the renowned pirate queen Grace O'Malley.

After another short stretch on the N59 turn inland and follow the red arrows of the Oghillies Loop to the greenway. Turn right and follow it back to Newport.

VARIATIONS

You could shorten the route by leaving the Rocky Mountain Way earlier to meet the greenway. Alternatively start at Burrishoole Bridge (53.9036, -9.5756) where there is parking for a few cars.

REFRESHMENTS

Newport has a number of restaurants, pubs and cafés. As does Mulranny which is only a few kilometres from the route. You also pass, shortly after the halfway mark, the Newfield Inn (nevinsinn.com) which serves food and drink.

DISTANCE	TOTAL		INSTRUCTION
0	0	S	From the centre of Newport follow the greenway north.
4.7	4.7	>	Turn right off the greenway following signs for the Rocky Mountain Way.
12.8	17.5	<	Meet the greenway and turn left (in the direction of Newport).
2.2	19.7	>	Turn right, leaving the greenway.
0.7	20.4	<	Turn left onto the N59.
0.8	21.2	>	Turn right.
3.4	24.6	>	Turn right.
3.1	27.7	>	Turn right onto the N59.
0.3	28.0	<	Turn left.
0.3	28.3	>	Keep right at the fork.
0.7	29.0	>	Turn right onto the greenway.
5.8	34.8	F	Arrive back at the finish in Newport.

The sweeping bends at Ashleam south of Dooega

ACHILL ISLAND
County Mayo
ROAD

82 km
1600 m

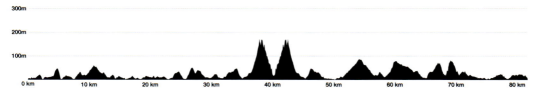

A tough circuit around the spectacular coast of the largest island on the west coast.

This route follows a figure of eight loop around the coast of Achill Island which is renowned for its rugged mountains and wide sandy beaches. Most of the route is reasonably gentle with the exception of the (optional) out and back to Keem Beach.

Achill is a cycling hub and this route follows sections of all three of the signposted routes, see page 25 for more information.

The island is very exposed to the wind so let it dictate the direction in which you tackle the route. Here it's described in an anti-clockwise direction starting and finishing at the bridge that connects the island to the mainland.

From Achill Sound (*53.9302, -9.9273*) head north, following Loop 2 along a network of quiet roads around the northeast of the island passing a number of fine sandy beaches. Shortly after the village of Doogort turn inland and climb the lower slopes of Slievemore.

Look out for the signs for the Deserted Village. If your bike is up to it then it's well worth diverting along the gravel road past the ruins. It's the same distance as the road but adds 100m of climbing.

At Keel you take the (optional but very worthwhile) out and back to Keem Beach. It's a steep climb in both directions as the road rises high above the sea before dropping down to the beach, but the views more than make up for it.

From Keel take the busy R319 east for a few kilometres before turning right and meeting the coast at the village of Dooega. Continue southeast along the coast past a potential shortcut across the headland. At the top of the steep hairpin climb there are amazing views along the coast.

A remote stretch of coast leads to the southern tip of the island where you turn north and follow the road back to Achill Sound.

VARIATIONS

This route could be combined with the Great Western Greenway (page 175) which links Achill Island with Westport. All three of the cycling hub routes are worthwhile shorter alternatives, see page 25 for more information.

REFRESHMENTS

There is a supermarket and a few cafés in Achill Sound. You also pass through a number of villages with pubs, shops and cafés. During the summer the island is busy but it can be quiet during the winter when many businesses close.

DISTANCE	TOTAL		INSTRUCTION
0	0	S	From Achill Sound head west along the R319.
0.9	0.9	>	Turn right.
3.5	4.4	<	Turn left at the junction.
1.8	6.2	>	Turn right at the crossroad.
1.6	7.8	>	Turn right at the junction onto the R319.
2.9	10.7	>	Turn right and follow the signs for Loop 2.
20.8	31.5	^	Continue through Keel on the R319 leaving Loop 2.
8.6	40.1	↶	At Keem retrace your steps back along the R319 to Keel.
8.5	48.6	^	Continue west along the R319.
9.4	58.2	>	Turn right.
9.1	67.3	>	Turn right.
13.2	80.5	>	Turn right.
1.0	81.5	F	Finish at Achill Sound.

CROSS LAKE
County Mayo
GRAVEL

8km
40m

300m				
200m				
100m				
0 km	2 km	4 km	6 km	8 km

A short flat circuit on a mix of sandy beaches, tracks and minor roads that is ideal for families.

This route follows a slight variation of the Cross Beach Loop which is signposted with blue arrows. A hybrid is ideal for this route's mixed terrain but most road bikes will also manage the grassy tracks and sections of hard sand. There are plenty of places along this short route to linger and take in the excellent views over to the Inishkea islands and the tiny island of Inishglora, the resting place of the mythical Children of Lir.

The route starts overlooking the beach beside the old graveyard (*54.2092, -10.0806*) that surrounds the ruins of Cross Abbey. Park here, or if it's busy, park on the grass beside the more modern graveyard. Head back the way you arrived, turning right at the junction. Follow the road anti-clockwise around the lake (past a number of picnic benches).

At the end of the road turn right and follow the track through the dunes to the beach where, at any time other than high tide, it's possible to cycle south along the hard-packed sand near the water. If the tide is very high you might have to push your bike along the stony upper section of the beach or else follow the grassy path that runs through the dunes. But take care as it runs very close to a barbed wire fence.

0 — kilometres — 2

Modern Graveyard

S/F

Cross Lake

R313

Blacksod Bay

Look out for the tall black post that marks the point where you leave the beach and follow the track inland. At the end of the track turn right and follow the road anti-clockwise around the lake. You then retrace your steps back to the start.

VARIATIONS

The western shore of the Mullet Peninsula is basically one long beach and it may be possible, depending on the condition of the sand and the state of the tide, to continue further south along the coast before returning on the R313.

Another alternative would be to head south along the beach from the start of the route beside the old graveyard joining the route where it turns inland.

REFRESHMENTS

The nearby town of Belmullet has a good variety of shops, cafés and pubs.

DISTANCE	TOTAL		INSTRUCTION
0	0	S	Start at the old graveyard and head east along the road.
0.6	0.6	>	Turn right at the junction.
0.4	1.0	>	Turn right at the fork.
1.0	2.0	>	Turn right at the end of the road onto the track through the dunes.
0.6	2.6	<	Follow the beach south.
0.6	3.2	>	Leave the beach and follow the track.
0.5	3.7	>	Turn right the junction.
1.3	5.0	<	Turn left at the crossroad.
2.6	7.6	>	Turn right at the junction.
0.4	8.0	<	Turn left at the junction.
0.6	8.6	F	Finish at the old graveyard.

Near the highest point of the Sralagagh Loop

RATHLACKEN AND SRALAGAGH
County Mayo
GRAVEL

30 km
510 m

300m			
200m			
100m			
0 km	10 km	20 km	30 km

A figure of eight route following minor roads and tracks around the hills and coast of North Mayo.

This route combines two quite short signposted loops to create a more substantial cycle. While this isn't a very hilly route there are still excellent views over Sligo Bay from the route's higher points.

Some of the route follows rough tracks that are more suitable for a hybrid or mountain bike than a road bike.

Both loops are well signposted so turn by turn directions aren't necessary. They could be tackled in any order but are described with Rathlacken first and Sralagagh second.

From the main street of Ballycastle (*54.2799, -9.3734*) head east before turning left (opposite the Seaview Lounge) onto a quiet back road. At the crossroads turn right and after 3.7km you meet the Rathlacken Loop which is marked by blue arrows (the green arrows mark an 8km variation).

Continue down the road turning left and then right onto a gravel track. Look out for the strange four-legged tower, known as the Gazebo, on your left. There are excellent views from this late 18th century tower. On a clear day it's possible to make out the mountains of Donegal on the other side of the bay.

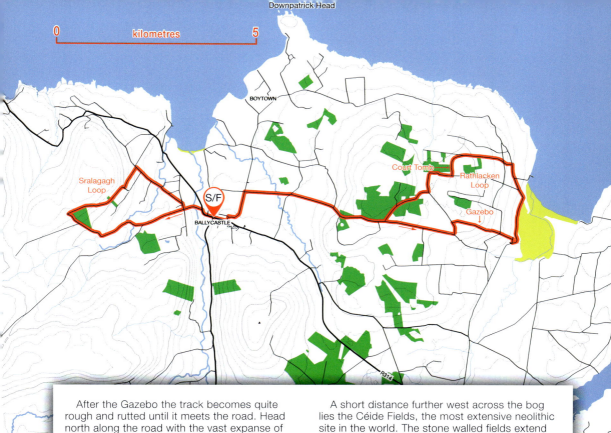

0   kilometres   5

BOYTOWN

Court Tomb

Rathlacken Loop

Sralagagh Loop

S/F

BALLYCASTLE

Gazebo

R314

KILLALA

After the Gazebo the track becomes quite rough and rutted until it meets the road. Head north along the road with the vast expanse of Lacken Strand to your right.

Turn left after just over a kilometre, leaving the shore and climb, steeply at first. As you gain height the views over Lacken Bay and the dunes at Kilcummin open up and the road becomes more of a track.

The track passes by the exceptionally well preserved Rathlacken court tomb. It's well worth a quick stop as it's one of the finest examples of a court tomb in the country and is over five thousand years old.

The route continues across the hillside on a mix of road and track to the point where you started the loop. Retrace your steps back to Ballycastle.

Back on the main street of Ballycastle you set off on the Sralagagh Loop which is signposted in a clockwise direction with green arrows.

Follow the R314 a short distance west before turning left onto a gently rising lane. After crossing the Bellanaminnaun River the road steepens until you reach the high point of the route at the edge of the forest. Above is open heather hillside and bog with plenty of signs of turf cutting.

A short distance further west across the bog lies the Céide Fields, the most extensive neolithic site in the world. The stone walled fields extend over thousands of acres and are almost 6,000 years old.

Follow the rough and in places muddy track along the edge of the forest. As you descend it turns into a grassy boreen and the view opens up revealing the iconic sea stack, Dún Briste, that lies just off Downpatrick Head.

A steep descent leads to the road where you continue downhill to complete the loop and retrace your steps back to Ballycastle.

REFRESHMENTS

There are no facilities on the route, but there is a café and a few pubs in Ballycastle.

VARIATIONS

Either of the loops could be done individually. The Sralagagh Loop is 9km with 160m of height gain while the Rathlacken Loop is 11km with 180m of height gain.

If you are looking for a longer route you could head north to Downpatrick Head and follow the coastline east to join the Rathlacken Loop.

Climbing the south side of Ladies Brae

OX MOUNTAINS
County Sligo
ROAD

35km
590m

A figure of eight route that crosses back and forth over the Ox Mountains.

The route, which starts and finishes in Coolaney (not to be confused with Collooney, the village just to the west), follows a series of narrow boreens, some of which can be a little rough, climbing over a pass between the mountains.

From the northern end of Coolaney (*54.1751, -8.6011*) turn left and cross the bridge over the Owenboy River before immediately turning left again onto a narrow, winding road. Climb gradually and turn right onto the road that cuts north through the hills.

Heading up the valley you pass a nice grassy spot where the Glenmore River runs alongside the road.

It's an ideal place for a break, there are even a few picnic benches.

Further up the valley the roads steepens before the top of the pass where you turn right and descend back down into the lowlands. At the junction turn left and head west to the foot of the climb back into the mountains, the Ladies Brae. From the bridge it's a steady 5% gradient to the top. About halfway up a break in the trees reveals the view north to Knocknarea and Benbulbin.

Retrace your steps descending southwards before turning left and following a quiet boreen back into Coolaney village.

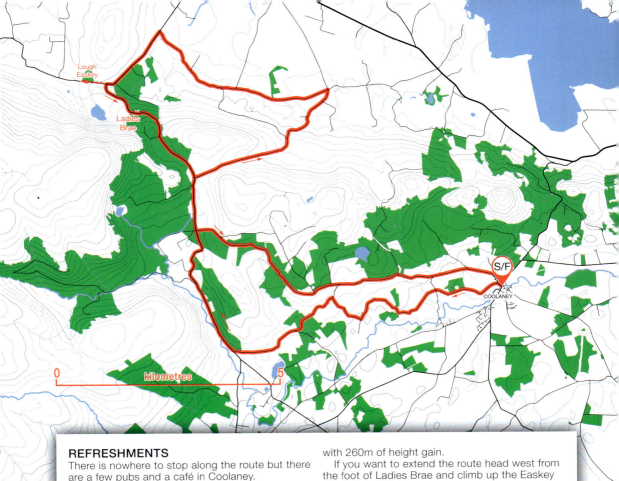

REFRESHMENTS

There is nowhere to stop along the route but there are a few pubs and a café in Coolaney.

VARIATIONS

Either of the loops could be done as a route in its own right. The northern loop is 14km with 280m of height gain while the southern loop is 19km with 260m of height gain.

If you want to extend the route head west from the foot of Ladies Brae and climb up the Easkey river valley past Lough Easkey. You would then descend the other side of the valley through Masshill before returning to Coolaney on quiet backroads. This gives a route of 63km with 750m of height gain.

DISTANCE	TOTAL	ARROW	INSTRUCTION
0	0	S	From bridge at the northern end of the village head north on the L2801.
0.05	0.05	<	Immediately turn left.
3.95	4.0	>	Turn right.
0.8	4.8	<	Turn left.
2.9	7.7	>	Turn right.
4.5	12.2	>	Turn right.
4.1	16.3	<	Turn left.
4.5	20.8	<	Turn left.
1.7	22.5	<	Turn left.
4.4	26.9	<	Turn left.
7.9	34.8	>	Turn right.
0.3	35.1	F	Arrive back to Coolaney.

Descending Baywatch, a section of the red trail

COOLANEY TRAIL CENTRE

County Sligo
MTB

22km
460m

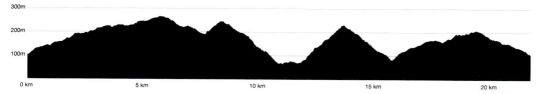

A range of purpose-built MTB trails that offer excellent views and engaging riding.

This trail centre in the Ox Mountains offers an unrivalled combination of impressive views, high-quality trails and some novel riding across open hillside rather than the more common forest setting.

There are plans for plenty more trails, and at the time of writing work is ongoing on three more trails - a blue, red and black. Bear in mind that the higher sections of the trails are exposed to the elements so if the weather is bad make sure you dress accordingly.

At first glance the trail network may look confusing, but it's very clearly signposted, however it might be an idea to take a photo of the map on the facing page or the map-board at the trailhead just in case.

All the trails share a common start along the climb up the Blue Trail. At the top of the climb you meet Two Way Junction where you have a choice to continue climbing up the Red Trail or else start the descent down the Blue Trail. After a short distance, at The Hub, you are faced with four options: continue along the Blue, take one of the two red trails or else tackle the black trail - No Delay.

The trails start from the large carpark (*54.1812, -8.6189*) 2km north of Coolaney village.

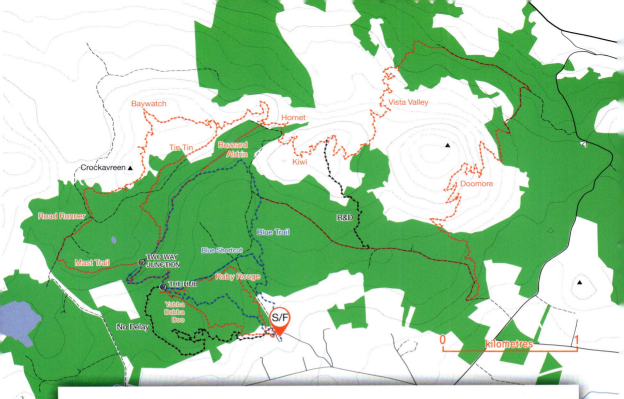

BLUE TRAIL

The Blue Trail is 5.3km with 90m of height gain. There is a shortcut option that leaves the climb near midway and follows a fire road to The Hub. It is 3.25km with 70m of height gain.

RED TRAILS

All three of the red trails start by climbing up the Blue Trail to Two Way Junction. They then continue climbing on the first section of red trail, which climbs through the trees and onto the open slopes of Crockavreen where there are excellent views over Sligo Bay and across to Slieve League and the distinctive summits of the Dartry Mountains.

After descending for 600m, just after a series of hairpins, you are meet a junction. Turning right onto Tin Tin is the shortest option, giving a route of 10.4km and 160m of height gain.

If you continue straight there is another junction after 900m. If you turn right onto Buzzard Aldrin gives a route of 11.3 and 180m of height gain.

Continuing straight on leads to the newest sections of trail on the slopes of Doomore. This option gives the longest possible combination, a route of 22km with 460m of height gain. It is the route depicted in the elevation profile.

Initially you climb slightly to the junction with the black trail, R&D, before dropping down Vista Valley to the gravel road. After 750m the trail climbs over the shoulder of Doomore hill, gaining 130m, before meeting another gravel road and following it for 2km to the join the climb up the Blue Trail.

BLACK TRAILS

There are two black trails: No Delay, which drops 90m over 2.6km, is more of a flowing trail; and R&D, which drops 90m over 1.1km, is steeper, rockier and more technical.

Combining the two black trails with the blue and red trails gives a route of 15.6km with a height gain of 280m.

REFRESHMENTS

There are a number of places to eat in nearby Coolaney village.

VARIATIONS

Obviously there is scope for much longer routes that cover some of the sections more than once.

The southeast corner of Lough Gill

LOUGH GILL
County Sligo/Leitrim
ROAD

39 km
450 m

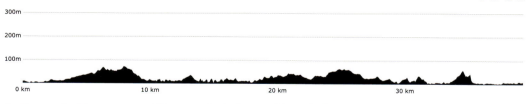

A signposted loop around the wooded shore of Lough Gill.

This route can either be blasted out in less than two hours or you could devote a whole day to exploring the many beautiful forests along the lakeshore.

Generally speaking the roads are quite busy with fast moving traffic so caution is required. The route is pretty flat, the highest point is a mere 73m so there aren't any long climbs. It's reasonably well signposted in a clockwise direction with markers every kilometre so you can track your progress.

From the bus/train station (*54.2714, -8.4819*) in Sligo Town the route follows the N4 north for a short distance before turning right onto the N16. Shortly after meeting the R286 the road starts to climb, passing the turn for Hazelwood Demesne on your right. The climb ends at a viewing point looking north over Colgagh Lough and the Leitrim hills.

The route then descends back to the lakeshore and you slip unnoticed across the border into County Leitrim. You pass the 17th century Parke's Castle set picturesquely at the water's edge and begin to climb inland to the village of Dromahair which marks the halfway mark of the cycle.

Leaving the village the road continues to climb before dropping down to the R287 which you follow over the shoulder of Killerry Mountain. A fast descent leads back to the lakeshore at Slish Wood.

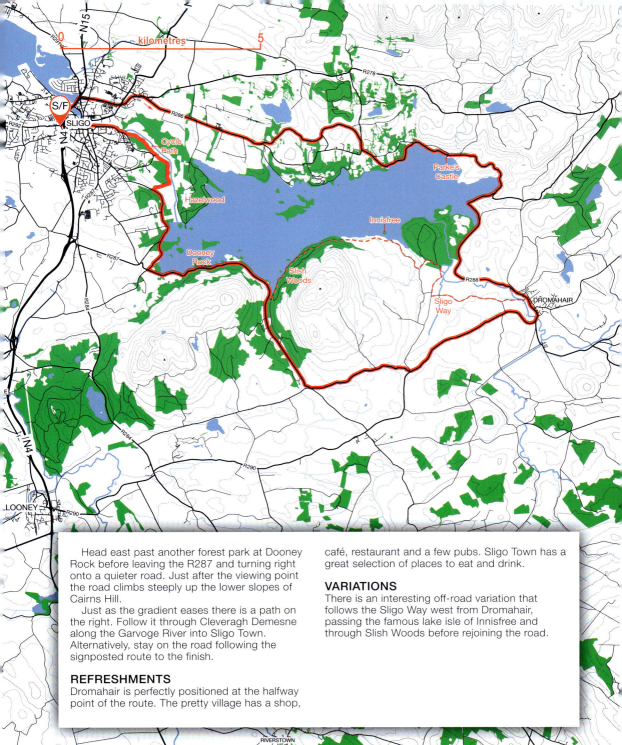

Head east past another forest park at Dooney Rock before leaving the R287 and turning right onto a quieter road. Just after the viewing point the road climbs steeply up the lower slopes of Cairns Hill.

Just as the gradient eases there is a path on the right. Follow it through Cleveragh Demesne along the Garvoge River into Sligo Town. Alternatively, stay on the road following the signposted route to the finish.

REFRESHMENTS
Dromahair is perfectly positioned at the halfway point of the route. The pretty village has a shop, café, restaurant and a few pubs. Sligo Town has a great selection of places to eat and drink.

VARIATIONS
There is an interesting off-road variation that follows the Sligo Way west from Dromahair, passing the famous lake isle of Innisfree and through Slish Woods before rejoining the road.

The impressive profile of Benwiskin

BENBULBIN
County Sligo/Leitrim
ROAD

55km
690m

A circuit of one of Ireland's most distinctive mountains.

While the steep slopes and flat top of Benbulbin dominate this route there are plenty of other impressive sights such as the Glencar Waterfall, the Devil's Chimney and the other-worldly Eagle's Rock. This is a quiet peaceful route with a fair amount of climbing but plenty of scenery to distract.

It is best done in an anti-clockwise direction in the hope that the prevailing wind will be at your back on the more exposed southern sections.

The route heads south from Grange (*54.3924, -8.5260*) and avoids the busy N15 by following a series of backroads. From the start there is a great view of Benbulbin.

Turning east it's a flat run to Glencar where huge limestone cliffs loom above the valley floor making it easy to see why it's known as the Swiss Valley.

Look out for the Devil's Chimney high on the left side of the valley. It's one of the highest waterfalls in Ireland and when the wind blows from the southwest the water appears to flow upwards and back over the edge.

At the end of the lake you pass the café and carpark beside Glencar Waterfall, which is only a short walk from the road and worth a visit.

After the lake the road begins to climb, gently at first, but just before the sharp left turn it steepens. You eventually reach the plateau, the highest point

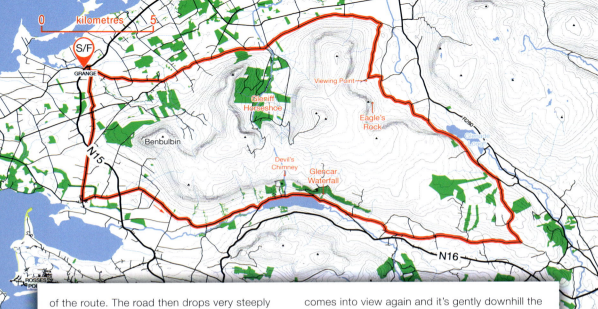

of the route. The road then drops very steeply down the other side and heads down the valley passing Glenade Lough. The left-hand skyline is dominated by more towering grey limestone walls.

As you make your way west a seemingly unremarkable rock face gradually reveals its true self. Eagle's Rock is a very impressive narrow fin of rock that stands separate from the main cliff. Look out for the viewing point beside the carpark.

A short distance later you turn the corner onto the final leg of the route. Here the mountain's sheer cliffs give way to distinctive fluted gullies. Shortly after passing the turn for the Gleniff Horseshoe the western profile of Benbulbin

comes into view again and it's gently downhill the rest of the way to Grange.

REFRESHMENTS

The only place to stop along the route is at the café beside Glencar Waterfall. There is a supermarket and a few pubs in Grange, but nearby Sligo Town has a wider range of places to eat and drink.

VARIATIONS

If you are looking for a shorter route then the Gleniff Horseshoe (page 192) is a good alternative. It could also be used to extend this route.

DISTANCE	TOTAL		INSTRUCTION
0	0	S	Starting from the bridge on the N15 in Grange village head north.
0.2	0.2	>	Turn right.
3.7	3.9	^	Go straight ahead crossing the N15.
2.4	6.3	<	Turn left.
8.7	15.0	<	Turn left at the t-junction.
4.4	19.4	<	Turn left at the fork.
7.9	27.3	<	Turn left.
3.3	30.6	<	Turn left.
1.0	31.6	<	Keep left at the fork.
3.1	34.7	<	Turn left.
1.2	35.9	<	Turn left.
2.0	37.9	<	Keep left.
0.2	38.1	<	Turn left.
3.1	41.2	<	Keep left.
10.3	51.5	>	Turn right.
3.2	54.7	>	Turn right.
0.3	55.0	<	Turn left onto the N15.
0.2	55.2	F	Arrive back in Grange village.

Just outside Mullaghmore with Classiebawn and Benbulbin in the background

MULLAGHMORE AND GLENIFF
County Sligo
ROAD

30 km
370 m

The route combines a coastal loop of Mullaghmore Head with a tough climb around the Gleniff Horseshoe.

While the two sections of this route are very different in character they both offer amazing views including what is probably Sligo's most iconic view, that of Classiebawn Castle backed by Benbulbin as seen from Mullaghmore Head.

Heading north from Mullaghmore village (*54.4667, -8.4479*) the route follows the road around the headland taking in the views of the fairytale castle of Classiebawn. At the junction turn onto the R279 but continue straight on where it turns right. You then cross the busy N15. Less than 100m north on the

N15 is Creevykeel Court Tomb. This well-preserved Neolithic tomb is worth a quick visit.

The flat road leads directly towards the hills and just as it starts to climb you meet a junction and follow the signs for the Gleniff Horseshoe.

You pass Barytes Mill (*54.3980, -8.4000*), an ideal place to stop for a break with picnic benches and a nice walk along the stream. As you climb you leave the woods and emerge into the upper valley with its steep grassy slopes.

The forestry plantation marks the end of the climbing and as you leave the trees a line of sheer limestone cliffs loom overhead. Look out for the

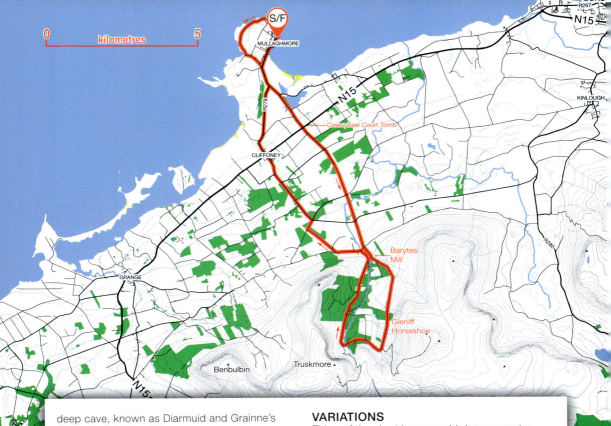

deep cave, known as Diarmuid and Grainne's Cave, set into the cliffs.

Just after the ruined schoolhouse the road begins to descend. At the junction turn left and follow more quiet roads back into Mullaghmore. Alternatively turn right and retrace your steps.

REFRESHMENTS
Mullaghmore has a number of pubs and restaurants. The only option you pass on the route is O'Donnell's pub in Cliffoney on the N15.

VARIATIONS
Either of the short loops could done as routes in their own right. The Gleniff Horseshoe is 9.5km with 200m of height gain. The best place to start is Barytes Mill (*54.3980, -8.4000*). The Mullaghmore Loop is 4.5km with 50m of height gain.

If the route is too flat for you then you could include the climb up Truskmore, Sligo highest mountain. It's a formidable 4.2km climb up the private road to the TV transmitter on the summit with 420m of height gain and an average gradient of 10%.

DISTANCE	TOTAL		INSTRUCTION
0	0	S	From the mini-roundabout head north along the coast road.
3.4	3.4	>	Turn right.
2.5	5.9	^	Continue straight, across the N15.
4.7	10.6	^	Straight through at the junction, signposted 'Gleniff Horseshoe'.
9.2	19.8	<	Turn left at the junction.
0.8	20.6	>	Turn right.
1.2	21.8	>	Turn right.
0.4	22.2	<	Turn left.
2.8	25.0	^	Continue straight, across the N15 through Cliffoney onto the R279.
2.5	27.5	<	Turn left.
1.9	29.4	F	Arrive back in Mullaghmore.

The top of the climb up the Gates of Glan

GLENANIFF
County Leitrim
ROAD

25km
480m

This route, while short, offers some challenging climbs and excellent views.

Leitrim is Ireland's least populated country and the glens in the northern half of the county have some wonderful cycling on beautiful boreens, that climb through these valleys, featuring great views over the surroundings.

This route is a prime example of the genre, with some stiff climbs and rough, in places, roads. You will notice some useful cycling specific signposts on this route, see for details of more routes in the area cycleleitrim.ie.

From St. Aidan's Church (*54.3788, -8.1123*) head north, descending gently, on the R282 before turning left and crossing the bridge. This signals the start of the route's main climb, over the next 8km there is 270m of height gain.

As you climb you pass the rushing waters of Fowley's Falls on your right before continuing up the right-hand side of Glenaniff valley, passing a number of cottages and farmhouses. Near the head of the valley the angle increases, signalling the start of the section known as the Gates of Glan. A final steep stretch (>10%) leads of the top.

Here you enter a barren mountain pass before starting the descent down to the R281. Don't let the views across Lough Melvin and Donegal Bay distract you as the road drops steeply, and watch out for wandering sheep.

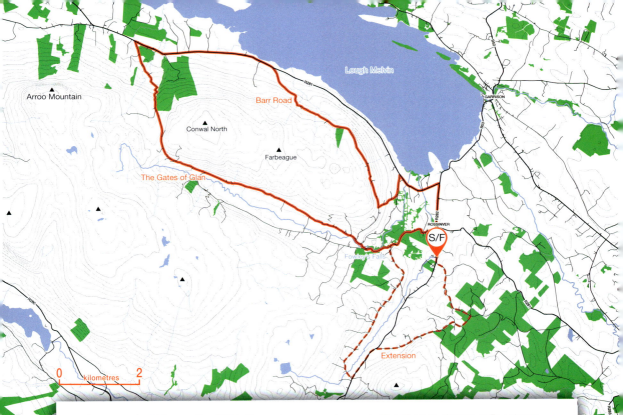

After a gentle 3.5km on the R281, if your legs are up, you turn right onto the second climb, signposted "Barr Climb". It's steepest at the start, and as you gain height Lough Melvin comes into view. The road emerges out onto open hillside and as you pass the viewing point it starts to descent.

After 2km you turn sharply left onto a gravel lane that drops incredibly steeply back down to the R281. From here it's an easy last few kilometres back to the start.

REFRESHMENTS
Near the end of the route you pass the entrance to The Organic Centre in Rossinver (54.3924, -8.1189), currently the café is closed for refurbishments, so check the website (theorganiccentre.ie) before visiting.

VARIATIONS
It's possible to extend this route to into a figure-of-eight by adding on an extra loop to the south of the start/finish. This clockwise loop is similar in character, following quiet lanes and boreens, and adds 12km and 190m height gain.

You could reduce the route by staying on the R281 rather than tackling the second climb, this saves about 1.7km and 140m of height gain.

DISTANCE	TOTAL		INSTRUCTION
0	0	S	From the church head north on the R282.
0.85	0.85	<	Turn left.
3.1	2.25	>	Turn right.
12.0	8.9	>	Turn right onto the R281.
15.5	3.5	>	Turn right.
20.4	4.9	<	Turn sharply left down very steep lane.
21.1	0.7	<	Turn left.
21.6	0.5	>	Turn right onto the R281.
22.8	1.2	>	Turn right onto the R282.
24.7	1.9	F	Arrive back at the church.

The descent down to the R207

DRUMSHANBO
County Leitrim
ROAD

38km
540m

A circuit through the quiet hills of Leitrim.

This route loops through the hills north of Drumshanbo village. Following a network of boreens and mountains roads it's very quiet, you could easily not meet a single car all day.

From the large carpark opposite the church (*54.0490, -8.0379*) in Drumshanbo the route heads north along a small boreen that rises and falls almost constantly. As well as been much quieter than the R207, which it runs parallel to, the boreen is a little higher giving a much better view over Lough Allen. This stretch of road is also used by the Leitrim Way and Kingfisher Trail.

After just under 10km you reach a junction. The Leitrim Way carries straight on following a series of small muddy paths. This is a more direct route but there are half a dozen stiles and the ground is very soft so it's better to divert briefly to the R207.

At the junction there are a few picnic benches and a sign pointing to a sweat lodge a short distance upstream. This is worth a quick look if you are curious.

The right turn off the R207 signals the start of the 12km climb over the saddle between Benbrack and Bencroy. Initially the road follows the Yellow River upstream before breaking out onto open hillside. The gradient is never too bad, averaging 3%, and it eases near the top when the masts come into view.

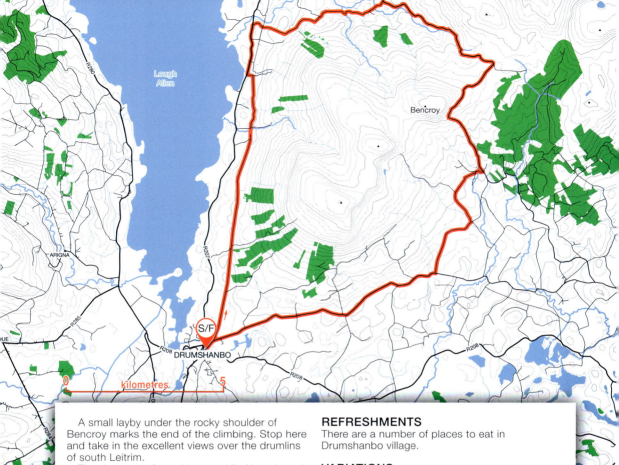

A small layby under the rocky shoulder of Bencroy marks the end of the climbing. Stop here and take in the excellent views over the drumlins of south Leitrim.

The descent is fast with some blind bends and gravel so take care. As the angle eases turn right and follow quiet roads back into Drumshanbo.

REFRESHMENTS

There are a number of places to eat in Drumshanbo village.

VARIATIONS

Cory Mountain on the western side of Lough Allen has great potential for a similar length route on a mix of boreens and gravel roads. The described route is effectively a shorter variation of the 58km Ride 5, a variant of the Kingfisher Trail. See page 252 for more information.

DISTANCE	TOTAL		INSTRUCTION
0	0	S	From the carpark opposite the church in Drumshanbo head north
0.3	0.3	<	Turn left.
8.9	9.2	<	Turn left.
0.2	9.4	>	Turn right onto the R207.
1.7	11.1	>	Turn right.
4.8	15.9	<	Turn left at the junction.
0.7	16.6	>	Turn right at the junction.
8.8	25.4	>	Turn right.
0.3	25.7	<	Keep left at the fork.
2.1	27.8	>	Turn right at the junction.
2.3	30.1	>	Turn right at the junction.
8.2	38.3	F	Arrive back at the carpark.

NORTH

The Ring of Gullion, Armagh see page 246

FAMILY CYCLING IN THE NORTH

The following routes are traffic-free and reasonably short so are ideal for families and younger children. See the Cycling NI website (cycleni.com) for further information.

DONEGAL

1 ROSSNOWLAGH BEACH *54.5526, -8.2106*
With over 3km of hard sand this beach is the perfect place for beginners to build their confidence. Be aware that it can get busy in the summer.

2 THE GAP TRAIL *54.77921, -8.3280*
This purpose-built 2.8km (each way) walking and cycling trail follows an old railway line that served as a Bord na Mona turf extraction facility.

DERRY

3 BEECH HILL *54.9691, -7.2701*
There are five signposted multi-use trails on the 12 hectare grounds of Beech Hill Country House Hotel between 300m and 1.6km in length.

4 CLAUDY COUNTRY PARK *54.9060, -7.1577*
This 3km trail travels up one side of the Faughan and Glenrandal Rivers before crossing over and descending the other side.

5 GARVAGH FOREST *54.9793, -6.6889*
The park has four cycling trails including a 1.3km multi-use trail, a 1.3km skills loop, a 2.8km blue trail and a 4.8km red trail. See visitcausewaycoastandglens.com for details.

ANTRIM

6 ANTRIM TOWN LOOP *54.7149, -6.2398*
This 7.2km route runs along the shore of Lough Neagh and through Rea's Wood before returning along the course of the Six Mile Water.

7 DIVIS RIDGE *54.5991, -6.0421*
This 8km route through the Belfast Hills has great views over the city. It's follows a mix of tarmac and gravel over Black Mountain and Black Hill.

8 BARNETT DEMESNE *54.5484, -5.9686*
This park in south Belfast has three mountain bike trails, a gentle 3.4km green trail and a more challenging 3.9km blue trail which has three red variations for more experienced riders.

DOWN

9 CASTLE WARD *54.3697, -5.5824*
On the shores of Strangford Lough the demesne has three easy green trails for beginners as well as a flowing 13km blue trail for more experienced riders.

10 TOLLYMORE MOUNTAIN BIKE SKILLS COURSE *54.2245, -5.9403*
This 1.5km course is designed to help riders develop their technique with a variety of challenging features.

ARMAGH

11 CRAIGAVON LAKES MOUNTAIN BIKE TRAIL *54.4500, -6.3830*
This purpose-built trail weaves a 10km course around the lakes.

12 GOSFORD FOREST PARK *54.3048, -6.5186*
A 6.5km family trail through magnificent woodland which has a number of technical and skills variations and a pump track. See getactiveabc.com for details.

MONAGHAN

13 ULSTER CANAL GREENWAY *54.2598, -6.9552*
This 4.2km greenway crosses Monaghan Town. It is entirely traffic-free with the exception of a short section in the town centre.

TYRONE

14 BLESSINGBOURNE MOUNTAIN BIKE TRAILS *54.3831, -7.3156*
This trail centre has a number of trails including a 4km blue trail that is ideal for beginners.

CAVAN

15 KILLYKEEN FOREST PARK *54.0057, -7.4672*
This 240 hectares woodland park has a 3km family cycling trail which runs close to Lough Oughter, part of the River Erne system.

FERMANAGH

16 CROM ESTATE *54.1631, -7.4328*
A flat 5.5km trail that leads around the grounds of the Crom Estate on the shores of Upper Lough Erne.

17 CASTLE ARCHDALE *54.4783, -7.7331*
A 9.5km signposted route through the Country Park's 95 hectares of mature forest. The mix of singletrack and forest roads is ideal for beginners.

Killykeen Forest Park

CAVAN LAKES

County Cavan
ROAD

32km
220m

300m			
200m			
100m			
0 km	10 km	20 km	30 km

A tour around the lakes and drumlins of County Cavan.

This route explores the unique landscape northwest of Cavan Town. The small hills and lakes were formed during the last ice age when glaciers deposited large quantities of boulder clay which were moulded by the movement of the glaciers into oval shapes, known as drumlins.

While there aren't any major climbs there are a lot of short hills but, with a few notable exceptions, they aren't too steep. The route is described in a clockwise direction.

From the main carpark in Killykeen Forest Park (*54.0057, -7.4672*) a short section of gravel track leads to a footbridge that crosses a narrow channel of Lough Oughter to Gartanoul.

After crossing the bridge follow the road through the forest. Turn right onto the R201 and after a short distance turn right again.

Follow the quiet road, which weaves between the lakes, north to the edge of Milltown before turning east and crossing the stone bridge over the River Erne.

Turn south and cross Annalee River on a narrow metal bridge before tackling a number of short climbs. Shortly after passing Farnham Lough turn right onto a slightly busier road that weaves its way around a number of small but steep wooded drumlins. You then turn into the Forest Park and follow the road back to the carpark.

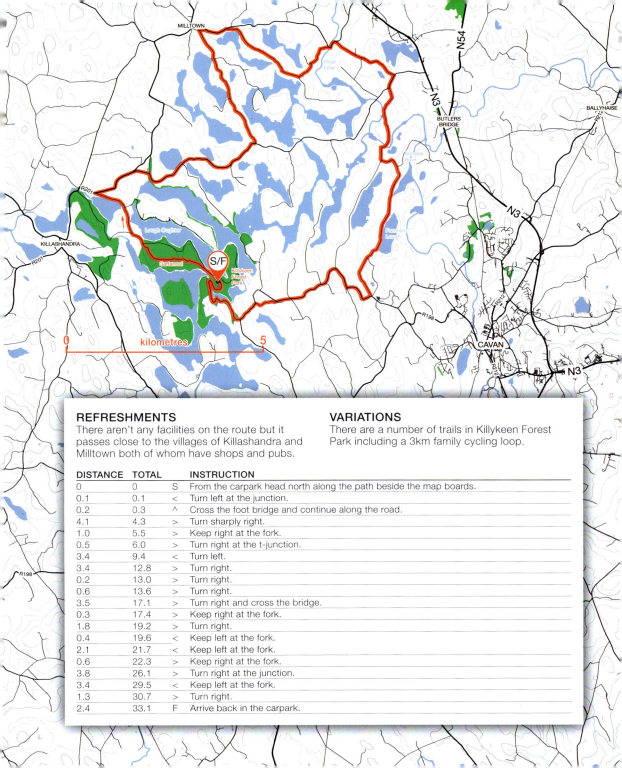

REFRESHMENTS

There aren't any facilities on the route but it passes close to the villages of Killashandra and Milltown both of whom have shops and pubs.

VARIATIONS

There are a number of trails in Killykeen Forest Park including a 3km family cycling loop.

DISTANCE	TOTAL		INSTRUCTION
0	0	S	From the carpark head north along the path beside the map boards.
0.1	0.1	<	Turn left at the junction.
0.2	0.3	^	Cross the foot bridge and continue along the road.
4.1	4.3	>	Turn sharply right.
1.0	5.5	>	Keep right at the fork.
0.5	6.0	>	Turn right at the t-junction.
3.4	9.4	<	Turn left.
3.4	12.8	>	Turn right.
0.2	13.0	>	Turn right.
0.6	13.6	>	Turn right.
3.5	17.1	>	Turn right and cross the bridge.
0.3	17.4	>	Keep right at the fork.
1.8	19.2	>	Turn right.
0.4	19.6	<	Keep left at the fork.
2.1	21.7	<	Keep left at the fork.
0.6	22.3	>	Keep right at the fork.
3.8	26.1	>	Turn right at the junction.
3.4	29.5	<	Keep left at the fork.
1.3	30.7	>	Turn right.
2.4	33.1	F	Arrive back in the carpark.

Passing the route's highpoint

SLIEVE BEAGH
County Monaghan/Fermanagh/Tyrone
ROAD

44 km
700 m

A circuit on quiet roads around the gentle rolling hills.

The Slieve Beagh mountains are a raised area of blanket bog that straddles the border between County Monaghan, Fermanagh and Tyrone. The windswept uplands are an important habitat and home to a number of birds including curlew, hen harrier, red grouse, plover and snipe.

This route follows very quiet roads, rough in parts, in an anti-clockwise loop, but could just as easily be done clockwise.

Start in Knockatallon, County Monaghan from the church carpark (*54.3058, -7.1298*). Head northeast descending gently along the L1002 for 2.5km. You then turn left, onto the route's main climb, which has 190m of height gain over 4.5km.

Initially you climb on quiet roads through farming countryside which gives way to rough scrub and forestry before After the junction the road levels off and you cross open heath, passing areas of turf cuttings.

You then descent to the R186 which becomes the B83 as it crosses the border. Turning left you follow a network of very quiet roads, meeting a few sections of the Carleton Cycle Trail along the way.

After 27km you turn south and begin to climb gradually until, just after crossing the border, a fast descent leads to the crossroads at Knockatallon. Here you turn left and climb back to the church carpark where you started.

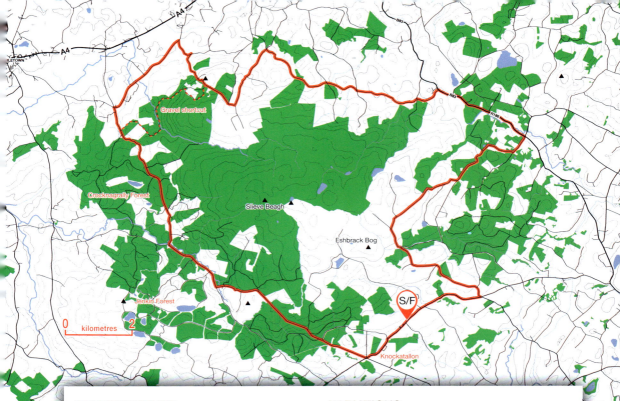

REFRESHMENTS

There are only two options on or near the route, the first is the Sliabh Beagh Hotel at the start/finish and the second is the small shop a hundred meters south of the crossroads at Knockatallon (*54.2944, -7.1506*).

VARIATIONS

Part of this route follows the Carleton Cycle Trail. This route is signposted but there is very little information about it online.

The Slieve Beagh mountains offer great scope for gravel riding and there is potential for a very worthwhile gravel variation of this route.

DISTANCE	TOTAL		INSTRUCTION
0	0	S	From the church carpark head northeast.
2.51	2.51	<	Sharp left at the junction.
3.33	5.84	<	Keep left
4.45	9.29	<	Turn left at the junction.
2.41	11.7	<	Turn left at the junction.
0.6	12.3	<	Turn left onto the R186.
3.1	15.4	<	Turn left onto Corleaghan Road.
0.8	16.2	<	Turn left at the junction.
5.5	21.7	<	Turn left at the crossroad onto Fardross Road.
2.1	23.8	>	Turn right.
0.2	24.0	^	Continue straight onto Slatmore Road.
2.3	26.3	<	Turn left at the junction.
0.7	27.0	<	Turn left at the junction onto Kelly Road.
2.9	29.9	<	Turn left at the junction onto Alderwood Road.
5.1	35.0	<	Turn left at the junction.
2.1	37.1	<	Turn left onto Mullynavale Road.
5.4	42.5	<	Turn left
1.7	44.2	F	Arrive back in the church carpark.

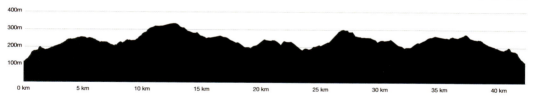
Passing Lough Formal on the return leg

SCARPLANDS LOOP
County Fermanagh
GRAVEL

42km
560m

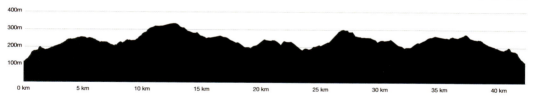

One of the few official gravel routes on the island.

The corner of County Fermanagh that lies between Lower Lough Erne and the border is an empty place, the low-lying forested hills are connected by a network of gravel roads and tracks.

The Scarplands Cycle Trail is a 38km linear trail that links the village of Belcoo to Lough Navar passing through the Cuilcagh Lakelands Geopark (cuilcaghlakelands.org). It is one of the only official signposted gravel routes on the island. There are also two loops that can be done separately or integrated into the Cycle Trail, the Aghanaglack Loop and the Lough Navar Loop (see page 208).

The Scarplands Cycle Trail also forms the backbone of the Lakeland Gravel Grinder

(lakelander.co.uk), Ireland's original gravel race, which runs every October.

The route described here is a variation of the Scarplands Cycle Trail (blue arrows), modifying it into a loop, albeit with some out-and-back sections. It's over 95% gravel and, with the exception of the start, the climbs are all pretty gentle.

The quality of the gravel varies, it's mostly quite smooth, but there are sections of fresh gravel that are quite draggy, watch out for them, particularly on the descents as they always seem to appear at the worst possible moment. Note that the gravel is particularly sharp, punctures are common, so carry at least one spare tube!

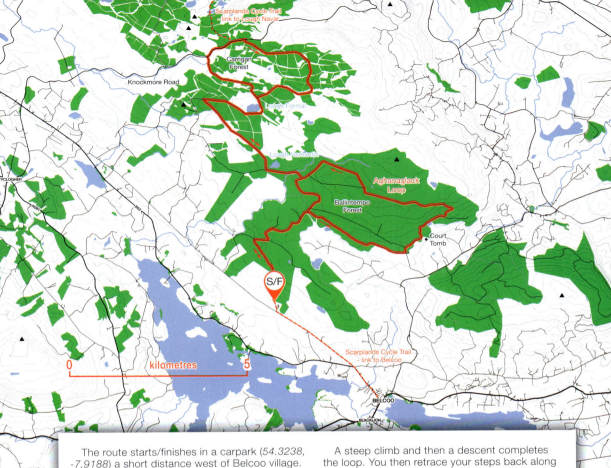

The route starts/finishes in a carpark (*54.3238, -7.9188*) a short distance west of Belcoo village. From the start you climb steeply, gaining 140m, but the angle eases after a while.

After 4.3km you meet the Aghanaglack Loop (red arrows) and turn right onto it, following it anti-clockwise. Initially you descend gently for a few kilometres as far the Ballintempo carpark. Here you start to climb again, gaining 130m over the next 5km. One kilometre into the climb you pass the sign for the Aghanaglack Court Tomb, which is just a short distance off the track and worth a quick detour.

From the route's highpoint you descend to the junction with the Scarplands Cycle Trail where you turn right, following it northwest. The next 6.3km leads, generally downhill, past Lough Namanfin. Just after Lough Formal, you begin the second 8.4km loop.

Just over 2km of fast gravel leads to Knockmore Road where you turn right and follow the smooth tarmac for 1.3km before turning right again, back onto the gravel.

A steep climb and then a descent completes the loop. You then retrace your steps back along the out-and-back section to the Aghanaglack Loop. A final descent then brings you back to the start in no time.

REFRESHMENTS
There aren't any facilities on the route but the villages of Belcoo and Blacklion are close to the start/finish.

VARIATIONS
The Scarplands Cycle Trail could be done as an out-and-back route. At 91km (with 1230m of height gain) it could be done as bikepacking overnight, camping along the way.

The Aghanaglack Loop is a shorter variation, it's 21km with 300m of height gain.

It's possible to start the route at the Ballintempo Forest carpark (*54.3360, -7.8594*), this means you skip the tough climb at the start, reducing the distance to 33km with 420m of height gain.

Approaching the viewpoint at Magho

NAVAR FOREST
County Fermanagh
GRAVEL

20km
340m

This loop on tarmac roads and gravel tracks has some spectacular views over Lower Lough Erne.

On a quiet day when you have the roads to yourself this vast expanse of lakes and lush mossy pine forest has a real wilderness feel.

The route is described in an anti-clockwise direction but could be done in either. The tarmac road that loops through the forest is quite narrow so watch out for cars particularly on the blind bends.

Half of this route is on gravel tracks so you will need tyres that are at least 30mm with a bit of thread. However a road bike will be fine on the shorter tarmac loop but watch out for places where the forestry vehicles have pushed gravel onto the road.

From the carpark (*54.4406, -7.8865*) just off the Glennasheevar Road head north along the tarmac road. After just over a kilometre the climbing begins in earnest and it's 3.5km at an average gradient of 5% to the highpoint of the route. A short descent leads north to the viewpoint overlooking the Magho cliffs and Lower Lough Erne.

After taking in the expansive view retrace your steps and turn right. A short distance later turn right onto a gravel track. This leads to a junction where you turn right onto a potholed gravel road that leads past Meenameen Lough to the Glencreawan viewpoint. Retracing your steps back to the lake

Lower Lough Erne

A46

kilometres
0   2

Magho Viewpoint

Glencreawan Viewpoint

Shortcut

Meenameen Lough

Lough Achork

Lough Navar

S/F

Glennasheevar Road

Ulster Way

follow the gravel road west then south around Lough Navar before rejoining the tarmac road. Turn right descending to Glennasheevar Road which leads east back to the carpark.

REFRESHMENTS
There is nowhere to stop en route. The nearest village is either Garrison to the west or Derrygonnelly to the east.

VARIATIONS
There is plenty of scope to extend this route by following the gravel tracks of the Ulster Way south into Conagher and Big Dog Forest.

The shorter variation that sticks to the tarmac road, signposted as Lough Navar Scenic Drive, is 13km with 260m of height gain.

DISTANCE	TOTAL		INSTRUCTION
0	0	S	From the carpark head north up the road.
4.1	4.1	>	Keep right at the fork.
1.0	5.1	⮌	From Magho viewpoint retrace your steps.
1.2	6.3	>	Turn right.
0.1	6.4	>	Turn right onto the gravel track.
2.1	8.5	>	Turn right at the t-junction.
1.2	9.7	>	Keep right at the fork.
0.7	10.4	⮌	From Glencreawan viewpoint retrace your steps.
0.6	11.0	>	Turn right.
5.7	16.7	>	Turn right at the junction.
1.4	18.1	<	Turn left onto the Glennasheevar Road.
1.8	19.9	F	Turn left off Glennasheevar Road into the carpark.

Glengesh Pass

GLENCOLMCILLE
County Donegal
ROAD

66km
1120m

A tough loop around Donegal's southern western peninsula.

The Glencolmcille Peninsula is a wild and windswept place and this route has a number of exposed sections that would be tough in the wind. This combined with plenty of height gain makes for a testing route.

This route starts with one of Ireland's steepest road climbs, the legendary Glengesh Pass, but there are also three tough climbs later in the route.

The road surface is generally good and it isn't too busy. It is best done in a clockwise direction, tackling Glengesh early in the day and availing of the prevailing wind on the homeward stretch.

From Ardara (54.7619, -8.4132) head south along the N56 for just over two kilometres before turning right onto the R230 which leads into Glengesh. The 5km climb has an average gradient of 4% and starts gently but the final section around the hairpins is tough with a gradient of 11%.

From the top it's a downhill run across the hillside into Carrick. Climbing out of the village leave the R263 and take the back road to Malin More. Turn right and head north along the coast with great views of the sea cliffs below Glen Head.

Passing through the village of Glencolmcille turn left on the R230 following it for a few kilometres before turning left into the long river valley. You then turn right climbing steeply over the shoulder of Meenacharvy Hill.

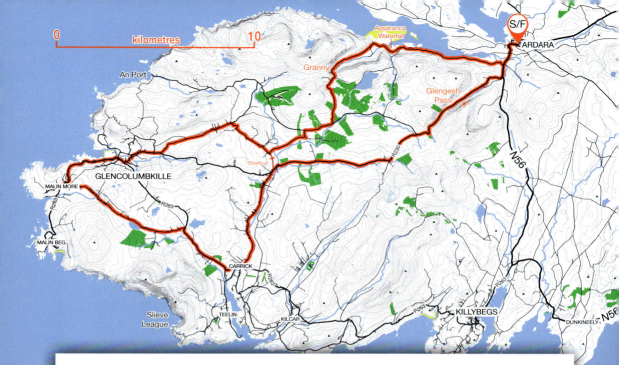

Descend to the far side of the valley and head northeast then north climbing a boreen. Eventually the road levels before dropping steeply into a narrow rocky valley, known as Granny, which leads down to the sea at Maghera.

Follow the southern shore of the bay past Assaranca Waterfall, an impressive sight after rain, before meeting the N56 and taking it back into Adara.

REFRESHMENTS

Carrick and Glencolmcille villages both have plenty of places to stop for a snack or drink. There are also a few options at the start in Ardara.

VARIATIONS

Skipping the western section and heading north towards Granny gives a 36km route with 600m of climbing.

There a number of worthwhile linear extensions including a visit to the Slieve League viewing point at Bunglas (adding 12km and 350m of height gain) or the isolated beach at An Port (adding 13km and 150m of height gain).

DISTANCE	TOTAL		INSTRUCTION
0	0	S	From Ardara head south along the N56.
2.2	2.2	>	Turn right onto the R230.
14.3	16.5	<	Keep left where the R230 forks right.
5.7	22.2	>	Turn right onto the R263.
4.1	26.3	<	Turn left.
7.2	33.5	>	Turn right onto the R263.
4.4	37.9	<	Turn left onto the R230.
0.5	38.4	<	Keep left.
0.1	38.5	>	Turn right at the junction.
1.6	40.1	<	Turn left.
3.9	44.0	>	Turn right.
3.0	47.0	<	Turn left.
2.6	49.6	>	Turn right.
1.4	51.0	<	Turn left.
13.2	64.2	<	Turn left onto the N56.
1.6	65.8	F	Arrive back in Ardara.

Looking over Lough Agannive to the northern slopers of Errigal

ERRIGAL
County Donegal
ROAD

39km
560m

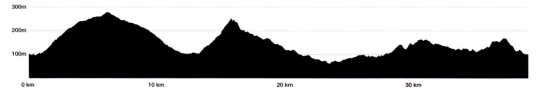

A circuit around the iconic Donegal peak following a mix of roads and rough boreens.

The conical summit of the 751m Errigal dominates the skyline of this part of Donegal and this route loops around the mountain with the first half featuring two climbs on good surfaces while the second half is more rolling on rougher roads.

The route is described in an anti-clockwise direction but could be done in either way. While it features a few rough roads it is suitable for a road bike.

From the hostel in Dunlewey (*55.0300, -8.1415*) head northeast along the R251 which climbs up the valley. To the left are the scree slopes of Errigal while on the right are the massive granite cliffs of the Poisoned Glen. The road is a little busy but the surface is excellent. The climb has a steady gradient and eases gradually before starting to descend.

At the foot of the descent turn left onto the R256, climbing again over the narrow pass between Errigal and its distinctive flat topped neighbour, Muckish. While this climb isn't as long as the previous climb it is steeper.

A rolling descent leads down the valley before you turn left off the main road. The next section of the route forms part of the Donegal Cycle Route (page 251) and follows a network of small roads through rolling farmland past a number of small lakes and hills.

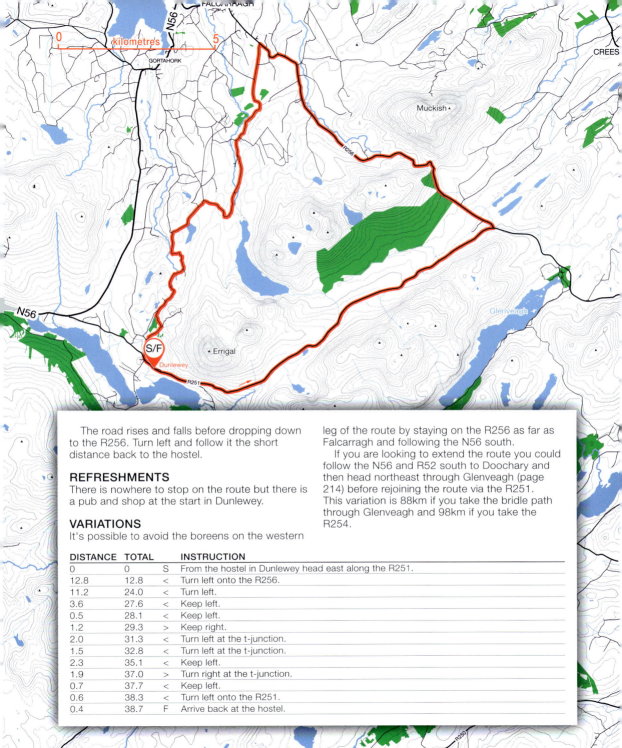

The road rises and falls before dropping down to the R256. Turn left and follow it the short distance back to the hostel.

REFRESHMENTS
There is nowhere to stop on the route but there is a pub and shop at the start in Dunlewey.

VARIATIONS
It's possible to avoid the boreens on the western leg of the route by staying on the R256 as far as Falcarragh and following the N56 south.

If you are looking to extend the route you could follow the N56 and R52 south to Doochary and then head northeast through Glenveagh (page 214) before rejoining the route via the R251. This variation is 88km if you take the bridle path through Glenveagh and 98km if you take the R254.

DISTANCE	TOTAL		INSTRUCTION
0	0	S	From the hostel in Dunlewey head east along the R251.
12.8	12.8	<	Turn left onto the R256.
11.2	24.0	<	Turn left.
3.6	27.6	<	Keep left.
0.5	28.1	<	Keep left.
1.2	29.3	>	Keep right.
2.0	31.3	<	Turn left at the t-junction.
1.5	32.8	<	Turn left at the t-junction.
2.3	35.1	<	Keep left.
1.9	37.0	>	Turn right at the t-junction.
0.7	37.7	<	Keep left.
0.6	38.3	<	Turn left onto the R251.
0.4	38.7	F	Arrive back at the hostel.

Climbing past Lough Inshagh

GLENVEAGH
County Donegal
GRAVEL

32km
400m

This route follows a mix of roads, tracks and paths through the Derryveagh Mountains.

Glenveagh National Park is home to 16,000 hectares of rugged mountains, lakes and beautiful native oak woodland in the heart of the Derryveagh Mountains. This route is evenly split between roads and tracks, some of which are rough, so a gravel bike is ideal but a hardy hybrid should manage.

The trails are popular and shared with walkers so take extreme care, particularly on the descents. The route can be done in either direction but is described here as a clockwise loop.

From the carpark in the National Park (*55.0574, -7.9387*) follow the cycling/walking path along the southern shore of Lough Beagh towards the castle.

After just over two kilometres turn left onto the gravel track (signposted 'Lough Inshagh Walk'). The 2.5km climb is steep (the average gradient is 5%) with plenty of loose gravel on the initial section through the trees. The angle eases when the track emerges out of the woodland onto the open heather hillside. There are excellent views across the flat boggy plateau to Lough Inshagh and north to the distinctive flat top of Muckish.

After passing through a gate in the deer fence you make the fast, but not too rough, descent to Lough Gartan. Back on the road follow a boreen southwest overlooking the northern shore of Lough Gartan. Almost immediately after turning onto the R254 the

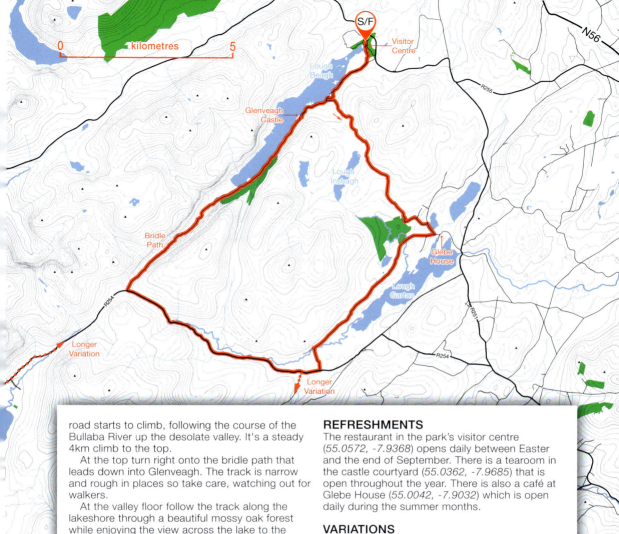

road starts to climb, following the course of the Bullaba River up the desolate valley. It's a steady 4km climb to the top.

At the top turn right onto the bridle path that leads down into Glenveagh. The track is narrow and rough in places so take care, watching out for walkers.

At the valley floor follow the track along the lakeshore through a beautiful mossy oak forest while enjoying the view across the lake to the granite cliffs. At the castle follow the footpath (bikes should be walked) through the ornamental garden before meeting the cycle path and following it back to the carpark.

REFRESHMENTS

The restaurant in the park's visitor centre (*55.0572, -7.9368*) opens daily between Easter and the end of September. There is a tearoom in the castle courtyard (*55.0362, -7.9685*) that is open throughout the year. There is also a café at Glebe House (*55.0042, -7.9032*) which is open daily during the summer months.

VARIATIONS

A 64km variation follows a rough gravel track to the R250 which it takes to Fintown before rejoining the route at the top of the bridle path via the R252 and R254.

DISTANCE	TOTAL		INSTRUCTION
0	0	S	From the carpark head south along the gravel path (not the road).
2.4	2.4	<	Turn left onto the gravel track (signposted 'Lough Inshagh Walk').
5.8	8.2	>	Turn right at the t-junction.
0.4	8.6	>	Turn right.
0.2	8.8	>	Keep right at the fork.
5.0	13.8	<	Turn left.
0.7	14.5	>	Turn right on the R254.
6.5	21.0	>	Turn right onto the bridle path.
11.1	32.1	F	Arrive back at the carpark.

Climbing the north side of Mamore Gap

INISHOWEN
County Donegal/Derry
ROAD

164km
2260m

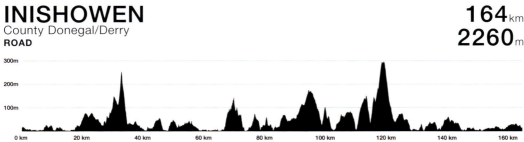

A challenging tour of the Inishowen Peninsula.

As well as appealing to riders looking for a really challenging day in the saddle this route will be of interest to cyclists who want to travel at a more leisurely pace. Tackling the route over a weekend will leave plenty of time to check out the many sights along the way.

Every summer a popular sportive called the Inishowen 100 follows this route. There is also a signposted drive of the same name that takes a slightly different route.

The route is described in a clockwise direction in the hope that the prevailing wind will help on the first half, it also leaves you with an easy finish as the last 30km are pretty flat.

There are two notable climbs - Mamore Gap and Kinnagoe Bay - as well as plenty of smaller hills.

As this is a long route it isn't practical to include turn-by-turn directions. The best approach is to download the GPX file from threerockbooks.com/cycling and follow it on your smartphone or GPS.

From the Templemore Sport Centre (55.0245, -7.3385) in the northwest suburbs of Derry City head west on the A2, crossing the border and passing through the villages of Bridgend and Burnfoot. The route meets the shore of Lough Swilly near the wildlife reserve of Inch Island and follows the R238 north to Buncrana. Past the town a few short hills

216

warm you up for the first of the two big climbs, Mamore Gap. Rising in a straight line through the Urris Hills the climb starts gently and keeps getting steeper, the last kilometre has an average gradient of 12%.

From the top it's a winding descent back to sea level and flat roads lead through the villages of Ballyliffin, Carndonagh and Malin.

Just after Malin the road climbs again and there is a great view of Five Fingers Strand. Following the road over rolling hills leads to Malin Head, the most northerly point in Ireland. It's worth making the short diversion to Banba's Crown which marks the start point of the Malin to Mizen cycle and offers great views over the headland.

Heading east on quieter roads climb over the shoulder of Glengad Mountain and then drop down into Culdaff. After the village two short climbs sap the legs before the final test of the day, the climb out of Kinnagoe Bay. Steepest at the start, the gradient averages 5.6% over 4.3km. Once you emerge onto open moorland you are

treated to great views across Lough Foyle to the Causeway Coast.

After a fast descent head northeast to Strove before meeting the coast road and following it southwest through Greencastle, Moville, Redcastle and Quigley's Point. Shortly after the town of Muff you cross the border and arrive back at your starting point in the Derry suburbs.

REFRESHMENTS
There are plenty of towns and villages along the route. Derry also has a wide range of accommodation and services.

VARIATIONS
The 48km loop around Malin Head would be worthwhile as a ride in itself. Starting and finishing in Culdaff and looping around the coastline before returning via Malin village.

This route could easily be linked up with the Causeway Coast (page 228) or the Wild Atlantic Way (page 270).

The climb to Glenlark Forest

THE SPERRINS
County Tyrone
ROAD

51km
790m

A testing loop through the valleys and hills of the Sperrin Mountains.

This route follows the signposted Gold Cycle Route through the Sperrin Mountains, deviating from that route in one section in order to stay on quieter roads.

The Gold Cycle Route is reasonably well signposted (with a brown signs and white text) but directions have been included. While there is one section of muddy track a road bike will manage. There aren't any particularly long climbs but what makes this route feel hard is the sheer number of short climbs throughout.

The route can be done in either direction but is described as a clockwise loop starting from the village of Gortin.

From Gortin (*54.7186, -7.2372*) head north along the B48 before turning right onto a quiet road and climbing across the southern slopes of the hills, looking down over the Owenkillew Valley. A 2km section of muddy track leads to Barnes Gap where you cross onto the northern side of the ridge.

Continue east traversing the hillside and tackling a number of short climbs while enjoying the view across the Glenelly Valley to the largest peaks of the Sperrin range.

After continuing straight past the point where the Gold Cycle Route drops down to the B47 turn south and start climbing up the valley. It's a steady 4%

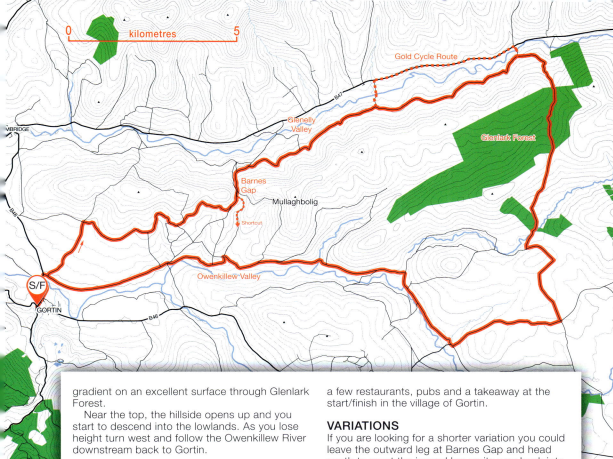

gradient on an excellent surface through Glenlark Forest.

Near the top, the hillside opens up and you start to descend into the lowlands. As you lose height turn west and follow the Owenkillew River downstream back to Gortin.

REFRESHMENTS

There is nowhere to stop en route but there are a few restaurants, pubs and a takeaway at the start/finish in the village of Gortin.

VARIATIONS

If you are looking for a shorter variation you could leave the outward leg at Barnes Gap and head south to meet the inward leg on its way back into Gortin. This route is 20km with 250m of climbing.

DISTANCE	TOTAL		INSTRUCTION
0	0	S	From the village of Gortin head north along the B48.
1.2	1.2	>	Turn right.
0.1	1.3	<	Turn left.
2.1	3.4	>	Turn right at the junction.
3.8	7.2	^	Continue straight ahead onto the track.
2.2	9.4	<	Turn left.
0.4	9.8	^	Continue straight through the crossroads.
1.2	11.0	>	Turn right.
9.9	20.9	>	Keep right.
7.2	28.1	<	Turn left at the t-junction.
3.3	31.4	>	Turn right at the crossroads.
3.6	35.0	>	Turn right at the t-junction.
0.1	35.1	>	Keep right at the fork.
2.7	37.8	<	Turn left.
5.8	43.6	<	Turn left.
6.0	49.6	<	Turn left onto the B48.
1.2	50.8	F	Arrive back in Gortin.

Dropping down Sika's Run

GORTIN GLEN TRAIL CENTRE
County Tyrone
MTB

17km
610m

500m
400m
300m
200m
100m

0 km   5 km   10 km   15 km

This mid-sized trail centre offers a selection of trails for beginner and intermediate mountain bikers.

Gortin Glen covers over 1500 hectares of coniferous forest on the southwestern edge of the Sperrin Mountains. The forest park, which is 11km north of Omagh, is owned by Forest Service NI and maintained by Fermanagh and Omagh District Council.

It's home to 14km of purpose-built mountain bike trails which include two blue trails and three red trails. The trails have seemingly been designed around park's tarmac roads and tracks so that uplifts are an option, however pedalling up these roads can be a slog.

Campbase Adventures offer bike and e-bike hire as well as an uplift service, for more information see campbaseadventures.com.

The full loop, taking in all the trails, which is depicted in the elevation profile above, is 16.6km with 610m of height gain.

BLUE TRAILS
Both blue trails share the same start (54.6834, -7.2440), climbing up the forest road. After a 1.5km climb you meet the start of the shorter of the two trails, The Roller Coaster, which drops directly down to the trailhead.

S/F

Sika's Run

The Mountain

Mullaghcarn Road

River Run

The Roller Coaster

Kelan's Chase

Kelan's Chase Climb

Ladies View Point

Mullaghcarn

The longer trail, Kelan's Chase, continues climbing on singletrack up to the Ladies Viewing Point (*54.6729, -7.2420*), a total height gain of 170m before a winding descent leads back to the trailhead.

The two trails can be combined into a figure-of-eight loop that is 8.1km with 310m of height gain. The best approach is probably to tackle the Kelan's Chase first as it has a lot more climbing.

RED TRAILS
There are three red trails. The first is River Run which branches off the blue trail, The Roller Coaster.

The other two are on the western slopes of Mullaghcarn. The climb to the highpoint of the upper trail, The Mountain, gains 170m over 3km, initially on the forest road before continuing upwards on single track. A winding descent drops down to the forest road and the start of the second trail, Sika's Run, which leads back to the trailhead.

REFRESHMENTS
In the main carpark there is a café, Brie's Barista Bar, that opens on weekends and serves coffee and sweet treats, see fb.com/Briesbaristabar for details.

VARIATIONS
Davagh Forest trail centre is a 30 minute drive to the west, see page 222.

One of the many technical rock slabs on the Red Trail

DAVAGH FOREST TRAIL CENTRE

County Tyrone
MTB

11 km
290 m

Davagh Forest in the foothills of the Sperrin Mountains is home to three purpose-built mountain bike trails.

Between Davagh's three trails there is something for all levels of rider from the gentle paths of the green trail to the red trail's impressive rock features which require plenty of nerve and technique to get down in one piece.

All three trails have a roughly 50:50 mix of singletrack and forest road. They are well signposted and must be followed in an anti-clockwise direction.

At the trailhead (*54.7194, -6.9232*) there are changing facilities, bike wash and toilets. Bike hire is available from Outdoor Concepts (outdoorconcepts.co.uk).

PUMP TRACK AND SKILLS AREA

The pump track and skills area beside the carpark is a great place to warm up before setting out on the trails. The pump track is a continous circuit of rounded bumps and berms that you ride by 'pumping' your arms and shifting your body weight rather than pedalling.

The skills area includes many of the features that you will encounter on the trails including boardwalks, climbing switchbacks, technical insides, rock rolls, drops offs, rock causeways and log rides.

GREEN TRAIL 3.3km 50m

This gentle trail is ideal for young families and beginners. The first half of the loop is on forest roads while the second half follows winding singletrack through the woods. Watch out for walkers on the trail. It's marked as the white dashed line on the map above.

BLUE TRAIL 6.5km 140m

From the upper carpark climb winding singletrack and forest roads to the high point of the trail. You then descend through a mix of flowing and rocky sections, with a few short climbs before meeting the green trail and following it back to the trailhead. Watch out for a number of optional rock slabs that should only be ridden by experienced riders.

RED TRAIL 10.8km 290m

This excellent trail initially follows the blue trail but continues much further up the slopes of Beleevnamore Mountain. At the top there is a choice of two descents, both offer a mix of singletrack, berms, drops and some tricky rock slab. The inner loop is slightly longer at 12.6km with 330m of height gain.

REFRESHMENTS

The hut at the trailhead serves tea, coffee and snacks. The nearest large town is Cookstown which has plenty of cafés, restaurants and pubs.

VARIATIONS

If you enjoyed Davagh then you should check out the other trail centres in Castlewellan (page 234) and Rostrevor (page 238) in County Down.

Whitewater Bridge

SLIEVE GALLION
County Derry
ROAD

41 km
580 m

A circuit of Slieve Gallion on the eastern edge of the Sperrins.

This route is identical to Sperrin Route 8 which is signposted sporadically, look out for the brown signs. It is best done in a clockwise direction so that you tackle the climb with fresh legs.

From the main street of Moneymore (*54.6911, -6.6699*) head north on the A29 before turning left onto a quieter road.

The climb starts almost immediately with some short steep sections as you head west through the rolling countryside. The second, more sustained, part of the climb leads to the heather covered upper slopes of Slieve Gallion.

The right turn onto Cuillion Road signals the end of the climbing and you traverse the hillside,

crossing Whitewater Bridge and turn left. There are good views of the surrounding countryside from the descent into the plantation town of Draperstown. From the town head east on the B40 before turning right and following quieter roads southeast tackling two more short climbs before the final descent back into Moneymore.

REFRESHMENTS
There is a café and shop in Draperstown at the halfway mark of the route.

VARIATIONS
You could reduce the route to 32km with 500m of

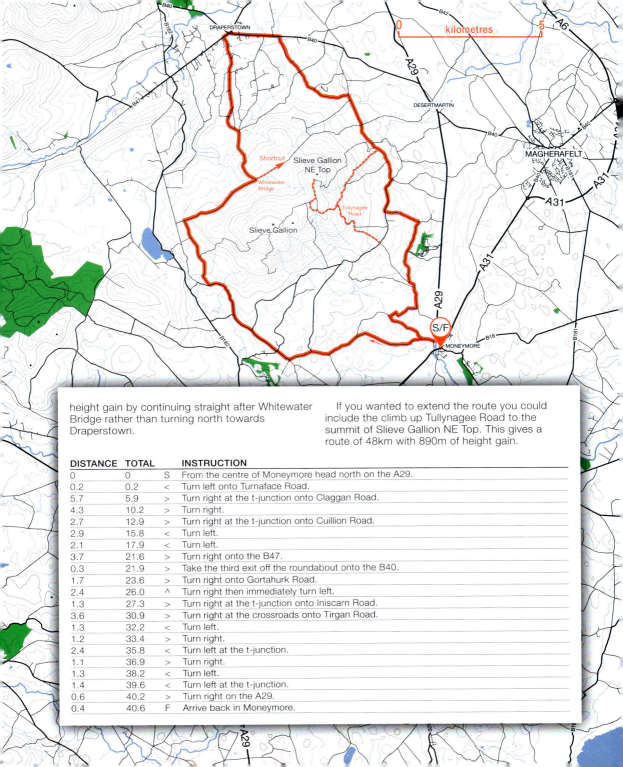

height gain by continuing straight after Whitewater Bridge rather than turning north towards Draperstown.

If you wanted to extend the route you could include the climb up Tullynagee Road to the summit of Slieve Gallion NE Top. This gives a route of 48km with 890m of height gain.

DISTANCE	TOTAL		INSTRUCTION
0	0	S	From the centre of Moneymore head north on the A29.
0.2	0.2	<	Turn left onto Turnaface Road.
5.7	5.9	>	Turn right at the t-junction onto Claggan Road.
4.3	10.2	>	Turn right.
2.7	12.9	>	Turn right at the t-junction onto Cuillion Road.
2.9	15.8	<	Turn left.
2.1	17.9	<	Turn left.
3.7	21.6	>	Turn right onto the B47.
0.3	21.9	>	Take the third exit off the roundabout onto the B40.
1.7	23.6	>	Turn right onto Gortahurk Road.
2.4	26.0	^	Turn right then immediately turn left.
1.3	27.3	>	Turn right at the t-junction onto Iniscarn Road.
3.6	30.9	>	Turn right at the crossroads onto Tirgan Road.
1.3	32.2	<	Turn left.
1.2	33.4	>	Turn right.
2.4	35.8	<	Turn left at the t-junction.
1.1	36.9	>	Turn right.
1.3	38.2	<	Turn left.
1.4	39.6	<	Turn left at the t-junction.
0.6	40.2	>	Turn right on the A29.
0.4	40.6	F	Arrive back in Moneymore.

Heading south just past the Gortmore viewing point

BINEVENAGH AND BENONE
County Derry
ROAD/GRAVEL

26km
460m

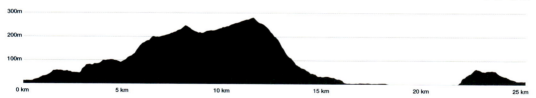

A varied loop across the slopes of Binevenagh Mountain and the sands of Benone Beach.

This route combines a section of Sustrans Route 93, which runs along the coast from Derry to Belfast, with a few kilometres along Benone Beach.

The route is described in a clockwise direction to get the climbing out of the way early. Any bike with tyres over 30mm should be able to handle the short stretch of gravel track and hard-packed sand on Benone beach.

From the promenade (55.1665, -6.7869) in Castlerock head south on Sea Road to the A2. Turn right and follow the busy road as far as the Bishop's Gate where you turn left into Downhill Forest. A gravel track leads through the woods to Burrenmore

Road. The climbing starts with a steep ramp before levelling out. After turning left onto Bishop's Road you start into the meat of the climb. For the first 1.5km the angle is a steady 7% before it eases back and a long straight leads to the viewing point at Gortmore.

While this isn't the high point of the route the worst of the climbing is over so you can relax and take in the incredible view over Lough Foyle, Inishowen and the Causeway Coast.

Back on the road descent briefly before a gentle climb leads into Binevenagh Forest. Turn right and descend around some tricky bends. Turn right at the junction and continue down to the A2. Follow it for

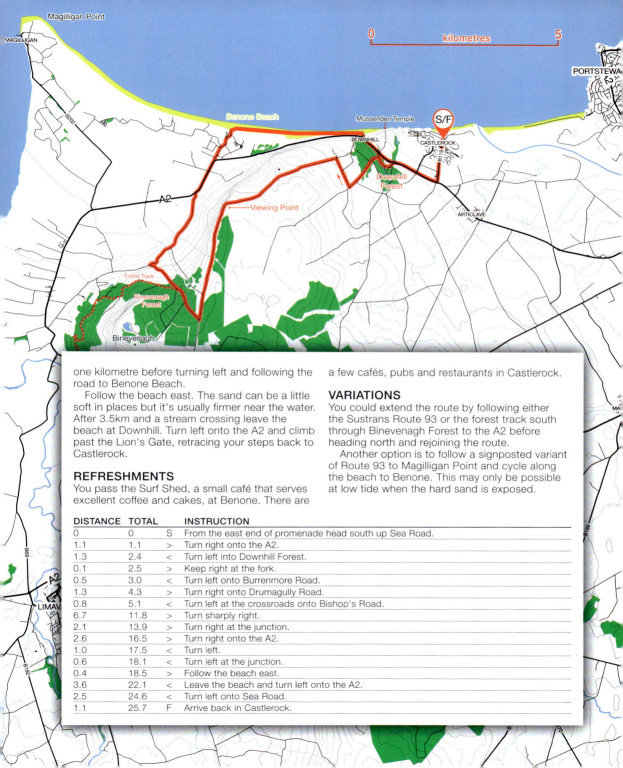

one kilometre before turning left and following the road to Benone Beach.

Follow the beach east. The sand can be a little soft in places but it's usually firmer near the water. After 3.5km and a stream crossing leave the beach at Downhill. Turn left onto the A2 and climb past the Lion's Gate, retracing your steps back to Castlerock.

REFRESHMENTS

You pass the Surf Shed, a small café that serves excellent coffee and cakes, at Benone. There are a few cafés, pubs and restaurants in Castlerock.

VARIATIONS

You could extend the route by following either the Sustrans Route 93 or the forest track south through Binevenagh Forest to the A2 before heading north and rejoining the route.

Another option is to follow a signposted variant of Route 93 to Magilligan Point and cycle along the beach to Benone. This may only be possible at low tide when the hard sand is exposed.

DISTANCE	TOTAL		INSTRUCTION
0	0	S	From the east end of promenade head south up Sea Road.
1.1	1.1	>	Turn right onto the A2.
1.3	2.4	<	Turn left into Downhill Forest.
0.1	2.5	>	Keep right at the fork.
0.5	3.0	<	Turn left onto Burrenmore Road.
1.3	4.3	>	Turn right onto Drumagully Road.
0.8	5.1	<	Turn left at the crossroads onto Bishop's Road.
6.7	11.8	>	Turn sharply right.
2.1	13.9	>	Turn right at the junction.
2.6	16.5	>	Turn right onto the A2.
1.0	17.5	<	Turn left.
0.6	18.1	<	Turn left at the junction.
0.4	18.5	>	Follow the beach east.
3.6	22.1	<	Leave the beach and turn left onto the A2.
2.5	24.6	<	Turn left onto Sea Road.
1.1	25.7	F	Arrive back in Castlerock.

The A2 between Portrush and Dunluce

CAUSEWAY COAST
County Derry/Antrim
ROAD

155km
1720m

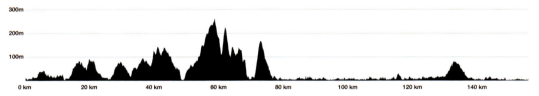

This route traverses the coastline of Counties Derry and Antrim linking Coleraine with Belfast.

F it cyclists may want to tackle this route in a long day, while others of a more leisurely disposition could spend a weekend, stopping along the way to take in some of the world famous sights such as the Giant's Causeway, Bushmills Distillery and the Carrick-a-Rede rope bridge.

For the most part the route follows the well signposted Route 93 of the National Cycle Network. The first half is increasingly hilly, culminating in the climb over Torr Head while the second half sticks close to the coast and is very gentle.

It's possible to get to the start of this linear route in Coleraine by train from Belfast. See page 34

for more details about taking a bike on the train. Tackling the route in this direction means that you are travelling on the side of the road closest to the sea.

Riders who are trying to complete the cycle in a day might be more inclined to stick to the A2. It's the most direct route but it can get quite busy. However those who aren't a hurry will be better served following the quieter roads of Route 93.

From the train station in Coleraine (*55.1338, -6.6630*) the route heads northeast meeting the coast at Portstewart. It passes through the resort towns of Portrush and Bushmills, with its

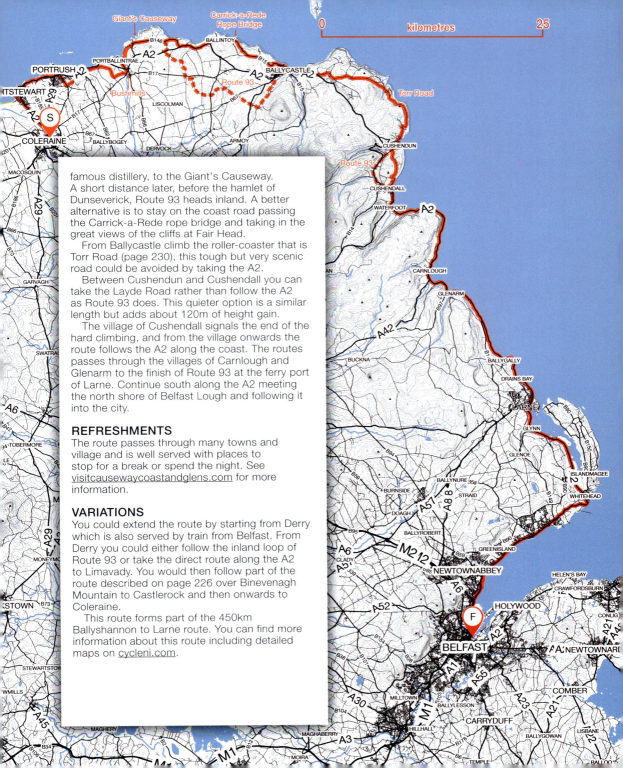

famous distillery, to the Giant's Causeway. A short distance later, before the hamlet of Dunseverick, Route 93 heads inland. A better alternative is to stay on the coast road passing the Carrick-a-Rede rope bridge and taking in the great views of the cliffs at Fair Head.

From Ballycastle climb the roller-coaster that is Torr Road (page 230), this tough but very scenic road could be avoided by taking the A2.

Between Cushendun and Cushendall you can take the Layde Road rather than follow the A2 as Route 93 does. This quieter option is a similar length but adds about 120m of height gain.

The village of Cushendall signals the end of the hard climbing, and from the village onwards the route follows the A2 along the coast. The routes passes through the villages of Carnlough and Glenarm to the finish of Route 93 at the ferry port of Larne. Continue south along the A2 meeting the north shore of Belfast Lough and following it into the city.

REFRESHMENTS

The route passes through many towns and village and is well served with places to stop for a break or spend the night. See visitcausewaycoastandglens.com for more information.

VARIATIONS

You could extend the route by starting from Derry which is also served by train from Belfast. From Derry you could either follow the inland loop of Route 93 or take the direct route along the A2 to Limavady. You would then follow part of the route described on page 226 over Binevenagh Mountain to Castlerock and then onwards to Coleraine.

This route forms part of the 450km Ballyshannon to Larne route. You can find more information about this route including detailed maps on cycleni.com.

The highpoint of Torr Road

TORR HEAD AND GLENDUN
County Antrim
ROAD

58 km
1070 m

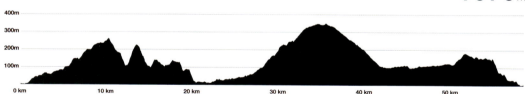

A tough loop along the Antrim coast and glens.

There is some amazing scenery on this route but to enjoy it you will have be prepared to climb. The first half follows Route 93 from Ballycastle to Cushendun along Torr Road. It then turns inland to climb Glendun and then descend Glenshesk, two of the famous glens of Antrim.

The route is described in a clockwise direction to get the steepest climb out of the way early.

From the roundabout at the eastern end of the seafront in Ballycastle (*55.2048, -6.2398*) head east along the A2.

The climbing starts almost immediately. It's steady at first but steepens just before the turn for Murlough Bay. At the highpoint of Torr Road the sea

and the Scottish coast come into view, but don't relax as there are three shorter but very steep climbs to come. A quick descent into a valley leads to the first, and worst, of the climbs. With an average gradient of 11% over a kilometre it's brutal and the steepest section through the hairpins will have all but the strongest and most determined riders walking.

A very steep descent leads to the next climb, which is a similar distance but only half as steep. Finally the route eases off and there is one more short climb before the descent into Cushendun.

Almost immediately you ease into the long (10km) but steady (3%) climb up Glendun which

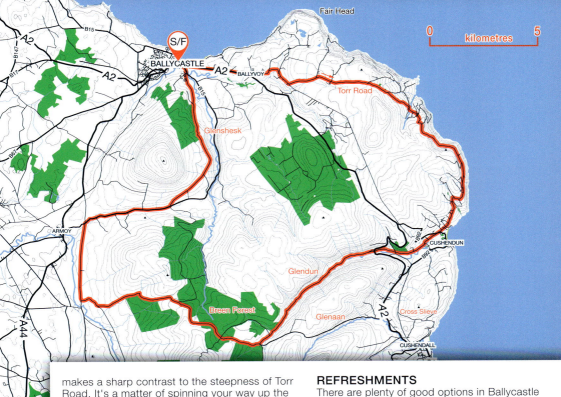

makes a sharp contrast to the steepness of Torr Road. It's a matter of spinning your way up the valley enjoying the views of the stream and the surrounding hillside. You pass under the arches of the Glendun viaduct which carries the A2 over the valley. After the junction you emerge into the uplands and continue climbing through Breen Forest until the angle eases and you start to descend.

Turning north onto Coolkeernan Road the route levels out for the first time and after 4km of the B15 you descend Glenshesk back into Ballycastle.

REFRESHMENTS
There are plenty of good options in Ballycastle including Thyme & Co Café and the Bay Café. In Cushendun there are a few pubs and a café.

VARIATIONS
If Torr Road has got the best of you then return to Ballycastle via the A2, reducing the route to 37km with 800m of height gain.

An interesting shorter alternative would be to start in Cushendun and climb up Glendun before descending down Glenaan into Cushendall. You would then return to the start by climbing over the shoulder of Cross Slieve. This route is 28km with 500m of height gain.

DISTANCE	TOTAL		INSTRUCTION
0	0	S	From the roundabout at the eastern end of the seafront in Ballycastle head east on the A2.
3.4	3.4	<	Turn left onto Torr Road.
2.4	5.8	<	Turn left.
14.7	20.5	>	Turn right at the junction.
0.2	20.7	<	Keep left.
10.8	31.5	>	Turn right.
10.5	42.0	>	Turn right at the t-junction.
3.7	45.7	>	Turn right onto the B15.
4.2	49.9	<	Turn left.
6.0	55.9	>	Keep right.
1.7	57.6	<	Turn left onto the B15.
0.6	58.2	F	Arrive back at the roundabout.

Passing Sketrick Island on the eastern side of the Lough

STRANGFORD LOUGH
County Down
ROAD

130 km
1180 m

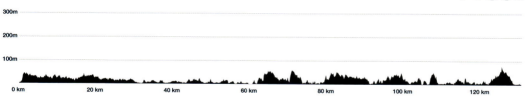

300m
200m
100m

0 km   20 km   40 km   60 km   80 km   100 km   120 km

A circuit of Strangford Lough, a designated Area of Outstanding Natural Beauty.

This route follows quiet roads around the shores of the Ards Peninsula and one of Europe's richest wildlife habitats, Strangford Lough, a haven for marine life, butterflies and wild flowers. While the hight point of the route is a mere 62m, there is a lot of climbing as it's rarely flat.

The route is described in a clockwise direction from Newtownards which is reached easily from Belfast.

This is a long and wandering route so it isn't practical to include turn-by-turn directions. The route is signposted as Route 99 of the National Cycle Network and Sustrans have published a detailed map of the route that can be bought from sustrans.org.uk. Alternatively download the GPX file from threerockbooks.com/cycling and follow it on your smartphone or GPS.

From Newtownards (*54.5889, -5.6871*) the route heads east towards the coast where it passes through the fishing villages of Ballyhalbert and Portavogie on the eastern shore of the Ards Peninsula. On a clear day you can see across the Irish Sea to the Isle of Man and Scotland.

Heading south along the coast you pass Quintin Castle and loop around Ballyquintin Point before arriving in Portaferry.

The short crossing from Portaferry to Strangford village departs at a quarter to and a quarter past

232

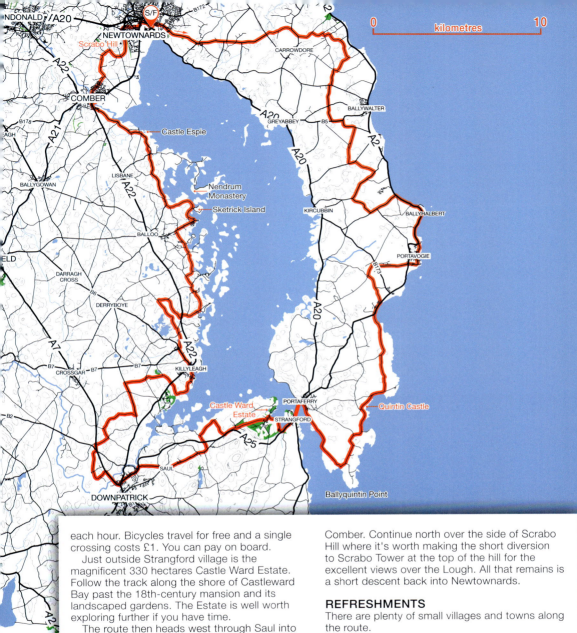

each hour. Bicycles travel for free and a single crossing costs £1. You can pay on board.

Just outside Strangford village is the magnificent 330 hectares Castle Ward Estate. Follow the track along the shore of Castleward Bay past the 18th-century mansion and its landscaped gardens. The Estate is well worth exploring further if you have time.

The route then heads west through Saul into the historic town of Downpatrick, the burial site of Saint Patrick. From Downpatrick head north through the village of Killyleagh with its château-style castle.

Shortly after Whiterock you pass Sketrick Island, Nendrum Monastery and Castle Espie Wetland Centre before arriving at the town of Comber. Continue north over the side of Scrabo Hill where it's worth making the short diversion to Scrabo Tower at the top of the hill for the excellent views over the Lough. All that remains is a short descent back into Newtownards.

REFRESHMENTS

There are plenty of small villages and towns along the route.

VARIATIONS

The route could be started from Belfast following the traffic-free Comber Greenway meeting the route in Comber just south of Newtownards.

The Blue Trail

CASTLEWELLAN TRAIL CENTRE

County Down
MTB

15km
320m

300m
200m
100m

0 km   5 km   10 km   15 km

A compact and very family-friendly trail centre.

Set on the grounds of a Victorian castle, Castlewellan is ideal for beginner and intermediate riders. While there aren't any big hills in the park the trails make excellent use of the terrain and there is plenty of flowing singletrack. The forest park doesn't have the same mountain feel as some of the other trail centres, its slopes are covered with a wider variety of trees giving it a lush, almost tropical, feel.

The park is a very family-friendly venue with plenty to entertain the kids including a pump track, maze and picnic area. There is also (paid) car parking, toilets and a bike wash, showers and café. Life

Adventure Centre onegreatadventure.com offer on-site bike hire.

The park is also used by families, walkers and horse riders so watch your speed on the forestry roads and the points where the mountain bike trails meet or cross other trails.

PUMP TRACK
The pump track beside the carpark (*54.2605, -5.9529*) is a great place to warm up before setting off on the trails. A pump track is a continous circuit of rounded bumps and berms that you ride by 'pumping' your arms and shifting your body weight rather than pedalling.

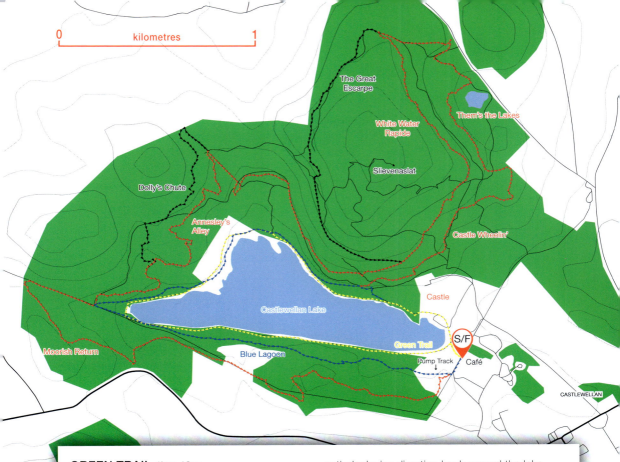

CASTLEWELLAN

GREEN TRAIL 4km 40m
This gentle trail makes a clockwise circuit of the lakeshore passing Castlewellan Castle. It's an easy flat route on a wide trail that is ideal for young kids (marked in yellow on the map).

BLUE TRAIL 4.5km 90m
The blue trail is perfect for building confidence in riders who are relatively new to mountain biking. It also offer great views over the lake. The first half, which winds its way through the woods south of the lake, is gentle but great fun with plenty of rollers. It then joins the Green Trail and follows it the rest of the way around the lake.

RED TRAIL 14.8km 320m
The Red Trail weaves its way around the slopes overlooking the lake. It starts off along the blue trail before climbing up and over the eastern slopes of Slievenaslat. Around the back of the hill the trails makes a long descent before following a sequence of short climbs and descents in an anti-clockwise direction back around the lake.

BLACK TRAIL
The two variations of the Red Trail are graded black which means they are only suitable for advanced riders. Dolly's Chute and the Great Escarpe are both tight, fast trails with plenty of rock gardens.

REFRESHMENTS
There is a café at the trailhead as well as plenty of other options nearby in Castlewellan village.

VARIATIONS
If you enjoyed Castlewellan then you should check out the other trail centres in nearby Rostrevor (page 238) and Davagh Forest (page 222) in County Tyrone.

Slievenaman Road

MOURNE MOUNTAINS
County Down
ROAD

43km
660m

500m
400m
300m
200m
100m

0 km   10 km   20 km   30 km   40 km

A road circuit of the high Mournes.

As no roads cut through the Mournes the best way to appreciate them from a bike is to cycle around the perimeter of the mountains. There are great views in all directions from this route. You look into the Mournes themselves, south along the coast, inland over the North Down countryside and across Carlingford Lough to the Cooleys.

The route is described in a clockwise direction so that you are on the same side as the sea on the busy A2.

Heading south from the southern end of the promenade (*54.2065, -5.8927*) in Newcastle follow the A2 south along the coast. To the right are the slopes of Slieve Donard, Ulster's highest mountain.

Turn away from the coast onto Quarter Road and climb north following the Annalong River. The road then contours westwards across the slopes of Slieve Binnian which is easily recognised by the granite tors on its summits. Just after the entrance to Silent Valley Mountain Park the road kinks right and the main climb of the route begins. It's a 10km climb with an average gradient of 3%.

After a short distance turn right onto the B27 and follow it up the valley between Pigeon Rock Mountain and Slieve Muck.

Near the top the angle eases and Spelga Reservoir comes into view. A short while later the B27 forks left but keep right descending

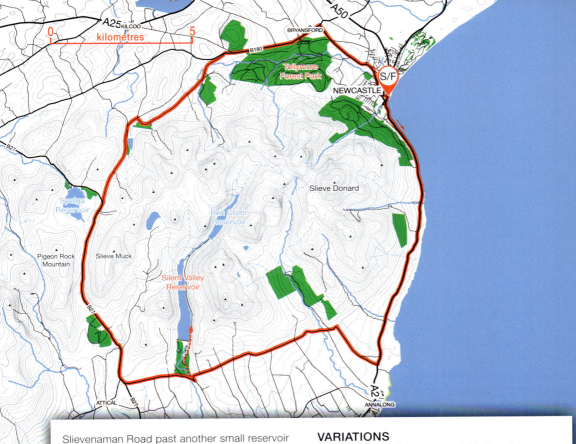

Slievenaman Road past another small reservoir before turning right onto Trassey Road. This leads east to the B180 which passes Tollymore Forest on the way back into Newcastle.

REFRESHMENTS

There are plenty of options in Newcastle but the only place on the route is a small shop where you turn off the A2 onto Quarter Road.

VARIATIONS

It would be possible to extend this loop into a 71km figure of eight by combining it with the Western Mournes route on page 240.

Western Mournes route on page 240.

Another very worthwhile extension is the out and back climb up the Silent Valley to Ben Crom reservoir. This round trip adds 11km and 120m of height gain.

DISTANCE	TOTAL		INSTRUCTION
0	0	S	From the promenade in Newcastle head south on the A2.
10.1	10.1	>	Turn right onto Quarter Road.
7.8	17.9	>	Turn right.
2.5	20.4	>	Turn right onto the B27.
7.2	27.6	>	Keep right.
3.0	30.6	>	Keep right.
0.4	31.0	>	Turn right.
4.4	35.4	>	Turn right onto the B180.
3.6	39.0	>	Turn right.
2.5	41.5	>	Take the second exit off the roundabout.
1.0	42.5	>	Turn right and right again.
0.5	43.0	F	Arrive back at the promenade.

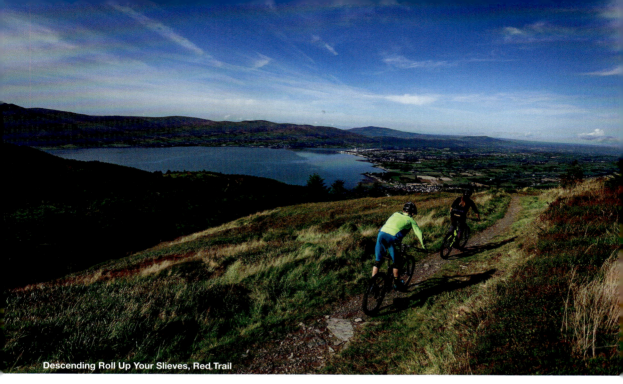

Descending Roll Up Your Slieves, Red Trail

ROSTREVOR TRAIL CENTRE

County Down
MTB

25 km
700 m

500m
400m
300m
200m
100m

0 km 5 km 10 km 15 km 20 km 25 km

A great venue for intermediate and advanced mountain bikers.

Lying on the south western corner of the Mourne Mountain just above Carlingford Lough, Rostrevor combines great singletrack with excellent views. It's pitched at more advanced riders with a brilliant 25km red trail, a black variation and two downhill tracks. The trails in nearby Castlewellan (page 234) are much more suitable for beginners.

East Coast Adventure (eastcoastadventure.com) offer bike hire and an uplift service from the carpark in Kilbroney.

RED TRAIL 25km 700m
An excellent long trail that will test your endurance.

The trail starts to climb as soon as it leaves the lower carpark (54.0973, -6.1872), the first section to the upper carpark is the steepest. After that the angle eases and a number of switchbacks lead around the slopes of Cloughmore past Kodak Corner where there are amazing views over Carlingford Lough to the Cooley Mountains.

On the slopes of Slievemeen the trail reaches its highpoint and from there on it's mostly downhill interrupted by a few short climbs.

The trail leads north across the mountain slopes gradually losing height. One outstanding section that seems to go on forever is Yellow Brick Road. It has a

238

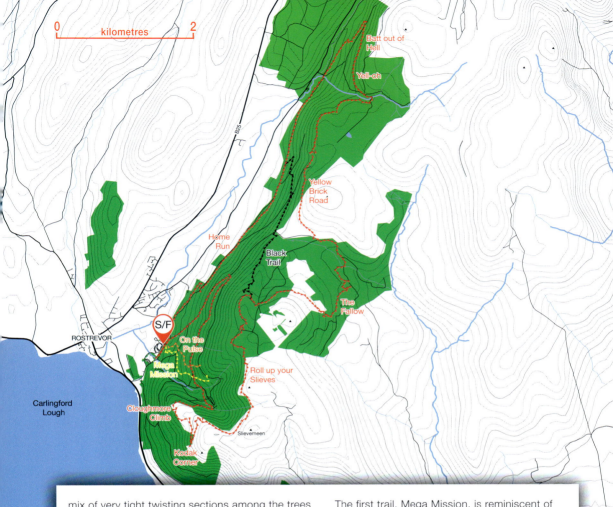

Map labels (top to bottom, left to right):

kilometres 0 — 2

Batt out of Hell
Yell-oh
Yellow Brick Road
Home Run
Black Trail
The Fallow
ROSTREVOR
S/F
On the Pulse
Mega Mission
Roll up your Slieves
Cloughmore Climb
Kodak Corner
Slievemeen
Carlingford Lough
B25
R173

mix of very tight twisting sections among the trees and fast open hillside with plenty of rocky drops.

Shortly after crossing Yellow Water River the trail turns south and descends the Kilbroney Valley back to the carpark.

BLACK TRAIL 3.1km 0m

A shorter, but harder, variation of the Red Trail that reduces the loop to 19km. There are a number of very technical sections and lots of rock gardens so it's only suitable for experienced mountain bikers.

DOWNHILL TRAIL

There are two purpose-built downhill trails. Both are graded as orange/extreme so they are very technical and only suitable for highly experienced riders on appropriate bikes.

The first trail, Mega Mission, is reminiscent of a BMX track with a relatively smooth surface and plenty of huge berms and big jumps. The second trail, On the Pulse, is very different in style. It has a more natural feel with plenty of steep tightly winding singletrack and lots of rocks.

REFRESHMENTS

There is a café beside the lower carpark in Kilbroney and plenty of other options nearby in the village of Rostrevor.

VARIATIONS

If you enjoyed Rostrevor then you should check out the other trail centres in nearby Castlewellan (page 234) and Davagh (page 222) in County Tyrone.

Yellow Road

THE WESTERN MOURNES
County Down
ROAD

28km
510m

400m
300m
200m
100m

0 km   10 km   20 km

A short loop around the hills on the western edge of the Mourne Mountains.

From the seaside town of Rostrevor on the north shore of Carlingford Lough this route loops through the rolling hills in an anti-clockwise direction.

From the Main Street (*54.1009, -6.1999*) head north climbing up the Kilbroney Valley. It's steepest at the start and the angle eases as you gain height, but is never much over 4%. Just after the point where the river crosses the road is the Yellow Water picnic site, a pleasant place to stop among the tall pines.

You then descend into the Shankys River valley and the distinctive granite tors that cap the summit of Hen Mountain come into view. Turning left,

continue descending until a short steep climb leads into the village of Hilltown. After a very short stretch on the busy B8 turn left onto Yellow Road.

Now the climb up Glenmore begins in earnest. The 5km climb has an average gradient of 5% with a number of steep ramps interspersed with more gentle sections. Near the top you pass another picnic area with good views north over the patchwork fields of north Down.

One final steep section leads over the shoulder of Slieve Roe where there are great views over the Mournes to the west, the jagged skylines of the Cooleys to the south and a glimpse of the waters of Carlingford Lough.

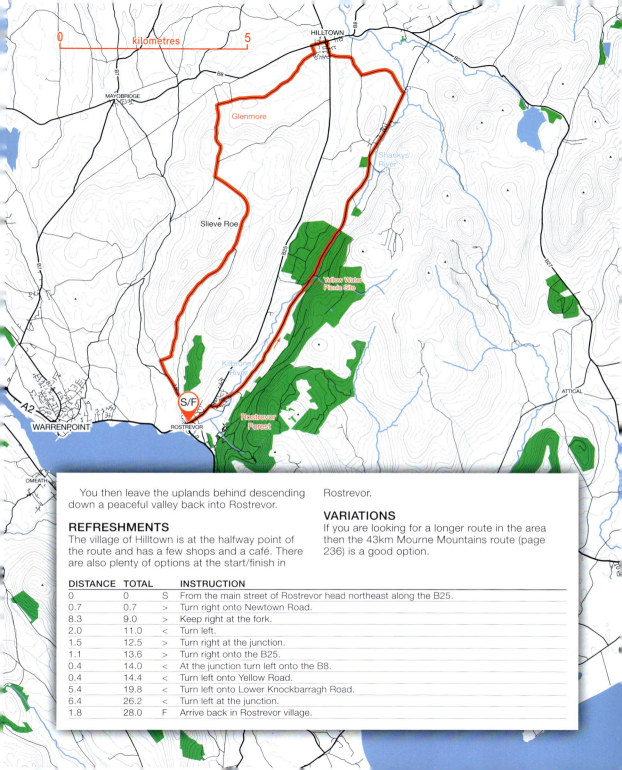

You then leave the uplands behind descending down a peaceful valley back into Rostrevor.

REFRESHMENTS

The village of Hilltown is at the halfway point of the route and has a few shops and a café. There are also plenty of options at the start/finish in Rostrevor.

VARIATIONS

If you are looking for a longer route in the area then the 43km Mourne Mountains route (page 236) is a good option.

DISTANCE	TOTAL		INSTRUCTION
0	0	S	From the main street of Rostrevor head northeast along the B25.
0.7	0.7	>	Turn right onto Newtown Road.
8.3	9.0	>	Keep right at the fork.
2.0	11.0	<	Turn left.
1.5	12.5	>	Turn right at the junction.
1.1	13.6	>	Turn right onto the B25.
0.4	14.0	<	At the junction turn left onto the B8.
0.4	14.4	<	Turn left onto Yellow Road.
5.4	19.8	<	Turn left onto Lower Knockbarragh Road.
6.4	26.2	<	Turn left at the junction.
1.8	28.0	F	Arrive back in Rostrevor village.

Midway between Jerrettspass and Poyntzpass

NEWRY CANAL
County Down/Armagh
ROAD

32km
80m

300m			
200m			
100m			
0 km	10 km	20 km	30 km

A popular easy route along the canal towpath between Newry and Portadown.

This linear route should be within the abilities of even the most casual of cyclists as, like most routes along waterways, it is dead flat and mostly traffic-free.

It's a route that is well suited to a leisurely approach. There are a number of restored buildings along the route that offer an interesting insight into the history of the canal which was built in 1742 so that coal could be transported from the sea at Newry.

Returning to the start by train is straightforward as both ends of the canal are on the main Belfast to Dublin line. Bicycles are permitted free of charge on a first come first served basis at all times with the

exception of before 9.30 from Monday to Friday. See translink.co.uk for details.

The towpath is predominantly tarmac with some short sections of gravel and is suitable for all bikes. As it is shared with walkers keep to a reasonable speed and use a bell to alert others of your presence.

The route can be done in either direction but is described from south to north to take advantage of the prevailing wind. Navigation is straightforward and there are plenty of signposts so detailed directions aren't necessary.

From New Street (*54.1795, -6.3367*) in the centre of Newry head north on Canal Quay along the

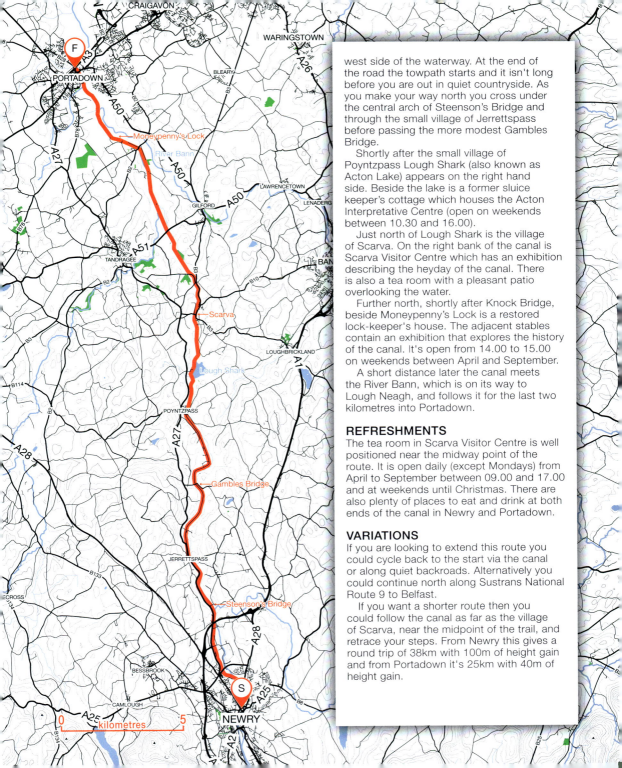

west side of the waterway. At the end of the road the towpath starts and it isn't long before you are out in quiet countryside. As you make your way north you cross under the central arch of Steenson's Bridge and through the small village of Jerrettspass before passing the more modest Gambles Bridge.

Shortly after the small village of Poyntzpass Lough Shark (also known as Acton Lake) appears on the right hand side. Beside the lake is a former sluice keeper's cottage which houses the Acton Interpretative Centre (open on weekends between 10.30 and 16.00).

Just north of Lough Shark is the village of Scarva. On the right bank of the canal is Scarva Visitor Centre which has an exhibition describing the heyday of the canal. There is also a tea room with a pleasant patio overlooking the water.

Further north, shortly after Knock Bridge, beside Moneypenny's Lock is a restored lock-keeper's house. The adjacent stables contain an exhibition that explores the history of the canal. It's open from 14.00 to 15.00 on weekends between April and September.

A short distance later the canal meets the River Bann, which is on its way to Lough Neagh, and follows it for the last two kilometres into Portadown.

REFRESHMENTS

The tea room in Scarva Visitor Centre is well positioned near the midway point of the route. It is open daily (except Mondays) from April to September between 09.00 and 17.00 and at weekends until Christmas. There are also plenty of places to eat and drink at both ends of the canal in Newry and Portadown.

VARIATIONS

If you are looking to extend this route you could cycle back to the start via the canal or along quiet backroads. Alternatively you could continue north along Sustrans National Route 9 to Belfast.

If you want a shorter route then you could follow the canal as far as the village of Scarva, near the midpoint of the trail, and retrace your steps. From Newry this gives a round trip of 38km with 100m of height gain and from Portadown it's 25km with 40m of height gain.

Lough Neagh Discovery Centre

LOUGH NEAGH
County Armagh/Tyrone/Derry/Antrim/Down
ROAD

180 km
1030 m

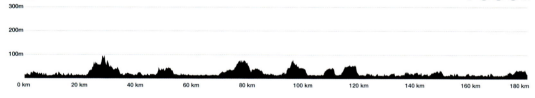

A gentle circuit of Lough Neagh, the largest freshwater lake in Britain and Ireland.

This route follows mostly quiet roads around the vast lake, which is nearly 400 square kilometres. Never straying far from the shore, it passes a number of interesting sights including the Ardboe High Cross, Annagariff Wood, Clotworthy House and the railway viaduct at Randalstown. This route is well suited to the leisure cyclist, who is looking for a fairly flat route to savour over a few days.

The route is also known as the Lough Shore Trail which is part of Route 94 of the National Cycle Network. It is signposted in places but as there are some signs missing they can't be relied on. However it isn't practical to include turn-by-turn directions so

the best approach is to download the GPX file from threerockbooks.com/cycling and follow it on your smartphone or GPS.

The route can be done in either direction but it is described clockwise starting from Portadown.

From the bridge over the Upper Bann (*55.2048, -6.2398*) head north following the river downstream to the lake. After passing the village of Maghery and Mountjoy Castle turn slightly inland and tackle the biggest climb of the route before returning to the lakeshore.

Follow a weaving course north past Ballyronan Marina before crossing the Lower Bann at Toobe.

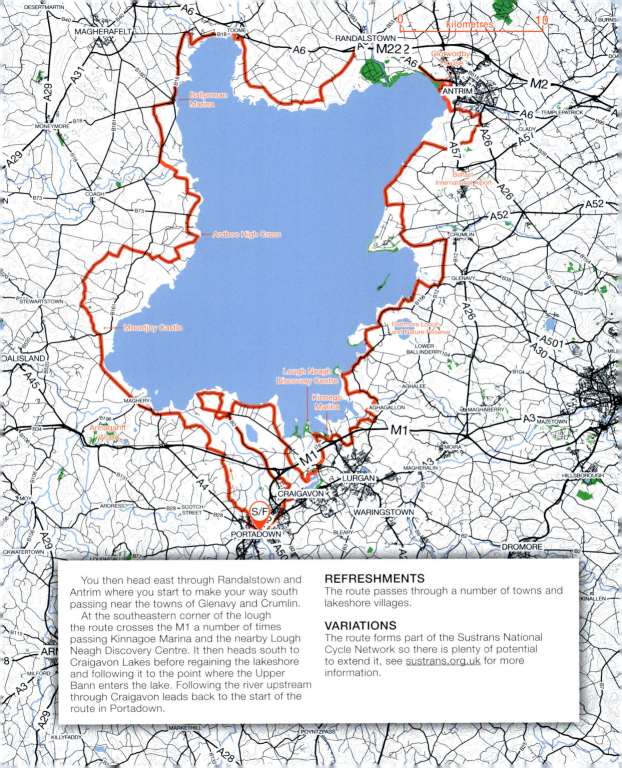

You then head east through Randalstown and Antrim where you start to make your way south passing near the towns of Glenavy and Crumlin.

At the southeastern corner of the lough the route crosses the M1 a number of times passing Kinnagoe Marina and the nearby Lough Neagh Discovery Centre. It then heads south to Craigavon Lakes before regaining the lakeshore and following it to the point where the Upper Bann enters the lake. Following the river upstream through Craigavon leads back to the start of the route in Portadown.

REFRESHMENTS

The route passes through a number of towns and lakeshore villages.

VARIATIONS

The route forms part of the Sustrans National Cycle Network so there is plenty of potential to extend it, see sustrans.org.uk for more information.

Approaching the highpoint of the route

RING OF GULLION
County Armagh
ROAD

13.5 km
370 m

A short but sharp road loop with plenty of climbing and great views

Slieve Gullion, Armagh highest mountain, is the centrepiece of the Ring of Gullion, a geological landform known as a ring dyke that is the remains of a huge volcano that erupted 60 million years ago.

This short route, which loops through Slieve Gullion Forest Park, packs a punch with plenty of brief but steep climbs. It also has some great views of the surrounding countryside. Navigation is straight-forward, as the forest drive, which is one-way, is well marked.

The surface is generally good tarmac, but watch out for patches of gravel and wandering sheep, both of which seem to appear out of nowhere at the worst possible moment.

The route starts and finished in the park's main carpark (*54.1166, -6.4087*) which opens at 09.00 and closes at dusk, check online for the exact closing time (visitmournemountains.co.uk).

Set off following the signs for the forest drive, immediately you are straight into a steep climb around a few bends before the angle eases. The road swings around the southern slopes of Slieve Gullion and the distinctive hills that make up the Ring of Gullion come into view. After a flat stretch the climbing continues and a series of steep ramps lead through pine trees onto more open hillside.

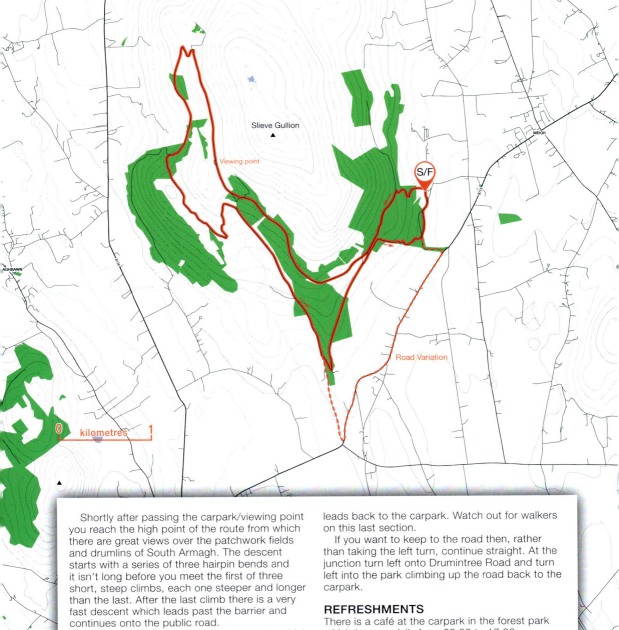

Slieve Gullion

Viewing point

S/F

Road Variation

AGHIBAWN

MEIGH

0 kilometres 1

Shortly after passing the carpark/viewing point you reach the high point of the route from which there are great views over the patchwork fields and drumlins of South Armagh. The descent starts with a series of three hairpin bends and it isn't long before you meet the first of three short, steep climbs, each one steeper and longer than the last. After the last climb there is a very fast descent which leads past the barrier and continues onto the public road.

Approximately 750m later take a left turn which leads back into the forest park. Go around the barrier, and continue on the tarmac path which although not perfectly smooth should be fine on even the skinniest tires. The path climbs gently through pleasant woodland before a brief descent leads back to the carpark. Watch out for walkers on this last section.

If you want to keep to the road then, rather than taking the left turn, continue straight. At the junction turn left onto Drumintree Road and turn left into the park climbing up the road back to the carpark.

REFRESHMENTS

There is a café at the carpark in the forest park which is open daily from 09.00 to 17.00.

VARIATIONS

This route could be significantly extended by linking it with the Cooley Mountains route which is just the other side of the M1 motorway. See page 46 for details.

Tassagh Viaduct

TASSAGH
County Armagh
ROAD

35km
500m

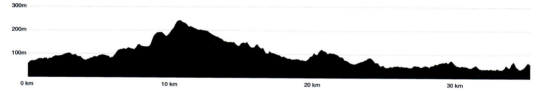

300m
200m
100m

0 km   10 km   20 km   30 km

A short loop through the rolling fields of south Armagh.

In spite of the presence of some short but very steep climbs, which there is no shame in walking, this route has a gentle pastoral feel. From the compact city of Armagh it loops clockwise over the hills and along the valleys past a number of interesting sights.

From the carpark (*54.3479, -6.6389*) beside the playground on the A51 follow the gravel path south through Folly Glen.

The path ends at the A28 and the route continues south on quiet country roads tackling a series of short steep climbs. From the high point of the route, a small hill marked with a stone cairn called the Vicar's Cairn, descend southwest passing Seaghan

Dam before a short stretch on the B31. Heading more west now you meet the Callan River north of Tassagh and follow it downstream passing the impressive 11 arched Tassagh viaduct which was built in 1910 for the railway linking Castleblayney in Monaghan with Armagh. However after partition in 1922 the line was no longer practical and services stopped in 1932 before it was finally closed in 1957.

You then turn west and climb, crossing the A29. You then turn north and cross the Callan River twice before arriving in the village of Milford.

From the village continue north crossing the A3 and A28 before turning east and passing the Navan

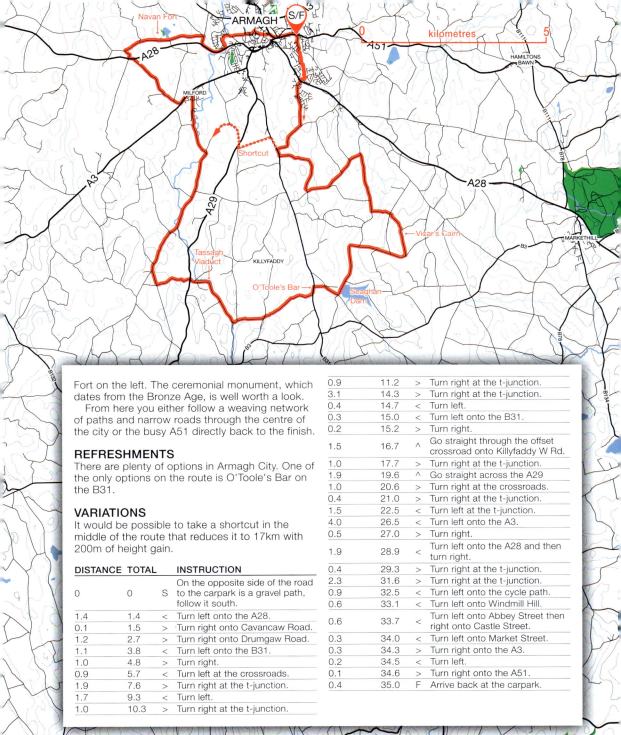

Fort on the left. The ceremonial monument, which dates from the Bronze Age, is well worth a look.

From here you either follow a weaving network of paths and narrow roads through the centre of the city or the busy A51 directly back to the finish.

REFRESHMENTS

There are plenty of options in Armagh City. One of the only options on the route is O'Toole's Bar on the B31.

VARIATIONS

It would be possible to take a shortcut in the middle of the route that reduces it to 17km with 200m of height gain.

DISTANCE	TOTAL		INSTRUCTION
0	0	S	On the opposite side of the road to the carpark is a gravel path, follow it south.
1.4	1.4	<	Turn left onto the A28.
0.1	1.5	>	Turn right onto Cavancaw Road.
1.2	2.7	>	Turn right onto Drumgaw Road.
1.1	3.8	<	Turn left onto the B31.
1.0	4.8	>	Turn right.
0.9	5.7	<	Turn left at the crossroads.
1.9	7.6	>	Turn right at the t-junction.
1.7	9.3	<	Turn left.
1.0	10.3	>	Turn right at the t-junction.
0.9	11.2	>	Turn right at the t-junction.
3.1	14.3	>	Turn right at the t-junction.
0.4	14.7	<	Turn left.
0.3	15.0	<	Turn left onto the B31.
0.2	15.2	>	Turn right.
1.5	16.7	^	Go straight through the offset crossroad onto Killyfaddy W Rd.
1.0	17.7	>	Turn right at the t-junction.
1.9	19.6	^	Go straight across the A29
1.0	20.6	>	Turn right at the crossroads.
0.4	21.0	>	Turn right at the t-junction.
1.5	22.5	<	Turn left at the t-junction.
4.0	26.5	<	Turn left onto the A3.
0.5	27.0	>	Turn right.
1.9	28.9	<	Turn left onto the A28 and then turn right.
0.4	29.3	>	Turn right at the t-junction.
2.3	31.6	>	Turn right at the t-junction.
0.9	32.5	<	Turn left onto the cycle path.
0.6	33.1	<	Turn left onto Windmill Hill.
0.6	33.7	<	Turn left onto Abbey Street then right onto Castle Street.
0.3	34.0	<	Turn left onto Market Street.
0.3	34.3	>	Turn right onto the A3.
0.2	34.5	<	Turn left.
0.1	34.6	>	Turn right onto the A51.
0.4	35.0	F	Arrive back at the carpark.

Inishowen 100

DERRY

Donegal Cycle Route

Ballyshannon to Larne

Causeway Coast

Lough Shore Trail

BELFAST

Strangfo Lough

Ballyshannon to Belfast

ARMAGH

North West Trail

Kingfisher Trail

Táin Trail

Royal Canal

Green Heartlands Cycle Route

DUBLIN

GALWAY

Grand Canal

Wild Atlantic Way

LIMERICK

The Barrow Navigation

The Kelly Comeragh Challenge

WATERFORD

The Norman Way

Tour of Iveragh

Ring of Kerry Cycle Route

CORK

Cork City to Glengarriff

Beara Way Cycle Route

50 km

LONG-DISTANCE ROUTES

In spite of the sometimes inclement weather, Ireland is a great cycle touring destination thanks to its compact size, spectacular scenery and extensive network of quiet roads. As the cycling infrastructure improves hopefully the number of visitors and locals travelling the country by bike will continue to grow. Currently there are over a dozen official signposted routes that will be of interest to the touring cyclist, ranging from 120km to 2,500km in length.

Some of these routes have short traffic-free sections, but the vast majority are on-road. And even through they try to avoid the busiest roads, it's essential to ensure that you are visible to the traffic and carry lights in case you are stuck out after dark.

All of the routes detailed in this chapter are signposted however some signs may point in the wrong direction or have disappeared altogether so it's unwise to rely solely on signposting to find your way. A GPS or smartphone is the best method of navigation (see page 14) on these long meandering routes. A GPX for each route can be downloaded from threerockbooks.com/cycling.

See page 34 for some general advice on touring and bikepacking in Ireland.

THE WILD ATLANTIC WAY

The 2,500km tourist route that runs the length of the west coast has been a great success since it was created in 2014. And even through it isn't a cycling route as such it is very popular with touring cyclists. See page 256 for a detailed breakdown of the route.

DONEGAL CYCLE ROUTE

The 200km Donegal Cycle Route starts in Newtowncunningham, halfway between Derry and Letterkenny, and finishes in Donegal Town. The Donegal Cycle Route takes a reasonably direct route, while the Wild Atlantic Way sticks closer to the coast and covers nearly twice the distance. Tourers who are following the Wild Atlantic Way might find that the Donegal Cycle Route offers some useful shortcuts.

The route is well signposted and mostly follows quiet minor roads although there are a couple of places where it's forced onto busier roads. The route forms part of the Eurovelo 1 (see page 254).

For more details including an interactive map see donegalcycleroute.ie.

THE NORTH WEST TRAIL

The North West Trail is a 329km loop through the northwestern counties of Donegal, Tyrone, Fermanagh, Leitrim and Sligo. This well signposted route (marked with a rather abstract titled triangle with a wavy line running through it) travels through a wide variety of scenic landscapes, including the Atlantic coast and remote uplands, along quiet country roads with traffic-free sections in some urban areas.

The route has 3,850m of height gain. The inland sections feature a number of tough climbs while nearer the coast the terrain is gentler.

The route is described starting and finishing in Enniskillen but it's possible to start anywhere and as it passes through a number of large towns including Sligo, Donegal, Lifford, Strabane and Omagh there are plenty of options.

From Enniskillen follow the Kingfisher Trail south then west passing Cuilcagh Mountain and the Marble Arch Caves. From the village of Belcoo the route crosses the border and continues west passing through the town of Manorhamilton before skirting Lough Gill (see route on page 188) and arriving in Sligo Town.

Between the towns of Sligo and Donegal the route follows the coast north, as does the Wild Atlantic Way. However for the most part they follow different routes with the North West Trail avoiding the busier roads taken by the Wild Atlantic Way.

Heading north through Yeat's Country the distinctive profile of Benbulbin (see route on page 190) dominates the skyline. Passing a number of long sandy beaches at Mullaghmore (see route on page 192), Streedagh, Bundoran, Rossnowlagh and Murvagh the route arrives in Donegal Town and turns inland. Climbing high into the Bluestack Mountains over the hardest climb on the route through Barnesmore Gap.

At Lifford the route crosses the river Mourne and follows it upstream into the foothills of the Sperrin Mountains and onwards to Omagh. It then heads southwest across rolling countryside gradually gaining height before dropping down into Enniskillen.

The official map of the trail is available to buy online from Sustrans (sustrans.org).

Climbing the north side of Healy Pass, Kerry, see page 119

THE KINGFISHER TRAIL

The 480km Kingfisher Trail weaves a rather complicated loop around the border counties of Fermanagh, Leitrim, Cavan, Donegal and Monaghan. For the most part the trail follows quiet roads, some of which are quite rough, through beautiful countryside characterised by rolling hills and myriad rivers and lakes. Developed as a cross-border initiative it was the first long-distance cycle trail on the island and is relatively popular.

The trail consists of two loops (the Northern and the Southern) joined back to back to form a figure of eight.

The 157km Northern Loop starts in Enniskillen and heads south before turning west passing the Marble Arch Caves and Cuilcagh Mountain. It then follows the border northwest past Upper Lough Macnean and Lough Melvin before heading north through Belleek. From the village it travels east then south around the shore of Lough Erne back into Enniskillen. The Northern Loop is quite hilly with 1,950m of height gain.

The 228km Southern Loop starts in Carrick-on-Shannon and travels east through the drumlin country of Cavan and Leitrim to Clones. It then heads west through the maze of lakes that make up Upper Lough Erne with a short ferry crossing (which must be arranged in advance) in Crom Estate in Fermanagh. Continuing west past Cuilcagh Mountain the route crosses the border at Blacklion. It then turns south passing the Shannon Pot, the source of Ireland's longest river, and along the shore of Lough Allen into Drumshanbo where it follows the Shannon south back to Carrick-on-Shannon. The loop is relatively flat with the exception of a trio of climbs in the northeastern corner where most of the 2,450m of height gain is concentrated.

The route features a number of optional shortcuts and variations:

- The West Fermanagh Link (Ride 3) is a 53km linear route that bisects the Northern Loop cutting east to west south of Lower Lough Erne.
- The Ballyshannon Loop (Ride 4) is identical to the 31km Ballyshannon Cycle Hub Loop 1 (page 25).
- Ride 5 is a 56km loop that shares a lot of the same ground as the Drumshanbo route on page 196.
- Ride 6 is a 36km loop around the countryside southwest of the town of Clones.

For the most part the trail is generally well signposted (by a brown sign with a kingfisher in white) however there are places where signs are missing or incorrect so carry a map or GPS/ smartphone as a backup.

The entire Northern Loop and most of the Southern Loop is covered by the Fermanagh Lakelands & Tyrone Cycle Map (sheet 50) which can be bought online from Sustrans (sustrans.org).

For further information check out kingfishercycletrail.com.

BALLYSHANNON TO LARNE

This 452km route is the first of two Sustrans routes that cross Northern Ireland, linking the west and east coasts.

From the town of Ballyshannon on the Atlantic coast the route heads east through the lakelands of Fermanagh and the Sperrins before following the River Foyle into Derry. From the city it passes though the Roe Valley to meet the north coast at the town of Castlerock. The route then heads east along the Causeway Coast (see page 228) to the ferry port of Larne. See cycleni.com for more details.

BALLYSHANNON TO BELFAST

The second of the two Sustrans cross-country routes takes a slightly shorter (390km) inland path.

From Ballyshannon the route crosses the border at Belleek and heads southwest along the shores of Lough Melvin and Lough Macnean. After Belcoo the route climbs across the northern slopes of Cuilcagh Mountain before turning north and passing through Enniskillen. It then heads northeast through Omagh and the foothills of the Sperrins, where there are a few tough climbs. From Cookstown the route veers south, passing through the city of Armagh before turning north. It then skirts the shores of Lough Neagh before finishing in Belfast. See cycleni.com for details.

THE TÁIN TRAIL

The 600km Táin Trail is a circular route that runs from Rathcroghan in Roscommon, through County Longford and around the Cooley Peninsula in County Louth before returning to the start via a more southerly route.

The trail retraces the route taken by Queen Maeve of Connacht and her armies in the mythical epic Táin Bó Cúailgne - The Cattle Raid of Cooley - the most famous of the Irish sagas. Connecting the Midlands

and the east coast the route will particularly appeal to cyclists interested in Irish folklore and mythology.

The route is signposted with distinctive Brown Bull signs however they may be missing in places so you will need other means to navigate. A number of different versions of the route exist both online and on the map boards in many of the towns along the route but the GPX file is based on the Longford Tourist Office map.

Note the trail shouldn't be confused with the walking route in the Cooley Mountains in Louth called The Táin Way.

THE GREEN HEARTLANDS CYCLE ROUTE

This 263km route loops around the south Roscommon countryside, passing through a number of small villages as well as the larger towns of Roscommon and Athlone. The route has been divided into six stages plus a link stage that cuts the loop in half. It does a good job of avoiding busy roads as it weaves its way through low-lying bog, forest and farmland. There is an app available that will be a great help with planning and navigating the route, see greenheartlands.ie for more information.

THE CANALS

The three waterways with extensive towpaths (the Royal Canal, Grand Canal and the Barrow) are covered elsewhere in this book (see page 32) but they are mentioned here as they are ideal long-distance off-road routes.

THE NORMAN WAY

This 140km heritage trail meanders along the coast of Wexford between Rosslare Harbour and the town of New Ross. This well signposted route follows quiet country roads visiting 30 historical sites and passing many small villages and excellent beaches.

EuroVelo 1 (page 254) runs along the 120km section of the Norman Way between Rosslare and Ballyhack Ferry. With a start/finish point at the ferry port of Rosslare it should become popular with visitors from abroad.

The route is also well positioned to be combined with other nearby routes. One possibility is to link it with the River Barrow towpath and the Grand Canal (page 60) making for an excellent route connecting Dublin City and Rosslare Harbour.

Another option is to take the ferry across the River Suir between Ballyhack and Passage East. This

Errigal as seen from the Donegal Cycle Route

leaves you only a short distance from the start of the Waterford Greenway (page 98) in Waterford City.

For more information about the route including a detailed map check out goo.gl/qyco2B.

THE KELLY COMERAGH CHALLENGE

This 160km route around the Comeragh Mountains in Waterford is popular with riders looking to test their endurance over one long day, however it can also be done as a weekend tour. The route, named in honour of Sean Kelly, one of Ireland's great bike racers, can be started from Clonmel, Carrick-on-Suir or Dungarvan. Be warned this is a tough route featuring a number of steep climbs amongst its 2,170m of height gain. The route described on page 100 follows the northern section of the Challenge route.

The Comeraghs and the Waterford coast are home to four other signposted loops as well as a greenway (page 98). See sportireland.ie for details.

EUROVELO

EuroVelo is a network of fifteen long-distance cycling routes across Europe. Two of these routes cross Ireland and even thought they are both in the early stages of development the plan is for them to connect existing routes where possible. For more details check out eurovelo.com.

EUROVELO 1
EuroVelo 1, known as the Atlantic Coast Route, runs for 9,000km along the western fringe of the continent from Norway to the Algarve via the west coast of Ireland between the ferry ports of Larne in Northern Ireland and Rosslare in the Republic.

It's worth bearing in mind that the EV1 was designed specifically for touring cyclists and as such it avoids busy roads where at all possible.

The route is 2,550km long in total, split between 2,300km in the Republic and 250km in Northern Ireland.

The route is fully signposted, the vast majority is on quiet roads with the exception of the stretches along the Great Western Greenway (page 175), the Limerick Greenway (page 136) and the Waterford Greenway (page 98). Currently 7% of the route in the Republic is traffic-free with the remainder on public roads, ultimately it is hoped that 22% will be traffic-free.

It also takes in a number of shorter signposted on-road routes such as the Sustrans network across Northern Ireland and the Donegal Cycle Route (page 251), the North West Trail (page 251) and the Norman Way (page 253) in the Republic.

For more information about the EV1 check out eurovelo.com and eurovelo1ireland.ie for more information specific to Ireland.

EUROVELO 2

Also known as the Capitals Route, EuroVelo 2 traverses the continent from Moscow to Dublin before continuing across the Midlands to meet the Atlantic at Galway City.

The eastern half of the 276km route between Dublin and Galway is in good condition, following the Royal Canal (see page 58) out of Dublin before taking the The Old Rail Trail (see page 50) from Mullingar to Athlone. However, the section between Athlone and Galway City is delayed and there is no completion date in sight. Follow its progress on galwaytodublincycleway.ie.

THE BEARA–BREIFNE WAY

The 500km Beara-Breifne Way runs from Dursey Island at the very tip of the Beara Peninsula in Cork through the middle of the country to the village of Breifne in Leitrim. The route retraces the course of the epic 14 day march undertaken in the winter of 1603 by Donal Cam, Chieftain of the O'Sullivan Beara clan, and a thousand of his followers.

The route links twelve walking trails (only ten are currently signposted) crossing plenty of rough ground where cycling mightn't be possible or permitted.

Work is ongoing on a cycling variation that will follow a similar course to the walking route but sticking to the roads. In a number of counties the signposts (brown signs with a chieftain on a red and yellow background, be aware that the image of the chieftain may be missing leaving a white curved square) are already in place, however they may be missing or wrong so don't rely on them.

In County Cork the route is signposted from the start at Dursey Sound to the town of Millstreet, a distance of 147km.

In County Tipperary the Ormond Way Cycling Route is fully signposted and in East Galway the Hymany Way is signposted between Portumna and Aughrim (see sportireland.ie/outdoors for details).

The Beara-Breifne Way forms part of an unofficial route called the Ireland Way which links it with the Ulster Way to create a 900km super route. For more information check out theirelandway.ie.

CORK CITY–BEARA

This 96km linear route links Cork City with Glengarriff on the Beara Peninsula. From the city it follows some busy roads west for 56km to Inchigeela (at time of writing there is no signposts until near Macroom). Here you have a choice, you can either take the longer alternative via Gougane Barra, which adds 12km, or take the more direct route via Kealkill. The two variations converge at the Coomhola Bridge before continuing west to the finish at Glengarriff.

The route is marked with brown signs, those pointing in the direction of Cork City have a crest while those pointing towards Beara feature a circle with Beara written inside it.

OFF-ROAD

Even through there isn't any official long-distance off-road cycling routes, with the notable exception of the canals, Ireland's vast network of tracks and paths has great potential.

For example many of the 43 National Waymarked Trails in the Republic and the Ulster Way in Northern Ireland, although intended for walkers, would be well suited to cycling.

Currently many of these trails see little footfall. This may be due, in part at least, to the time commitment required and the fact that many of them feature long stretches of road walking. Both these factors make them well suited to cycling and hopefully in the future some of them will be designated as multi-use trails. For more information about off-road cycling and the access situation in Ireland see page 21.

OTHER ROUTES

The following routes, which are described in detail in the main body of the book, could be done as multi-day tours:

- Beara Way Cycle Route, Cork/Kerry, page 120.
- Tour of Iveragh, Kerry, page 128.
- The Ring of Kerry Cycle Route, Kerry, page 127.
- Inishowen 100, Donegal, page 216.
- Causeway Coast, Antrim/Derry, page 228.
- Strangford Lough, Antrim/Down, page 232.
- Lough Neagh, Antrim/Down/Armagh/Tyrone/Derry, page 244.

THE WILD ATLANTIC WAY

For a long time prior to the launch of the Wild Atlantic Way Ireland's Atlantic coast attracted cycling tourers for its spectacular scenery, unique culture and fascinating history. However the packaging of the most scenic parts of Ireland into a well defined route has raised the region's profile significantly and the Wild Atlantic Way has been very popular with cyclists from its inception.

The route is well signposted and there are plenty of amenities en route. It's worth bearing in the mind that as the Wild Atlantic Way wasn't created specifically cyclists there are a number of sections on busy national and regional roads. However, in most cases, it's possible to find better, safer alternatives. Currently these variations haven't been documented but there is certainly scope for a cycling variation of the route.

There is a wide range of accommodation and places to eat and drink along the route, particularly in the more popular regions of West Cork, Kerry, the Burren and Connemara. In these areas it would be wise to book accommodation in advance during the tourist season, which starts in March and peaks in July and August before tapering off in September.

To cycle the entire 2,500km route requires serious commitment, in terms of both time and endurance, and even fit cyclists will need at least two weeks. Anyway most people don't have the time or inclination to race its full length and there is a lot to be said for choosing a section of the route and taking your time, exploring as you go and taking advantage of the freedom that cycling offers.

For those with only a weekend there are plenty of excellent shorter loops, the trio of Kerry peninsulas

Climbing Bóthar na gCloch on the southside of the Dingle Peninsula, Kerry, see page 134

for instance. If you have more time or want to cover a lot of ground then it makes more sense to take a linear approach, using public transport to access the start and/or finish.

The following cities and towns on or near the route are served by train: Kinsale, Killarney, Tralee, Galway, Westport, Ballina, Sligo and Derry. Bus Éireann, Ireland's national bus service, can also be used to reach many of the smaller towns along the route. For more information about public transport in Ireland see page 34.

Over the following pages the route is divided into six stages of approximately 300km. Each starts and finishes at a large town or city that is served by public transport.

The Wild Atlantic Way has many short loops and linear sections that add considerable distance to the route. Depending on circumstances it may not be possible to follow them all. However many of them visit some of the most spectacular parts of the route and if you have time they are well worth including. There are two distances listed for each stage, one for the direct route and the other including all the extensions.

The fifteen official signature points are marked on the map, these are the most popular sights on the route. However there are thousands of other sights to see so don't make the mistake of just rushing between the signature points.

The best direction to cycle the route is from south to north to take advantage of the prevailing southwesterly wind. This also means that you will be cycling on the side of the road closest to the coast and will have a better view. The route's six stages are listed and described in this direction.

If you are looking for general information about the Wild Atlantic Way and the surrounding area then check out *Exploring Ireland's Wild Atlantic Way* also published by Three Rock Books.

EUROVELO 1

Th EV1 starts in Rosslare and follows the Norman Way to Waterford, joining the Waterford Greenway and continuing west across East Cork to meet the Wild Atlantic Way in Kinsale.

It then makes it's way along the west coast, sharing some of the same ground as the Wild Atlantic Way, but generally speaking it takes a more direct route, rather than following as close to the coast as possible like the Wild Atlantic Way does.

For more information about the EV1 is see page 254.

OFF-ROAD OPTIONS

A number of waymarked trails cross paths with the Wild Atlantic Way including (from south to north) the Sheep's Head Way, Beara Way, Kerry Way, Dingle Way, North Kerry Way, Burren Way, Croagh Patrick Heritage Trail, Western Way and Slí Dhún na nGall. These trails feature a mix of quiet roads, tracks and paths, many of which may be suitable for mountain biking. However they aren't designated for this purpose so tread carefully. See sportireland.ie/outdoors for details.

The rugged topography of the west coast dictates the path taken by the Wild Atlantic Way and there are many places where it is forced away from the coast or around the mountains. These empty tracts, such as the coast of the Glencolmcille Peninsula in Donegal or the western slopes of Brandon in Kerry, offer a serious challenge for the adventurous mountain biker. There are also plenty of gentler tracks and paths that could offer pleasant diversions from the road, either to shorten or extend the route.

THE TRANS ATLANTIC WAY RACE

This 2,500km self-supported race along the Wild Atlantic Way has, since it first ran in 2015, attracted a field of elite cyclists from across the world. The race starts in Dublin, joins the Wild Atlantic Way in Derry and follows it south (into the wind!) to Kinsale before finishing at Blarney Castle just outside Cork City.

Currently the record stands at just over six days. The race's 200 places fill quickly so if you think you have what it takes then check out transatlanticway.com for more information.

ROUTES ON THE WILD ATLANTIC WAY

The following routes, which are described in detail in the main body of this book, share some ground with the Wild Atlantic Way (listed from south to north).

SOUTH

- Mizen Head, page 108.
- Sheep's Head, page 110.
- Glengarriff Woods, page 116.
- Healy and Caha Pass, page 119.
- Ring of Beara, page 120.
- Ring of Kerry, page 127.
- Tour of Iveragh, page 128.
- Slea Head, page 132.
- Dingle Peninsula, page 134.
- Loop Head, page 140.
- Black Head, page 144.

WEST

- Inishmore, page 152.
- Galway Wind Park, page 154
- Casla, page 157.
- Oughterard, page 158.
- Sky Road, page 164.
- Great Western Greenway, page 175.
- North Clew Bay, page 176.
- Achill Island, page 178.
- Cross Lake, page 180.
- Rathlacken and Sralagagh, page 182.
- Mullaghmore and Gleniff, page 192.

NORTH

- Glencolmcille, page 210.
- Inishowen, page 216.

A few kilometres north of Allihies village on the Ring of Beara, Cork, see page 120

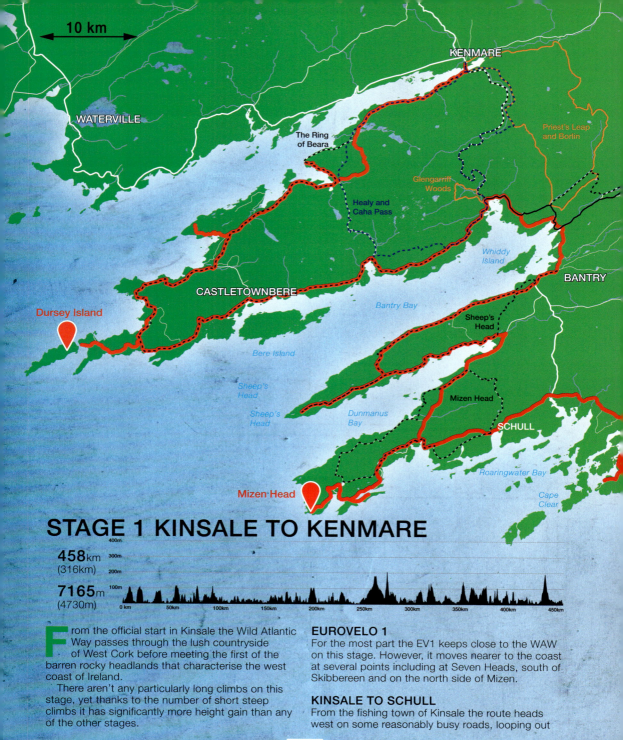

10 km

WATERVILLE

KENMARE

Priest's Leap and Borlin

The Ring of Beara

Glengarriff Woods

Healy and Caha Pass

Whiddy Island

BANTRY

CASTLETOWNBERE

Bantry Bay

Sheep's Head

Dursey Island

Bere Island

Sheep's Head

Sheep's Head

Mizen Head

SCHULL

Dunmanus Bay

Roaringwater Bay

Mizen Head

Cape Clear

STAGE 1 KINSALE TO KENMARE

458km (316km)

7165m (4730m)

From the official start in Kinsale the Wild Atlantic Way passes through the lush countryside of West Cork before meeting the first of the barren rocky headlands that characterise the west coast of Ireland.

There aren't any particularly long climbs on this stage, yet thanks to the number of short steep climbs it has significantly more height gain than any of the other stages.

EUROVELO 1

For the most part the EV1 keeps close to the WAW on this stage. However, it moves nearer to the coast at several points including at Seven Heads, south of Skibbereen and on the north side of Mizen.

KINSALE TO SCHULL

From the fishing town of Kinsale the route heads west on some reasonably busy roads, looping out

to the coast at some points and cutting inland at others. The weaving nature of the route means that there is plenty of scope for longer and shorter variations on quieter roads. One worthwhile diversion, that is overlooked by the official route, is to the wonderful area of Seven Heads.

From Rosscarbery the Wild Atlantic Way follows the R597 to Leap where it rejoins the busy N71 before following it along the coast into the town of Skibbereen. From Skibbereen a side route leads to Baltimore, the setting off point for the islands of Sherkin and Cape Clear, while the main route continues along the N71 through the town of Ballydehob to Schull.

MIZEN

Lying at the very tip of the Kilmore Peninsula is Mizen Head, the most southwesterly point in Ireland. It's well worth a visit for the spectacular views from the bridge that connects the lighthouse to the mainland. The northern section of the route described on page 108 could serve as a variation to the Wild Atlantic Way.

SHEEP'S HEAD

The Wild Atlantic Way follows the coast road along the shore of Dunmanus Bay to the lighthouse at the very end of the Sheep's Head before retracing its steps and climbing over the rocky spine of the headland to the quieter north coast. A 68km loop around this headland is described on page 110.

BEARA

Following the coastline north around Bantry Bay leads to Beara, the first of the three big peninsulas. The Wild Atlantic Way follows the Ring of Beara (see 120) from Glengarriff (see page 116 for an easy spin around Glengarriff Woods), diverting to the very tip of the peninsula to overlook Dursey Island which is linked to the mainland by Ireland's only cable car. The route then passes through some incredible rocky terrain between the villages of Allihies and Eyeries before a fairly flat stretch along the southern shore of Kenmare Bay leads to Kenmare.

Two roads climb through the mountains linking the north and south coasts of the peninsula. Both are challenging climbs through spectacular scenery. Healy Pass links Glengarriff and Kenmare, while further to the west is Caha Pass, a quieter and more spectacular alternative. A route that takes in both passes is described on page 119.

STAGE 2 KENMARE TO TRALEE

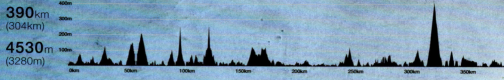

390km
(304km)

4530m
(3280m)

A s the Wild Atlantic Way loops around the Iveragh and Dingle Peninsulas it sticks quite closely to the coast. It's also reasonably flat with one notable exception, the Conor Pass, the highest point along the Wild Atlantic Way.

This section of the Wild Atlantic Way is very popular, and deservedly so, as the scenery is some of the best in the county. However it's still possible to escape the crowds by leaving the main route and exploring the quieter backroads.

EUROVELO 1

Between Kenmare and Waterville the EV1 diverts inland following the Tour of Iveragh (see page 128) through the spectacular Ballaghbeama Pass. It then continues north sticking close to the WAW for the remainder of the stage.

IVERAGH

The Iveragh Peninsula is home to the world famous tourist route, the Ring of Kerry. The traffic on the Ring gets particularly heavy during the summer, but every year in July it hosts thousands of cyclists taking part in the most popular sportive in the county. For more information about cycling the Ring see page 127.

A quieter alternative to the Ring is the 207km Tour of Iveragh (page 128), which explores both the coast and the interior of the peninsula, taking in a few classic mountain passes.

A shorter but still challenging variation of this route is the 68km Ring of the Reeks (page 130) which loops around Ireland's highest mountains, the Macgillycuddy's Reeks, passing through the beautiful Gap of Dunloe and the Black Valley.

There are plans for a greenway along the disused Great Southern & Western railway line that runs above the busy road between Glenbeigh and Cahersiveen. Unfortunately it has been beset by planning setbacks, but when it gets built it will be spectacular.

KILLARNEY

A number of routes start from the busy tourist town of Killarney including a short loop around Muckross Lake (page 122), a lap of the lakes that also takes in the spectacular Gap of Dunloe (page 124) and the Tour of Iveragh (page 128). Killarney is served by train and has a wide range of accommodation, pubs and restaurants.

DINGLE

From the town of Killorglin it's a flat run on busy roads along the south coast of the Dingle Peninsula until the road cuts inland passing just outside the village of

Annascaul and into Dingle Town. From the town the Wild Atlantic Way heads west around Slea Head, one of the most spectacular roads in the county, before returning to Dingle. This 43km loop is described in detail on page 132.

From Dingle Town the WAW climbs over Conor Pass to the northern coast of the peninsula. The Pass is probably more enjoyable when tackled from the north but the views are spectacular in either direction. Take particular care on the descent down the north side of the pass as there are some steep drops and it's extremely narrow in places.

A 68km loop that starts in Dingle Town and climbs over the peninsula to Camp and before returning over Conor Pass is described on page 134.

From the north side of Conor Pass the road heads east to Tralee. This section isn't the most inspiring on the route as it's quite monotonous and can be busy. A possible alternative may be to cycle along the vast beach that runs between Fermoyle Strand and Derrymore at low tide when the hard packed sand is exposed.

Brandon Point

Tralee Bay

TRALEE

CASTLEISLAND

Conor Pass

Dingle Peninsula

CASTLEMAINE

MILLTOWN

Inch Beach

KILLORGLIN

KILLARNEY

Bay

Muckross Lakes

Tour of the Reeks

CAHERSIVEEN

Killarney Lakes

Tour of Iveragh

Ring of Kerry

KENMARE

WATERVILLE

Kenmare Bay

10 km

STAGE 3 TRALEE TO GALWAY CITY

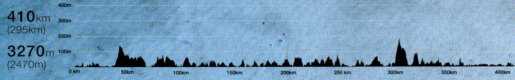

410km
(295km)

3270m
(2470m)

The gentle terrain along this stage allows the Wild Atlantic Way to follow the coastline fairly directly, making it the flattest stage of the route. The first half of the route through north Kerry and Loop Head is quieter with some spectacular cliff scenery while the northern section is much more popular with tourists, particularly the coast between Lahinch and Doolin.

Tralee and the Galway City are both on train lines so they are good starting or finishing points for a tour.

EUROVELO 1
North of Tralee the EV1 heads deep inland following the Limerick Greenway (page 136) and passing though Limerick City. It then follows the north shore of the Shannon Estuary west before rejoining the WAW just before Kilrush.

After Loop Head the EV1 continues slightly further inland than the WAW before making a diversion through the heart of the Burren.

NORTH KERRY
The coastline of north Kerry lies in sharp contrast to the more mountainous southern half of the county. The north is flatter and more pastoral yet the coast is still quite rugged in places, however this is less apparent from land.

At Tarbert the Wild Atlantic Way crosses the River Shannon via car ferry to Killimer in Clare. The roll-on/roll-off ferry operates daily and hourly throughout the year, see shannonferries.com for details. The alternative is to cycle around the Shannon Estuary crossing the river by the bridge in Limerick City (note bicycles aren't allowed to use the tunnel). This adds over 130km and isn't the most scenic so for most people the ferry is the best option.

LOOP HEAD
Thanks in a large part to Loop Head's position, squeezed between north Kerry and the popular sights of north Clare, it is much overlooked by tourists. Recently its profile has been raised a little but it's still quiet, certainly compared to its neighbours to the north and south.

From a cycling point of view this is a great plus and as an added bonus it's also very flat. A signposted route (page 140) loops around the headland following quiet roads southwest from Kilkee past impressive sea cliffs to the lighthouse at the very tip of the headland. It then heads east along the southern shore of the Shannon Estuary before cutting inland back to Kilkee.

MID CLARE
From Kilkee the Wild Atlantic Way continues north along the Clare coast through Doonbeg and Quilty to Lahinch. The route follows a fairly direct route along the N67 with limited scope for variation unless one wants to divert inland.

ARAN ISLANDS
The trio of islands in Galway Bay, while technically part of County Galway, are mentioned here as they are geologically so similar to the Burren and can be accessed from Doolin in Clare. The two smaller islands, Inisheer and Inishmaan, can easily be explored on foot, but the largest, Inishmore, requires a bike to complete the circuit in a day. See page 152 for details of an excellent loop that takes in the sights.

There are daily ferry crossings from Doolin in Clare (doolinferry.com) and Rossaveal in Galway (aranislandferries.com). During the summer they can get busy so it would be wise to reserve a ticket in advance online and there is a small additional charge to take your bike.

One interesting option would be to take the ferry to Inishmore from Doolin, cycle the loop there and then return to the mainland at Rossaveal in Galway.

THE BURREN
From Lahinch first time visitors will almost certainly want to follow the Wild Atlantic Way along the coast, visiting the Cliffs of Moher, Doolin and Black Head (see page 144 for details of a loop around Black Head).

And while the coast road offers beautiful views, to really appreciate the Burren's unique karst landscape you need to travel through its centre. There is an extensive network of very quiet boreens, some of which form part of the route on page 142.

The small seaside village of Kinvarra marks the northern limit of the Burren, from here the Wild Atlantic Way takes a fairly direct line north to Galway City along the N67. This road can be busy but most of it can be avoided by keeping to the quieter roads closer to the coast.

GALWAY

ATHENRY

LOUGHREA

Galway Bay

Black Head

Aran Islands

Inishmore

Black Head

GORT

LISDOONVARNA

Inland Burren

Cliffs of Moher

Liscannor Bay

ENNISTYMON

ENNIS

Mutton Island

SHANNON

KILKEE

LIMERICK

KILRUSH

Loop Head

River Shannon

FOYNES

RATHKEALE

LISTOWEL

Head

ABBEYFEALE

CHARLEVILLE

Tralee Bay

TRALEE

CASTLEISLAND

25 km

STAGE 4 GALWAY CITY TO BALLINA

793km
(454km)

6780m
(3650m)

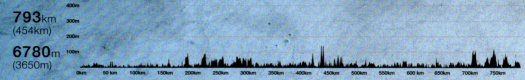

With no hard mountain passes this is another gentle stage of the Wild Atlantic Way. It also links some of the most popular sections of the route including Galway City, Connemara, Clew Bay and Achill Island.

And while the coast is reasonably flat, the mountains a short distance inland offer some interesting diversions as well as a spectacular backdrop.

EUROVELO 1

North of Galway City the EV1 take quite a direct line, further inland than the WAW, to Clifden. It then continues closer to the coast as far as Doo Lough where it follows a section of the Sheeffry Hills route (see page 170) towards Westport. From Westport it broadly follows the WAW along the North Mayo coast to Ballina.

GALWAY CITY TO CLIFDEN

From the City the Wild Atlantic Way follows the R336 west along the north shore of Galway Bay. It's a busy road but it gets quieter further from the city.

An alternative route between Galway and Clifden takes the N59 inland, and while the scenery is excellent, passing the Maamturk and Twelve Ben mountains, the road is very busy. There are plans to convert the old Galway to Clifden railway line into a greenway which will be hugely popular.

Shortly after Inverin the coast becomes much more featured with numerous bays and peninsulas. The route to Clifden weaves along the coastline passing many small villages and beautiful sandy beaches. See page 157 for details of a short route that starts in the village of Casla and explores the quiet backroads.

The indented nature of the coast means that there are plenty of possible shortcuts. For example cutting across the bog at Derryrush bypassing Carna, or following the quiet road across Roundstone Bog from Ballynahinch to rejoin the Wild Atlantic Way just outside Clifden.

There are two routes described in the main body of the book that could be combined to form a figure of eight that connects Galway Bay with Killary Harbour. The first route (page 158) links the village of Oughterard with the coast via a loop through the bogs of east Connemara. Follow it in either direction to Maam Cross where you meet the second route (page 162). This route, which loops around the Maamturk mountains, can also be taken in either direction to Leenane, the village at the head of the fjord.

CLIFDEN TO WESTPORT

North of Clifden the Wild Atlantic Way continues along the jagged coast around a number of headlands to Killary Harbour. The route described on page 164 loops around Sky Road, the first of the headlands just outside Clifden.

After winding along the shores of Killary Harbour the route passes through the narrow valley squeezed between Mweelrea and the Sheeffry Hills. The Wild Atlantic Way then continues north to Louisburgh before following the southern shore of Clew Bay past Croagh Patrick into Westport.

WESTPORT TO BALLINA

Cyclists should follow the Great Western Greenway (see page 175) rather than the road between Westport and Achill Sound. There is an interesting variation of the greenway called the Rocky Mountain Way (see page 176) that takes a slightly more adventurous route across the hillside on rough tracks.

From the end of the greenway the Wild Atlantic Way crosses the bridge onto Achill and loops around the island. This 82km circuit is described on page 178.

Back on the mainland the Wild Atlantic Way heads north skirting the vast Nephin Beg wilderness into the northwestern corner of Mayo known as Erris. Characterised by wide open spaces and long sandy beaches it is the quietest part of the stage.

A side branch of the route travels the length of the Mullet Peninsula passing close to Cross Lake where there is a short but interesting loop (page 180).

The town of Belmullet is the starting point for a signposted route called the Glinsk and Rossport Linear Route which follows some very quiet roads close to the coast. It could be a very worthwhile variation as it avoids a long stretch of the busy R314.

From Ballycastle (the starting point of the Rathlacken and Sralagagh route, see page 182) the Wild Atlantic Way heads north to the coast at Downpatrick Head, following quiet coastal roads through Lacken before rejoining the R314 and following it into Ballina.

Mullet Peninsula

Erris Head

Glinsk and Rossport Linear Route

Downpatrick Head

Cross Lake

BELMULLET

Sralagagh

Rathlacken

Killala Bay

ENNISCRONE

Blacksod Bay

BALLINA

FOXFORD

Keem Bay

Achill Island

North Clew Bay

NEWPORT

CASTLEBAR

KNOCK

Clew Bay

Great Western Greenway

WESTPORT

Clare Island

LOUISBURGH

Owenwee Bog

Inishturk

Sheffrey Hills

Inishbofin

Killary Harbour

Maamturks

TUAM

Sky Road

CLIFDEN

Derrigimlagh

OUGHTERARD

Slyne Head

Oughterard

ATHENRY

GALWAY

Gorumna Island

Galway Bay

Inishmore

Aran Islands

25 km

STAGE 5 BALLINA TO BUNBEG

382km
(303km)

4420m
(3390m)

This is another reasonably flat stage with the exception of the 100km stretch between Donegal Town and Ardara which accounts for nearly half the total height gain.

EUROVELO 1
From Enniscrone the EV1 heads east through the Ox Mountains and then keeps close to the coast as it makes its way north to Donegal Town.

From Donegal Town it follows the Donegal Cycle Route (see page 251) through Donegal as far as Newtowncunningham.

SOUTH SLIGO
From Ballina the Wild Atlantic Way heads north passing through the seaside town of Enniscrone before swinging east along Sligo Bay. This low-lying stretch of coast has dozens of small bays and coves and is very popular with surfers. The wave just outside Easkey village is internationally renowned.

The route on page 184 loops through the Ox Mountains which lie a short distance inland. There are plans for a large mountain bike trail centre in the forest on the south side of the mountains. The first 20km of trails are due to be built in late 2018 with another 60km to follow.

The Wild Atlantic Way continues along the coast around Ballysadare Bay, through Strandhill, another surfing village, and into Sligo Town.

Between Sligo and Donegal Towns the North West Trail (page 251) offers a quieter alternative to the Wild Atlantic Way.

NORTH SLIGO
A short distance inland of Sligo Town is Lough Gill, a popular route around the lake, see page 188. Heading north from Sligo Town the Wild Atlantic Way diverts to Rosses Point, a busy seaside resort during the summer months, before continuing north with the massive bulk of Benbulbin dominating the skyline. The route on page 190 follows a circuit around the iconic mountain passing Swiss Valley and Glencar Waterfall.

The Wild Atlantic Way continues north along the busy N15 with diversions to Streedagh beach and Mullaghmore Head. The short loop around Mullaghmore forms part of the route described on page 192 which also travels inland to the Gleniff Horseshoe.

SOUTH DONEGAL
Shortly after Cliffony the route briefly passes through County Leitrim and into County Donegal. A quiet road leads along the coast through the towns of Bundoran and Ballyshannon. It then passes the vast surfing beach at Rossnowlagh and close to another at Murvagh. The N15 and the R267 lead to Donegal Town.

North of Donegal Town the Donegal Cycle Route (see page 251) offers an alternative route that skips Glencolmcille and generally follows quieter roads than the Wild Atlantic Way.

GLENCOLMCILLE
From Donegal Town the Wild Atlantic Way heads west passing through the fishing town of Killybegs on its way to the Glencolmcille Peninsula. The 100km stretch between Donegal Town and Ardara is tough with nearly 2000m of height gain culminating in the climb over Glengesh Pass, albeit from the easier side.

The Wild Atlantic Way diverts from the village of Carrick to the Slieve League viewing point. It's a steep climb but worth it for the view. From Carrick the route crosses barren bog to Malinbeg before following the coast north to Glencolmcille village where it turns inland across more open ground to the climb over Glengesh. A very steep descent leads down the valley to Ardara.

As an alternative to Glengesh it's also possible to descend Granny Pass and follow the road alongside the tidal sands into Adara. This is a more scenic alternative as it takes in Maghera Beach and Assaranca Waterfall.

BÉAL AN MHUIRTHEAD

For more information about Glencolmcille see the figure of eight route on page 210 which covers much of the same ground as the Wild Atlantic Way.

NORTHWEST DONEGAL

The last leg of this stage is pretty flat, a welcome relief after the exertions of Glencolmcille. From Adara the route heads north to Portnoo beach before joining the road (with bike lane) along the Gweebarra River and crossing the bridge into the Rosses, a Gaeltacht region.

The route then cuts inland following the N56 to the town of Dungloe. From Dungloe it weaves along the R259 through a landscape of granite outcrops, small lakes and heather. Passing by Donegal International Airport in Carrickfinn, a brief stint along the N56 leads to the finish of the stage in Bunbeg.

THE MOUNTAINS

Two routes explore the mountainous interior of Donegal, both offering some great riding and amazing scenery. The first route loops through Glenveagh National Park on a mixture of road and gravel tracks, see page 214. The second follows the roads around Errigal, the iconic conical summit of Donegal, see page 212.

Bloody Foreland

FALCARRAGH   CREESLOUGH

BUNBEG

Errigal   Glenveagh

Arranmore Island   BURTONPORT

DUNGLOE   LETTERKENNY

Crohy Head

GLENTIES

Loughros More Bay

Granny Pass   ARDARA

Donegal Cycle Route   North West Trail

Glencolmcille

Slieve League   KILLYBEGS   DONEGAL

Donegal Bay   BALLYSHANNON

Mullaghmore Head   BUNDORAN

Kingfisher Trail

Inishmurray   Mullaghmore and Classie

Benbulbin

Sligo Bay   MANORHAMILTON

Killala Bay   SLIGO

ENNISCRONE   Ox Mountains   Lough Gill

COLLOONEY

BALLINA

25 km

STAGE 6 BUNBEG TO DERRY

371km
(344km)

4850m
(4540m)

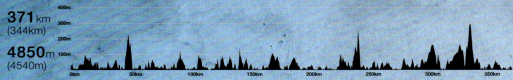

The final stage of the Wild Atlantic Way consists of two quite distinct sections. The first passes through wild and rocky terrain, taking in a number of exposed headlands, while the second, which starts as you make your way south along the shores of Lough Swilly, passes through more gentle, fertile land. That said, the fiercest climbs on the stage come towards the end at the top of Inishowen.

EUROVELO 1

The EV1 follows the Donegal Cycle Route (see page 251) through Donegal as far Newtowncunningham where it heads east to Derry City.

BUNBEG TO CREESLOUGH

This region, known as Gweedore, is the most densely populated rural area in Europe. From the town of Bunbeg the route heads north as far as Bloody Foreland where it turns east passing the long curving beach at Magheraroart. The harbour beside the beach is the departure point for the islands of Inishbofin and Tory.

The route then veers slightly inland and there are great views across the bog to the distinctive flat summit of Muckish and the conical peak of Errigal. After passing through Falcarragh into Dunfanaghy the Wild Atlantic Way loops around Horn Head. This is a very worthwhile scenic 14km circuit with 330m of height gain including the out and back to the Horn Head viewing point (55.2148, -7.9783).

The route then heads southeast passing the wonderful forest park (55.1501, -7.9283) on the Ards Peninsula which has some interesting trails suitable for easy mountain biking.

CREESLOUGH TO FANAD

Passing through the village of Creeslough the route continues north before looping around the Rosguill Peninsula. The headland is home to a number

of spectacular beaches including Trá na Rossan (55.2246, -7.8141) and the Murder Hole (55.2399, -7.8067) as well as the busy village of Downing.

A short distance past Carrickart the Harry Blaney bridge crosses Mulroy Bay onto the Fanad Peninsula.

FANAD

The route heads northwest across Fanad through a land of small lakes and rocky hills to the coast near Ballyhiernan Bay (55.2469, -7.7274).

After the lighthouse at Fanad Head the route heads south along the western shore of Lough Swilly. After Portsalon there are spectacular views across the water to Inishowen from the top of the steep, switchback climb.

Continuing south the route passes through Rathmullan, Rathmelton and the large town of

Letterkenny before the Wild Atlantic Way veers northwest to start its circuit of the Inishowen Peninsula.

INISHOWEN

The route taken by the Wild Atlantic Way around Inishowen follows that of a driving route known as the Inishowen 100. A variation of this route is also popular with cyclists and is described on page 216.

Inishowen is connected on either side by ferries which raises the possibility of skipping some of the less interesting stretches of the coast if you are tight on time. The Lough Swilly ferry (swillyferry.com) links Buncrana on Inishowen with Rathmullan on Fanad. It saves 60km and runs daily between June and September. The Lough Foyle ferry (loughfoyleferry.com) runs between Greencastle on Inishowen and Magilligan Point on the Causeway Coast (see page 228). It saves

about 70km and runs daily between March and September.

After Buncrana the route tackles the first of the hard climbs, Mamore Gap. After taking in the impressive views at Malin Head, the most northerly point in Ireland, you head southeast over a number of tough climbs before the final sting in the tail, the steep climb out of Kinnagoe Bay. With that done all that remains is the flat final section along the western shore of Lough Foyle to the end of the Wild Atlantic Way at the border just outside Derry.

DERRY

Even though, technically speaking, the Wild Atlantic Way starts/finishes at the border between the Republic and Northern Ireland, it makes sense to continue your journey the short distance into Derry.

The city, the fourth largest on the island, has good transport facilities and a great range of accommodation and places to eat and drink.

Malin Head

Fanad Head

Glengad Head

10 km

Lenan Head

CARNDONAGH

Inishowen Head

Lough Swilly

MOVILLE

Route

MILFORD

BUNCRANA

Inishowen 100

RATHMULLAN

Lough Foyle

Inch Island

RAMELTON

LIMAVADY

NEWTOWNCUNNINGHAM

DERRY

Ballyshannon to Larre

INY

DUNGIVEN

ABOUT THE AUTHOR

David Flanagan is the author of a number of outdoor guides and maps which he publishes as Three Rock Books. Before embarking on his career in publishing he worked for ten years as a software engineer. Upon being made redundant he decided to take the opportunity to document the rock climbing areas that he and friends had developed, this lead to the publishing of *Bouldering in Ireland* in 2011.

One book led to another and in 2013 he started Three Rock Books and published his second title *Bouldering Essentials*. Since then he has gone on to write and publish a number of books with an active, outdoor focus including a guide to the best of Irish rock climbing, *Rock Climbing in Ireland*, a guide to Ireland's west coast, *Exploring Ireland's Wild Atlantic Way* with Richard Creagh, and *Cycling in Ireland*.

During lockdown he produced his first map, the *Adventure Map of Ireland*. In late 2022 he published *Exploring Ireland*, a guide to the Irish outdoors.

ACKNOWLEDGEMENTS

I'm very grateful to my family: Jenny, Hazel and Milo. Without their patience and understanding I would have never finished this book. Thanks to everyone who kept me company on the cycles, especially Quigs.

Thanks to Anna Connor, Ann Fitzpatrick, Ciarán Cannon, Daithi deForge, Doug Corrie, Eoin Hagan, Ethan Loughrey, Grant Fay, Helen Lawless, Patricia Deane, Rosaleen Ní Shúilleabháin, Triona O'Mahony and the readers: Diarmuid Smyth, Julie Flanagan, Marius Curtin, Martina Flanagan and Richard Creagh. A special thanks to my Dad for all his advice.

PHOTO CREDITS
Page 13, 140 Richard Creagh
Page 122 Hauke Musicaloris licensed CC BY 2.0
Page 234, 238 MountainBikeNI.com

The Back Road on Inishmore, Galway, see page 152